To

Usman H

CN00663782

By the blessings of what is contained in this book, may you taste the sweetness of loving the Messenger May Allah's Peace and Blessings be upon him. May your Eyes be Enabled by the Vision of the Messenger of Allah Peace and Blessing of Allah be upon him.

Muhammed Zakar Baig

Muḥammad ﷺ the Perfect Man

Muḥammad ﷺ the Perfect Man

by

Sayyid Muḥammad ibn ʿAlawī al-Mālikī al-Ḥasanī

Translated by Khalid Williams

Foreword by Dr Mostafa Badawi

VISIONS OF
REALITY
BOOKS

بسم الله الرحمن الرحيم

Published by
©Visions of Reality Books 1434AH, 2013
First Edition

All rights reserved. This book is in copyright. Subject to statutory exception and to the provisions of relevant collective licensing agreements, no reproduction of any part may take place without the written permission of the publishers.

The book is printed on Munken paper of archival quality and acid free.

Thanks are due to Abdassamad Clarke (Design and Typesetting), Muhammad Ansa (Indexing), Suraqah Abdul Aziz (Editing), Majid Hussain (proofreading) .

ISBN 978-1-909460-00-3

Book Distribution All Enquiries: sales@visions-of-reality.com
www.visions-of-reality.com

Printed and bound in Great Britain

VISIONS OF REALITY BOOKS

Contents

Publisher's Note

All praise is for Allah and the choicest of peace and blessings be upon His Beloved Messenger Sayyidina Muhammad.

It is with immense pleasure that we present the English translation of Sayyid Muḥammad ibn ʿAlawī's work *Muhammad Al-Insan Al-Kamil* The Perfect Man, to the general public.

This book comes at an important time when in the West the prevailing secular consumerism and selfishness seems to know few bounds resulting in an immorality – where even the elect of Allah's creation – the Prophets and Messengers, may the peace and blessings of Allah be upon them, are not safe from being openly mocked or their lives ridiculed. In the East, despotic rulers, the lack of leadership, external interference and sectarian division has opened up chasms of angst.

It is in this atmosphere that this phenomenal book written by the leading scholar of his time – Sayyid Muḥammad ibn ʿAlawī al-Mālikī al-Ḥasanī – is presented to the general readership in English for the first time.

It serves as a timely reminder to the characteristics of the greatest human being that ever lived, and presents an insight into the noble Prophetic way, the behavioural code of conduct – the Sunna – of the Perfect Man, that he, may the peace and blessings of Allah be upon him, left behind for all peoples for all times.

The author catalogues the Prophetic Perfections in great detail and provides scriptural evidence with meticulous scholarly authority. The book is further augmented by Khalid Williams' lucid and exemplary translation adding depth, breadth, clarity and making this within easy reach of the English speaking world.

The book is a modern day classic in the Arabic language – we pray that its translation becomes the same in English.

We pray that Allah accepts this work and makes it a source of eternal benediction - from the author, through to all who have had a hand in translating it, preparing it and publishing it as well as those reading it.

Amjid Illahi
January 2013/Safar 1434 AH

About the Translator

Khalid Williams is a translator specialising in traditional Islamic texts. He was born in the United Kingdom in 1983. After graduating from the University of Leeds with a First Class Honours Degree in Arabic Studies in 2006, he moved to Morocco where he currently resides with his family. There he had the honour of studying under the great jurist and grammarian of Salé, Shaykh Muṣṭafā al-Najjār al-Naḥwī, Allah have mercy on him.

His published works include:

Our Master Muḥammad ﷺ, the Messenger of Allah by Imam Sirajuddīn Ḥusaynī (Two Volumes, Sunni Publications 2008).

The following works have been completed and are due to be published by Visions of Reality Books:

Isnad min'ad Din by Abdal Fath Abu Ghudda

Sheikh Ahmad Zarruq's *Sharh on Hizb al-Bahr*

Virtues of Madina by Imam Janadi

Fadail Ahl Bayt – compilation from the works of Ibn Hajar Asqalani, Imam Nawawi, Imam Nasai', Ibn Shahin and Imam Suyuti

About Dr Mostafa Al-Badawi

Dr Mostafa Al-Badawi is a Consultant Psychiatrist and member of the Royal College of Psychiatrists. He studied under many shaykhs, foremost among whom is the late Habib Ahmad Mashhur al-Haddad. Dr Badawi is also one of the leading contemporary translators of Islamic books from Arabic into English.

Foreword

Muslims know that Prophets of God are born, that this is a God-given rank, not an acquired one, and that a Prophet is informed of his status and mission in clear terms by God, either directly or through the Angel Jibrīl. Prophets are of different ranks, the highest among them being the Divine Envoys (*Rusul*). Prophets occupy the highermost degrees of the human pyramid, for they represent the perfection of spirituality and virtue among human beings and their rank is unattainable by even the highest ranking saints, who come next in the pyramid. The summit of that pyramid is occupied by the most perfect and highest ranking being in the universe, Prophet Muḥammad – may God's blessings and peace be upon him and all other Prophets – Master and Seal of all Divine Envoys, whose spirit or light was the first to be created and whose physical form was the last to appear to earthly humanity. His perfection encompassed every conceivable aspect and has been described in detail in innumerable volumes over the centuries. There is however, one peculiarity that one needs to keep in mind when studying and reflecting on these perfections, which is that because the last revelation before Islam was Christianity and the Christians divinized their Envoy, the Qurʾān repeatedly emphasizes the human status of the Prophet of Islam, so as to annul from its roots any possibility of the same thing happening. Thus of the hundreds of miraculous events reported and authenticated in the life of the Prophet the Qurʾān mentions only one, the cleavage of the moon. The theme, 'I am but a human being like you' recurs both in the Qurʾān and the utterances of the Prophet. The great majority of orientalists, until recently openly hostile to Islam, although often claiming objectivity, chose to ignore the abundant material detailing the great spiritual merits of the Prophet, considering these no more than legends concocted by his followers. The obvious intention was to concede to him no more than the status of a social reformer and deny him that of a Divine Envoy. What is worse and certainly more incomprehensible is the tendency of certain narrow minded and rather materialistic Muslim scholars to deny or minimize these merits, and their efforts to portray the Prophet as no more than an ordinary man who just happened to have been charged with a Divine mission and to have received the revelation of the Qurʾān. The avowed intention there is to prevent the Muslims from divinizing him as the Christians divinized Jesus, but the hidden intention is to deny to his true heirs, the saints of the Muslim community, their superior spiritual states and inward knowledge.

When the Prophet is commanded in the Qurʾān to respond to the pagans' challenges by saying '*Am I but a mortal Envoy?*' [17:93] or '*Say: "I am but a mortal like you who receives revelation*" [18:110; 41:6] certain mentalities seem to stop at the first half of the proposition, which is that he is a mortal like us, while ignoring the second half which states that he is a Divine envoy, fit to receive revelation from God. God says, '*Were We to send down this Qurʾān on a mountain you would have seen it humble, cracking from the fear of God*' [59:21]. The descent of revelation is thus described to be so mighty that a mountain would crack were it to descend upon it. What then should the attributes of a human being be in order to survive such an event unharmed? The necessary qualities for a Divine Envoy to be capable of receiving revelation are precisely that dimension of being that differentiates them from common mortals and that scholars have felt the need to point out to their students over the centuries so that their attachment to the Prophet may grow stronger and thus more effective in guiding their behaviour and motivating their journey to God.

This book is devoted to reminding readers of the immense outward and inward perfections of the Prophet, while refuting certain malicious insinuations of orientalist origin and certain misinterpretations by literalistic minded Muslim authors. In these times of ours, when Islam is being misrepresented as a violent religion and knowledge of who the Prophet of Mercy really was is lacking in the West, such a book seeks to contribute to redressing the situation by drawing a detailed portrait of him in the light of the authentic historical sources of the Muslim tradition. Furthermore, because the love of God and His Prophet is the very core of faith in Islam, such works that acquaint Muslims more fully with their Prophet and increase their love and veneration for him by describing his perfection serve an essential function—for God says in the Qurʾān, '*Say: "If your fathers, your sons, your brothers, your spouses, your clan, your possessions that you have acquired, commerce you fear may slacken, and dwellings that please you, if these are more beloved to you than God and*

His Messenger, and to struggle in His way, then wait till God brings about His will'" [9:24]. For his part, the Prophet unequivocally declared that to love him and his family was the necessary complement of one's love for God and that no believer's faith would ever be complete until he reaches the stage of loving the Prophet more than his parents, his children, and his own self. Clearly, to read about the perfect attributes of the perfect man is one manner of accomplishing this. The second manner is to follow his Sacred Law and his *Sunna* as thoroughly as possible; the third to invoke blessings in abundance upon him; and the fourth to love and serve his descendants, especially the learned and virtuous among them, to whom belonged the author of this treatise Sayyid Muḥammad ʿAlawī al-Mālikī.

There are three kinds of claim to nobility in Islam: two outward (lineage and religious knowledge) and one inward (sanctity and inward knowledge). Over the years there were endless debates among scholars as to which is superior, the nobility of lineage, being a descendant of the Prophet through his daughter Fāṭima and *Imām* ʿAlī, or knowledge. These of course were always cordial scholarly debates, free of resentment or spite, for no Muslim scholar worth his while would dare challenge the nobility of the descendants of the Prophet. One of the most telling arguments produced by a famous scholar to conclude the textual evidence he arrayed was that should the scholar lose his mind, he would inevitably lose his knowledge, and thus his claim of nobility, while should a *sharīf* [descendant of the Prophet ﷺ] lose his mind, he would retain the honour of his lineage. The nobility of the latter was therefore concluded to be essential, while the former's was shown to be accidental. The essential being by definition superior to the accidental, the nobility of the *sharīf* was therefore demonstrated to be superior. The third kind of nobility, which is that of sanctity, although inwardly hidden, is related to lineage inasmuch as we know that the great majority of saints throughout the Muslim world come from a *sharīf* lineage. The author, Sayyid Muḥammad son of Sayyid ʿAlawī al-Mālikī, is himself an Idrīsī *Sharīf*[1] whose ancestors had emigrated to Mecca from Morocco. His father Sayyid ʿAlawī was

[1] Imam Idrīs the First, son of ʿAbdallāh, son al-Ḥasan al-Muthannā, son of Imam Ḥasan son of ʿAlī ibn Abī Ṭālib and Fāṭima daughter of the Prophet, emigrated from Iraq to Morocco in the second century A.H. His son, Imām Idrīs the Second, completed the foundation of the city of Fez, which remains to this day the capital of religious learning in Morocco. Their descendents are known as the Idrīsī *sharīfs* and a large number of them became over the centuries renowned scholars, saints, and sufis.

one of the most eminent and popular scholars of Mecca, as had been his grandfather, Sayyid ʿAbbās. Many of their direct ancestors had been teachers of religious sciences and orators who regularly delivered the Friday Sermon at the Sacred Mosque [*Masjid al-Ḥarām*]. He was therefore raised in a house of knowledge and spirituality and received tuition in all branches of Islamic knowledge, mainly from his father and then from the most eminent scholars in Mecca, Jeddah, and Medina at that time. As was traditional with his ancestors, he was trained to love and respect people of high spiritual rank and became deeply attached to the great saints of his time, such as Ḥabīb ʿAbdal-Qādir al-Saqqāf and Ḥabīb Aḥmad Mashhūr al-Ḥaddād in Jeddah and Sayyid Ḥasan Fadʿaq and Sayyid Muḥammad Amīn Kutbī in Mecca. When studying in Cairo he received special attention from masters such as Shaykh Ṣāliḥ al-Jaʿfarī, the leading Mālikī scholar of Egypt at the time, Shaykh al-Ḥāfiẓ al-Tījānī, the well known traditionist, and Shaykh ʿAbdal-Ḥalīm Maḥmūd, rector of al-Azhar University. He made special trips to Upper Egypt to visit the great Shaykh Aḥmad Riḍwān. He also had connections with numerous masters in Syria, Lebanon, Iraq, Morocco, India, and Pakistan. He obtained a PhD in Ḥadīth sciences from al-Azhar University in Cairo in 1391 A.H. Being much more proud of his title of Sayyid and that of *Shaykh al-Ḥadīth*, and the education he received at the hands of his father and other traditional teachers, than of his university degree, he never used the title Doctor in his books and always disliked being called so. Eventually, Sayyid Muḥammad became the foremost Sunni scholar of the Ḥijāz.[2] The generation of his father had been the last when Mecca was vibrant with brilliant scholars and students came from all over the world to acquire knowledge in the Sacred City. The prevalent political conditions made it very difficult for scholars other than those belonging to the official current to hold public teaching sessions, as had been the uninterrupted practice in the Two Sacred Sanctuaries of Mecca and Medina for over thirteen hundred years. As for those who held private sessions, they were frequently harassed, and many were forced to stop altogether.

2 The Idrīsīs, whose ancestor is Imām Ḥasan, as the Bā-ʿAlawīs, whose ancestor is Imām Ḥusayn, are eminent examples of families from the House of the Prophet who receive their knowledge of Islamic sciences from solid unbroken chains of ancestors. Both, as are countless other *sharif*ian families throughout the Islamic world, are staunch Sunnis, which categorically refutes the claims of the Shīʿa that knowledge transmitted through the descendents of the Prophet leads to Shīʿism.

This is how Sayyid Muḥammad found himself the only scholar to stand in open defiance to the Wahhābīs, although his opposition was invariably courteous and scholarly, as had always been and still remains the wont of true Muslim scholars. The campaign of vilification and slander to which he was subjected continued for most of his life, escalating at one time to the point where he was declared a *kāfir*, his passport was withdrawn from him, and he was prevented from travelling abroad. This happened despite his cordial relations with the late King Fahd, who ordered his passport returned to him, received him in his palace in Jeddah, and, after dinner, had his picture taken with him.

Sayyid Muḥammad achieved worldwide recognition and became loved and respected by Muslim scholars everywhere. They invited him to lecture and attend religious occasions in most Muslim countries, to some of which, such as Egypt, Syria, and Morocco, he was a regular visitor. He made several trips to Malaysia and Singapore, Indonesia, the Yemen, and East Africa, and travelled all over Europe and North America. He made one trip to South Africa and Pakistan. He was a man of great charisma whose radiant presence in the Ḥijāz made him the rallying point for all Ḥijāzis, young and old, who were proud of their teacher and considered him the leading figure of their community.

Most of the registered students at his school in Mecca were South East Asians, but his teaching sessions were attended by a great many local students from Mecca and Jeddah, a substantial number of Yemenis, and a few representatives of other nationalities. When he went to visit the Prophet in Medina, there were daily teaching sessions in his house, and he was invited by the people of Medina to attend gatherings practically every night. In Ramaḍān, when the late Ḥabīb Muḥammad Ṣāliḥ al-Meḥḍār held his Bukhārī reading sessions every afternoon in the Prophet's Mosque, he was always careful not to miss the closing session at the end of the month and share in the long *duʿāʾ* that concluded it.

Sayyid Muḥammad taught people to love God and His Messenger. His tremendous love for his ancestor the Prophet shone through his words, deeds, and attitudes. He set a good example for those who strove to acquire the prophetic virtues of tolerance, gentleness, compassion, and selfless devotion to the cause of God and Islam, together with uncompromising upholding of the truth and of justice. As a scholar he never stooped to the crude methods of his adversaries, always maintaining the traditional courteous stance that he had inherited from his teachers when defending his faith against often crude and spiteful attacks.

On two consecutive years before his death he visited his ancestor, Imām Idrīs, in Morocco, and wrote a long poem in his praise.

On Friday the 15th of Ramaḍān of the year 1425 A.H. we received news that Sayyid Muḥammad had died suddenly in Mecca. He was sixty three lunar years old. We learned subsequently that he had been putting his affairs in order for months before that, as if in preparation for his departure. Thousands attended his funeral, from Mecca and Jeddah, and from elsewhere in the Arabian Peninsula. Many more thousands came in the next few days from all over the Islamic World to offer their condolences to his brother Sayyid ʿAbbās, his son Aḥmad, and the rest of the family. He was buried in the Maʿlā Cemetery of Mecca – in the same enclosure where his father had been buried, as well as numerous other scholars and saints, at the northern end of the cemetery, to one's right as one approaches the tomb of the Prophet's first wife, the Lady Khadīja – leaving his son Aḥmad to run the school in Mecca and continue the regular teaching sessions in the tradition of their ancestors.

Mostafa Al-Badawi

Author's Introduction

PRAISE BE to Allah, Lord of the worlds; and blessings and peace be upon our master Muḥammad, the key to what was locked, the seal of what has passed, the helper of truth by truth, and the guide to the straight path, and upon his Household and Companions, as is truly merited by his status and magnificent rank.[3]

Much has been written on the prophetic biography (al-Sīra al-Nabawiyya) in its different aspects, not only in Arabic and Persian but also in many Western languages, including English, in which more works on the prophetic biography have been authored than in any other Western language. English literature is richly endowed with studies of this subject, because much effort was devoted by Western authors to producing biographies of the Trusted Prophet, thus providing clear proofs of the greatness of Islam's messenger and acknowledging that the Blessed Prophet had succeeded in freeing his society from the effects of slavery and ignorant customs, and from the yoke of base and degrading

---

[3] *The key to what was locked* means that the Prophet was the key with which the hearts of the pagans, once locked by false beliefs and prejudice to faith and religion, were opened, admitting the lights of faith and *tawḥīd*. At a higher level the Prophet was the key with which Allah unlocked the gates of His mercy, for he was, as the Qurʾān states, a 'Mercy to all beings.' He brought to humanity the knowledge of their Creator, His Oneness and Attributes, a Sacred Law that constitutes the first declaration of human rights and that guarantees social justice, an ethical system that promotes selfless compassion and sublime virtue, and a spiritual path that leads to the realization of inward knowledge of the Absolute. *The seal of what has passed* means that he is the very last in the long succession of Divine Envoys, his message being the synthesis and perfection of all previous ones and his rank being the Master and Seal of all Prophets. *The helper of the truth by the truth* means that he supported the truth of the message with the power of the Qurʾān, which is itself truth, and that when promoting both he did so in a truly upright manner and with true justice. *The guide to the straight path* is he who leads the way and with both his example and instructions shows others how to follow the shortest route to the mercy, forgiveness, and presence of their Lord, this being the straight path. *As befits his standing and magnificent rank* refers to his standing as Master and Seal of all Divine Envoys, and consequently Master of all human beings, and his rank as Allah's Beloved and supreme intercessor on behalf of humanity on Judgment Day. [Many thanks to Dr Mostafa al-Badawi for providing this commentary. Note: This is the famous Ṣalāt al-Fātiḥ, taught by Imam ʿAlī ؏ according to al-Ṭabarānī in *al-Awsaṭ* and Ibn Abī Shayba in his *Muṣannaf*.]

practices. One of them said that his ﷺ call raised the community (*umma*) from the pits of misery to the heights of happiness in only a few years. Nevertheless, their works are not free from misrepresentations and defamatory additions, and thus are not entirely trustworthy.

Yet no matter how much they write, and how many volumes they fill with descriptions of his virtues, they could never possibly encompass all the admirable qualities and pure, goodly attributes with which his person ﷺ was endowed; for he reached the heights of human perfection when his Lord elected him to convey His divine message; thus he spoke not of his own caprice, but his words were naught but Revelation being revealed. And his Lord praised him by saying: '*Verily, you are of a tremendous nature*' [68:4]; and He said: '*And had you been harsh and hard-hearted, they would have scattered from about you*' [3:159]; and there are many similar passages in this mightiest of books and finest of discourses. Thus it is beyond human power to enumerate every one of his perfections.

His virtues are perfect, and were he to gift
His resplendence to the moon, it would never be eclipsed.
Despite their skill, those who have described him
Need all of time to do so – and there is more they have not described.

And the more man develops his civilisation, and further ascends the ladder of progress, and the more his intellectual horizons broaden, he will perceive more and more of the benefits that Muḥammad ﷺ offered to all humanity.

Fourteen centuries have passed since the Messenger of Allah ﷺ passed on to the Supreme Assembly,[4] and his greatness continues to fill hearts and ears, and his remembrance remains the music of life for all those who thirst to drink from the spring of his holy inspiration, and to partake of the overflowing blessing of his unique valour and perfect greatness.

If the Muslims remember this Unlettered Prophet by way of sanctifying the message he bore and conveyed from Allah to the corners of the world, and through faith in the lofty doctrines and laws he brought forth, all of humanity might remember him for being their unique Messenger, noble, righteous and merciful, without compare in all of their long history.

[4] The assembly constituted by the superior angels and the spirits of past Divine Prophets in the higher heavens.

His ﷺ greatness was not drawn from any allegiance of kinship or any worldly prestige or wealth, nor from the greatness of the nation in which he appeared, nor from his high lineage or nobility. Rather, his greatness was drawn from the majesty of his personality, the perfection of his character and the broadness of his horizons, and from his being the highest paradigm of the perfect man. It was drawn from how he lived and died while struggling for Allah's cause, and from his being the Chosen Messenger elected by divine Providence from among all mankind to convey Allah's message to the world, after a time had passed wherein no messenger had come, and the people had gone astray and forgotten the guidance of Heaven which they had been given by the prophets and messengers in the past. Thus he came forth bearing the final message to unite all humanity on one doctrine, the primordial nature in which Allah created man.

The message called unto the doctrine of pure divine Oneness (*tawḥīd*), and affirmed the principles of justice, freedom, equality and fraternity among all people. In its lofty spirit, majestic teachings and noble goals, it constituted the religion of humanity, upholding human dignity and calling for love, mercy and cooperation, and for an awakening of the conscience, a sense of responsibility and the honouring of covenants and all that is sacred. It called for the spreading of knowledge and civility, and waged war on paganism, idolatry, misguidance, intolerance, wicked and evil practices, errant caprice, harmful delusion, unbridled lust, false superstitions and mindless customs. He gathered all people under one banner of divine guidance, in the shade of a perfect message – the law of Allah – and did not return unto his Lord until he had united the Arabs upon it and invited the kings and rulers to it, sending envoys to give glad tidings and warnings to Khosrau, to the King of Bahrain,[5] to the Abyssinians, to the ruler of Egypt, and to Heracles the Emperor of the Byzantines.

His successors after him continued to bear the burden of guiding other nations and setting humanity free, so that this message reached the corners of the earth. Upon it there arose an enlightened civilisation, and it still remains the doctrine of many nations and peoples, alive in both

[5] What is meant by Bahrain in ancient sources is not the current Kingdom of Bahrain but rather the whole territory along the western coast of the Gulf, which today would include the Eastern Province of Saudi Arabia, Kuwait, and the Emirates. [t]

its ethics and its laws, and will remain so until Allah calls back the earth and all upon it to Himself.

Once I was reading *sūrat al-Mā'ida* when I came to the Almighty's words: '*This day have I perfected for you your religion, and fulfilled My favour upon you, and have gladly chosen for you Islam as your religion*' [5:3]. I stopped at this verse and reflected on it, and began to repeat it again and again, tasting its sweetness and experiencing its eloquence, until my whole body was moved by it. From it I concluded the following:

1 – Allah intended for this religion to be the seal of all religions, so that no other religion would ever come after it to replace it, amend it or correct it, as He says: '*Muḥammad is not the father of any man among you, yet he is the Messenger of Allah and the Seal of the Prophets*' [33:40]. Because of this, He placed within this religion sufficient laws, ethics and teachings to ensure it would be lasting and unending, and fitting for all times and places, and able to give happiness to all mankind and to free humanity from its fetters, and establish justice and truth among all people. All this made this religion immutable, complete, preserved and unending.

As for its being immutable, Allah says: '*Turn, then, your face toward the religion in a pure fashion, in conformity with the primordial nature upon which Allah has created men; there is no changing Allah's creation. This is the immutable religion, but most men know it not*' [30:30].

As for its being complete, Allah says: '*We left nothing out of the Book*' [6:38].

As for its being preserved, Allah says: '*Falsehood comes to it not from before it, nor from behind it*' [41:42].

And as for its being unending, Allah says: '*We Ourselves have sent down the Remembrance, and We watch over it*' [15:9].

Completeness, preservation and endlessness are the primary qualities of perfection, and these qualities make it the perfect religion.

2 – If the message of Islam is complete, immutable, preserved, endless and perfect in every way, then the one whom Allah sends to bring it forth and invite others to it must also be at this level or indeed a higher one, and have this same rank or indeed a loftier one, and be of this status or indeed a greater one; for it is he who undertakes to bear the burden of this message, and it is only logical that a great load can only be borne by one who is greater than it.

3 – Leading on from this subtle point and this noble standpoint, I concluded that the Prophet Muḥammad ﷺ, who came forth with this perfect religion, must himself be a perfect man, and perfect in every way: perfect in his image and appearance, such that none who saw him ever saw the like of him, before or after:

He it is whose subtle and physical forms were perfected,
Then the Originator of souls chose him as His beloved.[6]

Perfect also in his character and nature, for his Lord said of him: '*Verily, you are of a tremendous nature*' [68:4]. Perfect too in his ethics and his way of life, for his Lord said of him: '*Did He not find you an orphan, and shelter you? And find you wandering, and guide you? And find you needy, and enrich you?*' [93:6-8] He is the perfect man in every way, both physically and spiritually, and free of all fault and blemish.

Created were you free of every blemish,
As though you were created just as you wished to be![7]

4 – I wanted to have a share in writing about this truth, a truth which is only denied by those who are guilty of grave folly and falsehood:

If the blind man denies that the sun shines,
He harms it not at all, but reveals his own folly.

So I endeavoured to write about the perfection of this man ﷺ, and thus I wrote this book, in which I have spoken about some aspects of his ﷺ person; and I ask the Lord Almighty to inspire us with the truth, and to guide us by His grace to that wherein there is goodness and righteousness. Praise be to Allah, Lord of the worlds; and blessings and peace be upon our master Muḥammad, his Household and his Companions.

Muḥammad ʿAlawī al-Māliki al-Makkī al-Ḥasanī

6 From the *Burda* of Imam Buṣayrī, chapter three. [t]

7 These lines are attributed to the Companion Ḥassān ibn Thābit ﷺ. [t]

PART ONE

THE PERFECTION OF HIS SUBLIME GIFTS AND EXALTED QUALITIES

'Have We not expanded your breast for you,
and lifted your burden from you,
which so weighed down your back?
And have We not exalted your remembrance for you?' [94:1-4]

The Perfection of His Pure and Noble Lineage

IBN ʿABBĀS ؓ reported that the Messenger of Allah ﷺ said: 'I was sired by no fornication of pagan ignorance; I was sired by naught but bonds of marriage, like the marriage of Islam.'

Hishām ibn Muḥammad al-Kalbī reported that his father said: 'I wrote five hundred ancestors of the Prophet ﷺ, and found in them no extra-marital bonds, nor any of the customs of the pagan ignorance.'

ʿAlī ؓ reported that the Prophet ﷺ said: 'I came from marriage, and never from fornication, from the time of Adam until my father and mother begat me. None of the fornication of pagan ignorance touched me.'

Ibn ʿAbbās ؓ reported that the Messenger of Allah ﷺ said: 'There were no bonds of fornication whatsoever among my forebears; Allah continued to pass me down from goodly loins to pure wombs, cleansed and refined. No two branches diverged save that I was in the best of them.'

Anas ؓ reported that the Messenger of Allah ﷺ recited '*There has come unto you a messenger from the best of you*[8]' [9:128], and then said: 'I am the best of you in lineage, kinship and ancestry; my forebears from Adam were unsullied by fornication.'

ʿĀʾisha, the mother of the believers ؓ, reported that the Prophet ﷺ declared that Jibrīl ؑ said: 'I searched the earth from East to West and saw therein no man finer than Muḥammad, and no tribe[9] finer than the sons of Hāshim.'[10]

Al-Bukhārī reports in his *Ṣaḥīḥ*, on the authority of Abū Hurayra ؓ,

8 The Arabic أنفسكم in this verse may be read *anfus*^{i}*kum* or *anfas*^{i}*kum*; the former reading, which is the more usual, means 'your own selves' (from *anfus*, meaning 'selves'); the latter (which the Prophet ﷺ recites in this narration, as is stated by Anas here) means 'the best of you' (from *anfas*, meaning 'most precious', 'most valuable'). [t]

9 Literally 'no sons of a man'. [t]

10 All these reports were narrated by al-Bayhaqī, al-Ṭabarānī and Ibn ʿAsākīr.

that the Prophet ☙ said: 'I was sent forth through the finest generations of the sons of Adam, generation after generation, until I arrived at the generation in which I am.'

Muslim reports in his *Ṣaḥīḥ*, on the authority of Wā'ila ibn al-Asqaʿ ☙, that the Prophet ☙ said: 'Allah elected Kināna from the sons of Ismāʿīl, and elected Quraysh from Kināna, and elected the sons of Hāshim from Quraysh, and elected me from the sons of Hāshim.'

Al-ʿAbbās ☙ reported that the Messenger of Allah ☙ said: 'Allah created mankind and placed me in their finest group, and the best of the two nations[11]. He then appraised the tribes, and placed me in the best household of them. Thus I am the best of them in person and the best of them in household'[12] – that is, the best of them in spirit and person, as well as the best of them in lineage.

Ibn ʿUmar ☙ reported that the Messenger of Allah ☙ said: 'Allah appraised His creatures and chose from them the sons of Adam, and then appraised the sons of Adam and chose from them the Arabs, and then chose me from the Arabs; and thus I remain a chosen one from chosen ones. Yea, whoso loves the Arabs, loves them because he loves me; and whoso hates the Arabs, hates them because he hates me.'[13]

Know that he ☙ was the only child of his mother and father, having neither brother nor sister, which meant that their superiority would pass to him alone, and their progeny would be confined to him alone, and he would be singled out with a lineage which Allah ordained for prophethood and chose for the ultimate nobility. Once you study his lineage and discover the purity of his birth, you will be certain that he is a descendant of noble forebears. He ☙ is the Prophet whose identity is of the Arabs, the Meccans, those of the Sanctuary, those of Hāshim, and those of Quraysh; he is the finest of the chosen sons of Hāshim, elected from the finest tribe of the Arabs and the noblest, purest, strongest, mightiest, most eloquent, most just, most pious, most honourable and most generous of them, on both his father's and mother's side; and he hailed from the dearest of lands to Allah.

Perhaps the great ḥadīth scholar Shams al-Dīn ibn Nāṣir al-Dīn al-Dimashqī said it best:

---

[11]   i.e. the Arabs and non-Arabs (*Tuḥfat al-Aḥwadhī*). [t]
[12]   Al-Tirmidhī.
[13]   Al-Ḥakim, al-Bayhaqī, al-Ṭabarānī, etc.

The forefathers of Muḥammad ﷺ,
To preserve the honour of his name,
Forsook all lewdness and were unblemished,
Till from Adam to his parents he came.

The Perfection of His Form, and His Beautiful Appearance ﷺ

Imam al-Buṣayrī, Allah rest his soul, said:

He it is whose subtle and physical forms were perfected,
Then the Originator of souls chose him as His beloved.[14]

Al-Qurṭubī said: 'He did not show all of his beauty to us; for had all his beauty been shown to us, our eyes would not have been able to see him ﷺ.'

There are countless prophetic ḥadīths and traditions which speak of the perfection of his ﷺ form and the beauty of his appearance; and thus part of the fullness of faith in him ﷺ is to believe that Allah ﷻ gave him a physical form of which the like had never been seen before him, nor was ever seen after him, on any human being.

HIS BLESSED FACE

The Prophet ﷺ had the most handsome of faces, as though the sun were shining in it. ʿAlī رضي الله عنه said: 'He was neither corpulent (*muṭṭaham*) nor round-faced (*mukaltham*); there was a slight roundness to his face.'[15] *Muṭṭaham* means very fat, and *mukaltham* means round-faced; that is, his face was not completely round, but there was a certain roundness to it.

ʿĀ'isha رضي الله عنها said: 'When the Messenger of Allah ﷺ was pleased, the features of his face would light up as though it was a piece of the moon.'[16]

Both Abū Bakr al-Ṣiddīq and Kaʿb ibn Mālik رضي الله عنهما said that the Messenger of Allah's ﷺ face was like the circle of the moon.

Abū al-Ṭufayl رضي الله عنه was asked to describe the Messenger of Allah ﷺ, and said: 'He was white and handsome of face. When he was pleased, it was

14 *Burda*, chapter three.

15 Al-Tirmidhī.

16 Al-Tirmidhī, *Shamā'il.*

as though his face were a mirror with the moon reflected in it.'[17]

Jābir ﷺ said: '[His ﷺ face was] like the sun and the moon, and it was round.'[18]

All the Companions who described the Messenger of Allah ﷺ agreed that his face was bright and filled with light which shone with resplendence and brilliance.

Al-Ḥasan ibn ʿAlī reported that his uncle Hind ibn Abī Hāla said: 'The Messenger of Allah ﷺ had great and stately attributes, and was honoured as such by others. His face shone like the light of the full moon.'[19]

Jābir ibn Samra ﷺ looked upon him one moonlit night, and said of it later: 'I began to look from him to the moon, and to me he was more beautiful than the moon.'[20]

Rubayyiʿ bint Muʿawwidh was asked to describe the Messenger of Allah ﷺ. She said: 'Had you seen him, you would have seen the sun rising.'[21]

Umm Maʿbad described him ﷺ thus: 'I saw a man of visible radiance, his appearance beautiful, his face bright; handsome and fair he was.'[22]

A woman of Hamdān who performed the pilgrimage alongside the Messenger of Allah ﷺ was asked to compare him ﷺ to something. She said: 'Like the moon when it is full. I saw neither before nor after him anyone like him.'[23]

HIS CHEEK

As for his ﷺ blessed cheek, it was perfectly smooth and long, without being high at its ball.

HIS EYES

As for his noble sight, his Lord described it by saying: '*The sight wavered not, nor did it stray*' [53:17]. It is affirmed by authentic narrations that the Messenger of Allah ﷺ could see as well by dark night as he could by

17 Muslim.
18 Muslim.
19 Al-Tirmidhī.
20 Al-Tirmidhī.
21 Al-Tirmidhi, al-Bayhaqī, etc.
22 Al-Bayhaqī, al-Ḥākim.
23 Al-Tirmidhī and al-Bayhaqī, etc.

bright day, and that he could see what was behind him as well as he could see what was in front of him.

The ḥadīth of Ibn Abī Hāla ✿ states: 'When he looked at something, he would turn to it with his whole body. He would lower his gaze, and he spent more time looking at the ground than he did at the sky. He would usually look at things casually, without staring.'[24] That is, he would glance at things from the corner of his eye nearest the temple.

Our master ʿAlī ✿ said: 'His ✿ eyes were large, his eyelashes full; there was a certain redness to his eyes.'[25]

Another narration says 'his ✿ eyes were deep black'[26], and another has it 'reddish eyes'[27] (*ashkal*); this means a slight redness in the whites of the eyes, which is attractive and desirable, as opposed to *shahla*, which means a redness in the pupil of the eye.

HIS HEAD AND BROW

As for his ✿ blessed brow, it was broad and full; this is what ʿAlī ✿ meant by describing it as 'smooth', or in another narration 'wide', or in another 'large'; they all mean essentially the same thing.

His ✿ head was large which is what ʿAlī ✿ meant when he described him ✿ as having 'an ample head'. His ✿ eyebrows were long and arched, but not so long that they actually met in the middle.

HIS NOSE

His nose was curved (*aqnā*), meaning that its top was high, its middle curved, and its lower part wide, or that the middle of the shaft curved outward and the nostrils were narrow.

HIS MOUTH

His mouth was wide; and the Arabs praised wide mouths and disliked small ones. His teeth were well-spaced[28], and his breath was fresh, and his incisors twinkled.

---

24 Al-Tirmidhī.
25 Al-Bayhaqī.
26 Al-Tirmidhī.
27 Muslim.
28 That is, not crammed together too tightly, but perfectly positioned. [t]

PROPHETIC BEAUTY

I T IS well-established that the Prophet 🌿 was endowed with absolute beauty; but this prophetic beauty is crowned by two immense things: the first is awe-inspiring majesty, and the second is resplendent light. This meant that those who saw him 🌿 were not bewitched by his beauty as they were with Yūsuf 🌿; although Yūsuf 🌿 was endowed with half of all beauty, when the women saw him they cut their hands and said '*Glory be to Allah! This is not a human, this is none other than a noble angel!*' [12:31]. A poet said:

Had Zulaykha's ladies seen but the Prophet's brow,
They would have not cut their hands, but cut their hearts.

As for the Prophet's 🌿 awe-inspiring majesty, Hind ibn Abī Hāla said of it: 'The Messenger of Allah 🌿 had great and stately attributes, and was honoured as such by others.'[29]

'Alī 🌿 said: 'Whoever saw him unexpectedly would be awe-stricken.'[30] Others said that the Prophet 🌿 was the most dignified of people in his gatherings.[31] Once a man came to him and was sorely awe-stricken by him and began to quake; so the Prophet 🌿 spoke words to set him at ease.[32] 'Amr ibn al-ʿĀṣ 🌿 said about the Prophet's 🌿 presence: 'I could not look at him directly because of the awe he struck in me; and were I to be asked to describe him, I would not be able to do so, because I never took a firm look at him.'[33] Ibn Abī Hāla further described him: 'When he spoke, his companions would bow their heads as though they were balancing birds upon them.'[34]

The Companions 🌿 were unable to look directly at him 🌿 because of how powerful the awe he inspired in them was, and how dignified his

---

[29]   Al-Tirmidhī.
[30]   Al-Tirmidhī.
[31]   Abū Dāwūd.
[32]   Al-Bukhārī, Ibn Mājah.
[33]   Muslim.
[34]   Al-Tirmidhī, Ibn Saʿd, al-Ṭabarānī.

bearing was. This is why all our descriptions of him ※ come from the youngest of them, or those who were in his care before the mission of prophethood began, such as Hind ibn Abī Hāla ※ and our master ʿAlī ※.

Another aspect of his awe-inspiring majesty and dignity was that those who sat with him ※ would be fearful and might begin to quake and tremble because of the awe he inspired in them; and so he ※ would be gentle and kind to them to still their quaking.

It is reported that Qayla bint Makhrama said: 'When I saw the Messenger of Allah ※ sitting humbly on his heels, I began to shiver in fear. A man said: "O Messenger of Allah, the poor thing is trembling!" The Messenger of Allah ※ said, without looking round to see me: "Poor girl, be at peace!" When he said it, Allah removed the fear that had entered my heart.'

Abū Masʿūd al-Badrī ※ said: 'I was beating a slave-boy of mine [for some offence], when I heard a voice from behind me say: "Watch out, Abū Masʿūd!" I ignored him, out of anger, until he was upon me, and I saw that it was the Messenger of Allah ※. When I saw him ※, the stick fell from my hand in my awe of him. He said to me: "By Allah, Allah has more power over you than you have over this boy!" I replied: "By Allah, O Messenger of Allah, I will never beat another of my slaves again!"'[35]

As for the resplendent light with which the prophetic beauty is crowned, we saw several aspects of it when we spoke of the description of his ※ blessed face. Now this resplendent light was an intrinsic part of him ※, and it was the first of all lights to be created, as is attested by the popularly well-known ḥadīth: 'The first thing Allah created was the light of your Prophet, O Jābir!'[36]

Al-Zarqānī said of this: 'Al-Bayhaqī also narrated it in a slightly different form.' This is not contradicted by the ḥadīth which al-Tirmidhī narrated: 'The first thing Allah created was the Pen', for the two may be synthesised by saying that primacy of the Pen is only relative to all else besides the Muḥammadan Light. It has also been postulated that the meaning of the primacy here is primacy of class; that is, 'The first light Allah created was my light.'

Another narration that affirms this Muḥammadan Light is what ʿAlī ibn al-Ḥusayn heard from his father, who heard from his grandfather

---

35   Muslim, Abū Dawūd, al-Tirmidhī.
36   Narrated by ʿAbd al-Razzāq al-Ṣanʿānī (cf. *al-Mawāhib al-Ladunniyya*).

that the Prophet ﷺ said: 'I was light in the hands of my Lord.' This ḥadīth is narrated by al-Ḥāfiẓ Abū al-Ḥasan ʿAlī ibn Muḥammad ibn al-Qaṭṭān in his *Aḥkām*; Ibn al-Qaṭṭān is well known for his strictness in grading ḥadīth, and for being one of the most diligent of scholars in narration, memorisation, and scrupulousness.

This resplendent Muḥammadan Light is further affirmed by Allah's words: '*There has come unto you from Allah a light, and a Clear Book*' [5:15]. Many scholars have stated that the meaning of 'light' here is Muḥammad ﷺ; this can be found in the exegeses of al-Ṭabarī, Ibn Abī Ḥātim, and al-Qurṭubī. Qatāda is reported as having said: 'By *light*, He means Muḥammad ﷺ.'[37]

Another proof of this Light is the story, affirmed by mass transmission, that when he ﷺ was born his mother saw a light, and there burst forth from him a light which illuminated the palaces of Syria.[38]

A further affirmation of this Light is found in the ḥadīth of al-Ṭabarānī: '...And we saw what seemed to be a light shining from his mouth.' It is reported that Ibn ʿAbbās ؓ said: 'When he ﷺ spoke, something like light could be seen shining from between his incisors.'[39]

It is further attested by the words of Ibn Abī Hāla, as narrated by al-Tirmidhī in his *Shamā'il*: 'He had a light which shone above him.'

It is also reported that our lady ʿĀ'isha said: 'Once I was sitting, and the Prophet ﷺ was mending his shoe. His forehead began to sweat, and light began to shine from the sweat. I started in amazement, and so he ﷺ said: "What makes you start so?" I replied: "Your forehead began to sweat, and the sweat gave off such bright light that if Abū Kabīr al-Hudhalī had seen you, he would have recognised you as more deserving of the poem in which he said:

Free of any recrudescence of menses,
Or corruption of nursing, or dangerous illness.[40]
And when you look at the features of his face,

37 Ibn Jawzī, *Tafsīr.*

38 See *al-Mawāhib.*

39 Al-Tirmidhī, al-Dārimī.

40 This describes a child who was not conceived during the end of a menstrual period, and whose mother did not become pregnant again whilst nursing him, which would have had an adverse affect on his nursing. [t]

They shine with the radiance of a shimmering cloud.'"[41]

Now some ignorant people imagine that the meaning of his ﷺ being light is that his body itself emitted light; this is a delusion and a poor understanding. It is as though they have made him ﷺ a lamp or an electric light; yet he ﷺ is far above being such a thing. Indeed, we have no objection to the assertion that a visible light may have shone forth from him ﷺ, just as it shines forth from radiant and light-emitting objects; but this was not a constant thing, but rather occurred at certain miraculous occasions when it was needed. Indeed, this has also been affirmed for those who were lower than him ﷺ, as it occurred to the great Companion Usayd ibn Ḥuḍayr:

Anas ﷺ is reported to have said: 'Usayd ibn Ḥuḍayr and ʿAbbād ibn Bishr were with the Messenger of Allah ﷺ one night dark as pitch. They spoke with him, and then when they left, one of their staffs lit up so that they could walk by its light. When they came to the point where they went their separate ways, each of their staffs lit up so that they each had a light to walk by.'[42]

Something similar happened to the great Companion al-Ṭufayl ibn ʿAmr al-Dawsī, who was nicknamed 'he of the light': One time he went to the Prophet ﷺ, who prayed for his people. He said, 'Send me to them, and give me a sign!' The Prophet ﷺ said: 'O Allah, illuminate him!', whereupon a light shone out from between his eyes. He said, 'Lord, I fear that they shall say I am ill!' So the light moved to the end of his whip, and thereafter would give him light on dark nights.[43]

41 Ibn ʿAsākir, Abū Nuʿaym, al-Khaṭīb.
42 Al-Bukhārī.
43 Ibn ʿAbd al-Barr.

The Perfect Care he took of his Blessed Appearance

The care he took of his body

The Prophet ﷺ would keep his body clean and command others to do the same. He bathed every week, washed his hands before and after eating, and cleaned his teeth with a tooth-stick (*siwāk*) very frequently.

He would take care to keep the extremities of his body clean and dirt-free, trimming his moustache and his nails, plucking his underarm hairs, and shaving his pubic hair.

He would enjoin and encourage cleanliness and warn against dirtiness, saying: 'Allah is goodly and loves what is goodly; clean and loves cleanliness; generous and loves generosity; munificent and loves munificence.'[44] He ﷺ also said: 'Keep as clean as you can, for Allah has founded Islam upon cleanliness; and none shall enter Paradise but all those who are clean.'[45]

The greatest sign of the cleanliness of his ﷺ blessed body was the sweet scent of his blessed sweat, which was finer than ambergris or musk, and the sweet scent that emitted from him in general, and diffused through any street he walked down; and there is no doubt that this was one of his ﷺ special and unique characteristics.

The care he took of his hair

He ﷺ would care for his blessed hair by cleaning it, combing it, and growing it long. Anas ؓ said: 'The Messenger of Allah ﷺ would often oil his head and comb his beard, and he frequently used a *qināʿ*.'[46] (A *qināʿ* is a piece of cloth placed on the head when using oil, to protect the turban from the oil.)

44 Al-Tirmidhī.

45 The like of it is narrated by al-Ṭabarānī and al-Rāfiʿī (see *Kashf al-khafāʾ*).

46 Al-Tirmidhī.

THE CARE HE TOOK OF HIS EYES

Ibn ʿAbbās ؓ said: 'The Prophet ﷺ used to apply *kohl* to his eyes every night, three applications to each eye.'[47]

THE CARE HE TOOK OF HIS TEETH

The Prophet ﷺ would take care to clean the food from between his teeth after eating. He ﷺ said: 'Ah, how fine are those of my community who clean in between (*al-mutakhallilūn*)!' It was said, 'Who are those who clean in between, O Messenger of Allah?' He ﷺ said: 'Those who clean in between when they make ablutions (*wuḍūʾ*), and those who clean in between after eating. As for cleaning in between when making ablutions, it is to rinse out the nose and mouth and wash between the fingers. As for cleaning in between after eating,[48] it is [praiseworthy] because there is nothing more grievous to the two [guardian] angels than to see food in their charge's teeth as he prays.'[49]

Another way he ﷺ would take care of his blessed teeth and breath was to make frequent use of the tooth-stick (*siwāk*) on all occasions: before praying, when making ablutions, before sleeping, after waking, when coming home, and when going out. He would enjoin and encourage it for others as well, saying: 'The tooth-stick cleans the mouth and pleases the Lord.'[50]

He ﷺ said: 'Were it not that I feared overburdening my community, I would command them to use the tooth-stick before every prayer.'[51] A version narrated by al-Bazzār and al-Ṭabarānī has it: '...I would oblige them to use the tooth-stick before every prayer just as I obliged them to make ablutions.'

THE CARE HE TOOK OF HIS CLOTHING AND COMPORTMENT

The Messenger of Allah ﷺ taught us that good comportment and beautiful clothing are among the traits and innate characteristics of the prophets. Our master Muḥammad ﷺ is the leader of the prophets, and

---

47 Al-Tirmidhī.
48 i.e. using a toothpick.
49 Al-Ṭabarānī.
50 Al-Nasāʾī.
51 Al-Bukhārī.

therefore is the cleanest of all Allah's creation in body, clothing, home, and company. It is reported that someone said of him: 'I never saw the like of this man, nor anyone of a more handsome face or cleaner clothes.'[52]

He ﷺ would ensure his appearance was beautiful, and encourage others to do the same, saying: 'Allah is beautiful and loves beauty.'[53]

He ﷺ would be concerned to dress well for occasions: if a delegation came to him ﷺ, he would make extra effort to receive them well, choosing a fine robe, shirt, or whatever he had to wear that was appropriate for whoever was coming and their status. On the days of Eid, he would wear a special cloak for it, as well as for Fridays. He would enjoin this upon others, saying: 'Beautify your clothes and make good your mounts, until you become, as it were, a blaze[54] among the people.'[55] He also ﷺ said: 'When Allah grants His servant a favour, He loves to see the effect of this favour show upon the servant.'[56] He ﷺ also said: 'One way for the believer to honour Allah is to keep his clothes clean, and to be content with a little.'[57]

The Messenger of Allah ﷺ forbade us from exposing our clothes to dirt, and commanded us to lift them above the ground, saying: 'Raise up your loincloth, for this will keep it cleaner and make it last longer.'[58]

The Care He Took of the Cleanliness of His Home and His Mosque

The Messenger of Allah ﷺ was also concerned with the cleanliness of his home, and loved for it to be clean, and encouraged others to do the same, saying: 'Keep your halls clean.'

He was also concerned with the cleanliness of the mosque, and would be pleased with anyone who undertook to do this task. When the woman who used to clean the mosque died and no one told him ﷺ of it until after she was buried, he was deeply affected and said, 'Why did you not tell me?' Then he went to her grave and prayed for her. There was a certain man who would burn incense in the mosque, who was given the

52 Abū Qarsāfa, al-Ṭabarānī.
53 Muslim, al-Tirmidhī, Aḥmad, etc.
54 The distinctive white stripe down the middle of a horse's face. [t]
55 Al-Ḥākim.
56 Al-Ṭabarānī, al-Bayhaqī.
57 Al-Ṭabarānī, Abū Nuʿaym.
58 Al-Bayhaqī.

name Naʿīm al-Mujammir because of how he would perform this task (*al-mujammir* means 'coal-burner').

He ﷺ did not show this concern for his own mosque only, but encouraged that this be done in all mosques. A ḥadīth reports: 'The Messenger of Allah ﷺ commanded us to build mosques in the neighbourhoods, and he commanded us to keep them clean.'[59] Another narration of this ḥadīth adds: 'And to perfume them [with incense].'

He also commanded that the places of ablution be kept outside the doors of the mosques so that people would not get the mosques dirty; and he forbade people from spitting phlegm in the mosque,[60] and told us that to clean mosques of even the smallest amount of dirt conceivable is an act greatly rewarded by Allah.

His blessed voice

The Messenger of Allah ﷺ had a beautiful voice; Anas ﷺ told us of this when he said: 'Every prophet Allah sent had a beautiful face and a beautiful voice; and your Prophet was the fairest of them in face and voice.'[61]

Al-Barrāʾ ibn ʿĀzib ﷺ said: 'The Messenger of Allah ﷺ recited *sūrat al-Tīn* one evening prayer, and I never heard a finer voice.'[62]

Jubayr ibn Muṭʿim said: 'He ﷺ had a beautiful tone of voice.'[63] His voice had a mellowness to it, as Umm Maʿbad said, meaning that it was soft and also clear. His ﷺ voice was also powerful, and could carry further than other voices: al-Barrāʾ said of it: 'The Messenger of Allah ﷺ addressed us with a voice so powerful it reached even the maidens in their chambers.'[64] Umm Hāniʾ said: 'We used to hear the Prophet ﷺ reciting in the middle of the night at the Kaʿba, whilst I was in my bed.'[65]

59 Al-Tirmidhī.

60 The floors of the mosques at the time would have been plain earth, not carpeted; until comparatively recent times, in Europe too floors were generally covered with straw, into which people would habitually spit. [t]

61 Al-Tirmidhī.

62 Al-Bukhārī, Muslim.

63 Al-Ḍaḥḥāk.

64 Al-Bayhaqī.

65 Ibn Mājah.

The Perfection of the Muḥammadan Heart

The heart of our master Muḥammad ﷺ is the best of all hearts, and the broadest, strongest, holiest, purest, softest, and gentlest. It is an illuminated and awakened heart, overflowing with the resplendent light of faith and the Qurʾān.

The best of hearts is his ﷺ blessed heart; Aḥmad and others narrate that Ibn Masʿūd ؓ said: 'Allah Almighty looked at the hearts of His servants and found the heart of Muḥammad ﷺ to be the best of their hearts; so He elected him for Himself and sent him forth with His message. Then He looked at the hearts of His servants and found that the hearts of his Companions to be the best of their hearts, so He made them the ambassadors of His Prophet ﷺ, sending them forth to struggle for His religion. Thus what the Muslims see as good is good in Allah's sight, and what the Muslims see as evil is evil in Allah's sight.'

His ﷺ blessed heart is also the purest and cleanest of hearts; for his blessed breast was opened in his youth, and all Satan's influence over his heart was removed. Muslim and others narrate that Anas ؓ said: 'Jibrīl ؑ came to the Messenger of Allah ﷺ [in his childhood] while he was playing with his friends. He laid him on his back, opened his chest, and removed his heart. He took a morsel of flesh from the heart, and said: "This is Satan's share [of influence] over you." He then washed the heart in a golden vessel with the water of Zamzam. He then repaired it, replaced it, and closed his chest. The boys went running to his (foster) mother, saying: "Muḥammad has been killed!" He then came to them, and they found that his colour had altered.' Anas added: 'I used to be able to see the mark left by the stitch in his chest ﷺ.'

The first time his ﷺ blessed breast was opened in this way was when he was still a child in the care of his foster-mother Ḥalīma. It happened a second time when he ﷺ was ten years old; the wisdom behind this is that ten is near the age of moral responsibility: his ﷺ heart was opened and sanctified so that it would not be marred by any of the flaws of men.

It happened again a third time when Jibrīl ﷺ came to him ﷺ to begin the transmission of the message. The wisdom behind this – as the rightly-guided scholars have said – was to honour and aid him ﷺ further, and to strengthen and prepare him so to receive what was about to be revealed to him with a firm heart, in the most perfect of sacred and praiseworthy states.

It happened again a fourth time on the night of the Miʿrāj,[66] as al-Bukhārī and Muslim narrate. The wisdom behind this – as the rightly-guided scholars have said – was to further honour and magnify him, and to further prepare him for the moment when he would stand before Allah and partake of intimate discourse with Him, and for the illuminations, mysteries and manifestations of divine Majesty and Beauty which he was about to behold.

Al-Ḥāfiẓ al-Qasṭallānī said, moreover, that all the reports of how his ﷺ blessed breast was opened and his heart removed, and so on, detail miraculous events which must be accepted as they are without any attempts to explain them metaphorically; for it is not beyond the divine power to do such things, and none of it is impossible for Allah.

He also mentioned that al-Suyūṭī spoke of claims made by certain ignorant people of his time that these events did not really take place, and that it is all a metaphor for the 'spiritual heart'; al-Suyūṭī said that such claims are manifest ignorance and grievous error, proving that Allah has forsaken these people because of their obsession with philosophy and their detachment from the subtleties of the Sunnah.

Allah gave His Messenger ﷺ wakefulness of heart, so that he was constantly aware of Allah and directed towards Him, and never overcome by heedlessness. His ﷺ heart was never heedless even as he slept; his dreams were continuations of the Revelation. His sleep did not vitiate his ritual purity as it does for the rest of us. This is attested to by authentic ḥadīths:

Al-Bukhārī and others narrate that 'Ā'isha ﷺ said: 'I said, "O Messenger

[66] The Night of Isrā' and Miʿrāj – the miraculous journey undertaken by the Prophet ﷺ on the mount Burāq and accompanied by Jibrīl ﷺ from Mecca to the Aqsa Mosque, where he ﷺ led a congregation of all previous Prophets in prayer, and from there onto the Seven Heavens and beyond.

of Allah, do you sleep before you offer the *witr* prayer?" He said: "O ʿĀʾisha, my eyes sleep, but my heart does not."'

Al-Bukhārī also narrated that Jābir ﷺ said: 'The angels came to the Prophet ﷺ while he slept. (The narration of al-Tirmidhī has it: 'The Messenger of Allah ﷺ came out to us and said: "I saw in my sleep as though Jibrīl were at my head, and Mikāʾīl at my feet"...') One of them said: "He is asleep." Another said: "The eye sleeps, yet the heart is awake." They said: "There is a similitude for your companion here." He said: "So give the similitude, then!" They said: "His likeness is that of a man who builds a house, and holds a great feast therein. He sends a messenger to invite the people. Those who answer the messenger enter the house, and partake of the feast; those who do not answer the messenger do not enter the house, nor do they partake of the feast." They said: "Explain it to him so he understands." One of them said: "He is asleep." Another said: "The eye sleeps, yet the heart is awake." They said: "The house is Paradise, and the Messenger is Muḥammad ﷺ: whoever obeys Muḥammad ﷺ has obeyed Allah, and whoever disobeys Muḥammad ﷺ has disobeyed Allah..."'

Al-Dārimī narrated in his *Sunan* that someone came to the Prophet ﷺ and said: 'Let your eye sleep, and your ear hear, and your heart perceive!' The Prophet ﷺ said: 'And so, my eyes slept, and my ears heard, and my heart perceived. It was said to me: "A lord built a house, and held a great feast, and sent a messenger to invite the people. Those who answered the messenger entered the house, and partook of the feast, and the lord was pleased with them. Those who did not answer the messenger did not enter the house, nor did they partake of the feast, and the lord was angry with them."

'He said: "Allah is the lord, and Muḥammad is the messenger, and the house is Islam, and the feast is Paradise."'

Lessons from the Story of the Opening of His ﷺ Blessed Breast

1 – The great scholar Ibn al-Munīr said: The opening of his ﷺ breast, and his ﷺ patient endurance of it, was akin to the trial which Allah sent to the Sacrificed One[67]; nay, it was even more difficult and trying, because that was only symbolic[68], whilst this actually happened. What is more, it was repeated, and it occurred to him when he ﷺ was still a young orphan, far from his family.

2 – Shaykh al-Islam Abū al-Ḥasan al-Subkī, Allah have mercy on him, was asked about the black morsel which was removed from his ﷺ heart when his breast was opened, and the angel's words: 'This is Satan's share [of influence] over you.' He answered:

Allah created, in the heart of every human being, a morsel which is receptive to what Satan casts into it. This morsel was removed from his ﷺ heart, so that there was no longer a place therein for Satan to cast anything. This is the meaning of the ḥadīth. Satan then had no influence over him in any case; as for what the angel negated, it was the thing which exists for the human race as a whole; the receptacle was removed, but its existence in the first place did not mean that any demonic insinuations would inevitably have been cast into the heart.

He was then asked, 'Then why did Allah create this receptacle in his ﷺ blessed being to begin with? Couldn't He have created him without it?' He answered:

It is part of the human being, and was created to complete the human form, and it had to be there; and its removal was a divine ennoblement which came later.

Others said that had Allah created His Prophet ﷺ in that way (without

[67] The son of Ibrāhīm ﷺ, affirmed by most scholars to have been Ismāʿīl ﷺ. [t]

[68] Because Allah did not actually make Ibrāhīm ﷺ go ahead with the sacrifice. [t]

the morsel), the human race would not have known anything about it; rather, Allah left it up to Jibrīl ﷺ to remove it, so that they would be able to see the perfection of his inner form, just as they could see the perfection of his outer form.

3 – Shaykh Abū Muḥammad ibn Abī Jamra said:

The wisdom behind the opening of his ﷺ breast, though his heart could have been filled with faith and wisdom without its being opened, was to increase the power of his certitude: in being allowed to see his own breast being opened without his being harmed, he was given an assurance that he was safe from all conventional dangers. This is why he ﷺ was the bravest of men in word and deed; and thus Allah described him by saying: '*The sight wavered not, nor did it stray*' [53:17].

4 – Concerning the wisdom of the repetition of this event, al-Ḥāfiẓ Ibn Ḥajar said, after mentioning the first, third, and fourth times:

Each of these three has its wisdom: The first was during the time of childhood, so that he ﷺ would grow up in the most perfect state of protection from Satan. Then when he ﷺ was sent forth as a prophet, it further honoured him so that he could receive what would come to him with a strong and perfectly pure heart. Then it happened again before he ascended to the heavens to prepare him for intimate discourse [with Allah].

Al-Ḥāfiẓ al-Shāmī said after mentioning and affirming the second time in his *Kitāb al-Tawḥīd*:

I was asked about the wisdom of this second time, and said that since eight is the age of reason and [near] the age of moral responsibility, his ﷺ breast was opened and sanctified so that it would not be marred by any of the flaws of men; and Allah knows best.

Al-Ḥāfiẓ Ibn Ḥajar also said:

The wisdom behind this [repeated] washing may have been to attain unto the thorough cleansing which occurs with the third washing, as was the Prophet's ﷺ custom [when performing ablutions].[69]

[69] That is, just as when we perform ritual ablutions (*wuḍū'*) we wash our limbs three times,

Ibn Abī Jamra, Allah rest his soul, said:

His ﷺ heart was washed even though it was already sanctified and ready to receive the goodness cast into it – and it was first washed when he was ﷺ still young, and the morsel was removed from it – as a veneration and a preparation for what he would experience there [on the Miʿrāj]. This same principle is found in other places, such as in the ablution for prayer; for the ablution is nothing but a veneration and a preparation for standing before Allah and partaking of intimate discourse with Him. This is why it is Sunnah to wash more than once, even if the first washing was sufficient; for the second and third washings are meant as veneration. The same is the case for the repeated washings of his ﷺ heart. Allah says: '*And whosoever venerates the sacraments of Allah – that comes from the piety of the hearts*' [22:32]. The washing of his heart ﷺ was of this nature, and was an allusion for his community to the veneration of sacraments, as is conveyed by these words.

Al-Burhān al-Nuʿmānī, Allah rest his soul, said:

It is a good action to bathe before entering the Sacred Precinct; so what think you of entering the Holy Presence? Since the Sacred Precinct is in the physical realm, it is fitting to bathe the physical body before entering it. And since the Holy Presence is in the spiritual realm, it is fitting to bathe the inner being before entering it. Now he ﷺ was taken up to the heavens to lead the angels in prayer, and prayer requires purity; so he ﷺ was sanctified both physically and spiritually.

Now you might say: 'Allah created him ﷺ as a light passed from one prophet to the next, and light is pure enough not to need physical cleansing. And wasn't the first washing enough, for otherwise this would imply that after his ﷺ prophethood began there was something in him that needed to be cleansed? Yet he is completely above being sullied by human flaws.'

We reply: the first [washing] was for the certain knowledge, the second for certain vision, and the third for true certainty.

5 – Al-Suhaylī said:

---

so the Prophet's ﷺ heart was also washed three times. [t]

The use of gold was especially apt on this occasion. If you look at the word *dhahab* [Arabic for 'gold'], you will see that it is connected to *dhahāb* ['to go', 'to remove']. Allah wanted to remove all impurity from him ﷺ and cleanse him completely. Furthermore, if you consider gold and its qualities, you will see that it is the cleanest and purest of materials.

6 – Ibn Abī Jamra said that the reason he ﷺ was not washed with the water of Paradise is that the water of Zamzam originated in Paradise and then settled on earth; this symbolises how his ﷺ blessing will always remain on earth.

Others say that the water of Zamzam was first bequeathed to Ismāʿīl ﷺ, and he was raised on it, so that his heart and his body grew by its nourishment, so that he became linked to it and to the blessed land from which it sprung. Because of this, it was appropriate that the same be true of his sincere and sincerely-accepted descendant ﷺ. It also symbolised how this would ever be especially associated with him; and on the day of the conquest of Mecca, when authority over the place became his ﷺ, he put al-ʿAbbās ؓ and his heirs in charge of watering the pilgrims, and ʿUthmān ibn Shayba and his heirs in charge of draping the Kaʿba, until the Day of Resurrection.

7 – The wisdom behind his ﷺ heart being washed with ice and cold water, besides the fact that it is healing and fresh and unsullied with impurities, is that it symbolised how the time had come for him ﷺ and for his community to arise, and that it was time for the refreshing arrival of his way and his noble law. It also symbolised the delight of his heart[70] in the victory he would be granted over his enemies, and the coolness of his heart, i.e. his tranquillity towards his community in the forgiveness and clemency he showed them, despite their sins.

Ibn Duḥayya said:

He washed his ﷺ heart with ice to symbolise the imparting of cold certitude to his heart. He used to say in the prayer, after reciting Qurʾān: 'O Allah, cleanse me of my faults with ice and cool water.' Allah wanted to cleanse his ﷺ heart with water borne from Paradise in a golden vessel filled with wisdom and faith, so that his heart would know the joy of

70 *Thulūj al-ṣadr*, an Arabic expression which literally means 'iciness of heart', used metaphorically to mean 'joy'. [t]

Paradise and taste its sweetness, which would make him all the more detached from this world and eager to call mankind unto Paradise. It was also because he had enemies who were saying evil things about him, so Allah wanted to remove from him the human traits of anxiety and offense caused by enemies; He washed his ﷺ heart to impart peace of mind to him, and rid him of any anxiety, as He says: '*Well We know that your breast is straitened by what they say*' [15:97]. With the repeated washings of his ﷺ heart, he became such that even if he were struck, or his head was split and his teeth broken, as happened at Uḥud, he would say: 'O Allah, forgive my people, for they know not.'

8 – The scholars differ over the meaning of the word 'wisdom' (*ḥikma*).[71] It has been said that it means knowledge that comprises gnosis of Allah, penetrating insight, refinement of soul, and acting in accordance with the truth and keeping away from its opposite; the wise man is the one who has all these things. Imam al-Nawawī said: 'This is the synthesis of the best we have heard said on the matter.'

The word *ḥikma* can also be used as a euphemism for the Qurʾān, which contains all of this, and as a euphemism for prophethood as well. It could also mean simply knowledge, or simply gnosis, or the like.

Al-Ḥāfiẓ Ibn Ḥajar said:

The most correct definition advanced for it is that it means to put things in their right places, or to understand the Book of Allah. According to the former[72] explanation, wisdom might exist apart from faith; according to the latter,[73] they are inclusive of each other, since faith indicates wisdom.

It is also worthy of note that the great Knower of Allah, al-Ḥabīb Imām Sayyid ʿAlī al-Ḥabashī, composed these lines concerning the opening of the prophetic chest and the removal of Satan's share from it:

The angels took no blemish from his heart;

[71] The occasion for this discussion is the ḥadīth narrated by Muslim wherein the Prophet ﷺ described the occasion when his heart was washed before the Miʿrāj, saying: '...[Jibrīl] brought forth a vessel of gold filled with wisdom and faith and emptied it into my chest.' [t]

[72] Ibn Ḥajar's expression here has 'second' (*thānī*), but I cannot see how he could be referring to anything but the former definition ('to put things in their right places'). [t]

[73] Ibn Ḥajar's expression here has 'first' (*awwal*), but I cannot see how he could be referring to anything but the latter definition ('to understand the Book of Allah'). [t]

They only increased the purity he already had!

Another meaning occurred to my heart as well, which is that the heart of our master Muḥammad ﷺ was filled with mercy – nay, it is the font and source of mercy, as Allah says: *'And We sent you not but as a mercy to the worlds'* [21:107]. This mercy was comprehensive and total, because it is the mercy of Allah Himself, which encompasses all things. But Allah ﷻ removed Satan, his aids, his brethren and all the damned from this mercy, so that they have no share of it. The meaning, then, is that the angels removed from his ﷺ heart Satan's share of his mercy, so that Satan will not partake of this mercy. Allah knows best.

The Perfection of His ﷺ Intellect

A PERFECT intellect is the root of good qualities and upright attributes, and by its means virtues are attained and vices avoided. It leads one to all that is good and virtuous. This is made clear by the ḥadīth which tells the tale of how Khālid ibn al-Walīd entered Islam. Khālid ﷺ told of how he went to the Messenger of Allah ﷺ and greeted him: 'He answered my greeting with a cheery face. I said, "I testify that there is no god but Allah, and that you are the Messenger of Allah." He said, "Come forward", so I went forward. The Messenger of Allah ﷺ said, "Praise be to Allah, who has guided you; indeed, I saw that you had an intellect which I expected would lead you only unto goodness."'[74]

Al-Ṭabarānī narrated, on the authority of Qurra ibn Hubayra ﷺ, that he went to the Prophet ﷺ, and said: 'We used to have gods and goddesses whom we worshipped instead of Allah ﷻ: we called them, but they did not answer us; and we asked them, but they did not give unto us. So we came to you, and Allah guided us through you, and now we worship Allah.' The Messenger of Allah ﷺ said: 'Successful indeed is he who is granted sagacity.'

The intellect of our Master Muḥammad ﷺ, the Messenger of Allah, reached a level of superiority and perfection not reached by anyone but he, by Allah's grace and favour over him ﷺ.

Allah ﷻ said: [Nūn. By the pen, and by that which they write, by the grace of your Lord, you are not mad] [68:1-2]. That is, you are at the highest level of intellectual brilliance and distinction, for Allah ﷻ has sworn by His word [Nūn], which is abundant divine assistance; and by the original, comprehensive pen; and by that which the recorders write in the highest of stations, the scratches of whose pens the Messenger of Allah ﷺ heard; and by that which is written by all the pens derived from the original one.

With this mighty oath, Allah bore witness to the extensiveness of the intellect of this noble Messenger ﷺ, and declared that there was no trace of

[74] Al-Bayhaqī.

madness in him, and that he was the possessor of nothing less than a perfect intellect, and superior breadth of knowledge. How should his intellect not be above all intellects, when Allah has blessed him, and favoured him, and chosen him for the final, comprehensive prophetic message, and the revelation of the Qur'ān, in which all knowledge is encompassed? Such a blessing cannot be borne except by one whom Allah has distinguished with the most complete and superior of intellects. For this reason, He said: [By the grace of your Lord, you are not mad.] That is, by virtue of your Lord's blessing you with prophethood and revelation, and the Qur'ān, which comprises the entirety of knowledge and wisdom, you are not mad. This negates what the Prophet's ﷺ enemies fabricated about him, and decisively confirms the superiority of his intellect and wisdom.

How can it be conceived that the one who received revelation of the Qur'ān, which comprises the entirety of knowledge and learning, and received revelation of the highest wisdom, above all others, could have had the slightest hint of imbalance, or imperfection?[75]

The upright *Tābiʿī*, Wahb ibn Munabbih, from whom Bukhārī, Muslim and others narrated ḥadīth, said: 'I read seventy-one scriptures (from previous revelations), and deduced from all of them that Allah ﷻ did not give to any of humanity, from the world's beginning to its end, intellects comparable to Muḥammad's ﷺ intellect, except as a single grain of sand compared to all the sand in the world; and [I deduced from them] that Muḥammad ﷺ is the most intelligent and soundest in judgement of all humanity.'[76]

The perfection of his ﷺ intellect was manifested in how he ﷺ confronted a world whose every realm was infested with ignorance to the extent that the people had utterly lost their minds, and changed this mentality into a sound and righteous mentality. To do this requires sound intellect and correct thought; and there is no doubt that this was achieved by means of the teachings of the Most Wise and the inspiration of the Lord of the worlds. But even divine teachings and inspirations require an illuminated and illuminating intellect, divinely prepared to convey them.

The perfection of his ﷺ intellect was also manifested in the way he

[75] Shaykh ʿAbdallāh Sirājuddīn al-Ḥusayni, *Our Master Muḥammad ﷺ The Messenger of Allah* (Sunni Publications 2008), vol. 1, pp. 119-120.

[76] *Sharḥ al-Mawāhib.*

ﷺ reasoned with the idolaters and presented his proofs to the Jews and Christians, and how he convinced them, dumbfounded them and frustrated their arguments.

The perfection of his ﷺ intellect was also manifested in the way he ﷺ taught the young man who came to him asking permission to fornicate, by saying: 'Would you like it if people fornicated with your mother, your sister, or your daughter?' The man said no. 'Other people hate this, too,' said the Prophet ﷺ. The man's only response was to say: 'I call you to witness that I have repented of fornication!'[77]

The perfection of his ﷺ intellect was also manifested in the wisdom he ﷺ displayed on the day that Quraysh bade him pass judgement over the issue of the Black Stone. The story is that when Quraysh rebuilt the Kaʿba, they disagreed as to who would have the task of setting the Black Stone in its place; every tribe wanted to have the honour of placing it alone. The dispute became heated, to the point where two tribes, ʿAbd al-Dār and ʿAdī, dipped their hands in a basin of blood and vowed to fight unto the death.[78] Quraysh were unable to resolve the conflict for four of five nights, until finally they gathered at the Sanctuary and reached a compromise, agreeing that they would bid whomever next entered the door of the Sanctuary to make the decision. It so happened that the first to enter was the Messenger of Allah ﷺ. When they saw him, they said, 'Ah, it is the Trustworthy One! We are happy to let Muḥammad decide.' When he ﷺ came to them and they explained what was to be done, he ﷺ bade them bring him a cloth. When it was brought forth, he placed the Black Stone in the middle of it and instructed each tribe to take hold of a piece of the cloth's edge and lift it up all together. They did so, and carried the Stone over to its proper place, and then the Prophet ﷺ set it in its place with his own hand.[79]

77 Aḥmad.

78 A pagan Arab custom. [t]

79 *Sharḥ al-Mawāhib*.

His ﷺ Vigilance

The perfection of his ﷺ intellect was further manifested in the vigilant way he dealt with those who declared enmity against him, and the precautions he took against them, and how he caused their schemes to backfire. One example of this is how he instructed Zayd ibn Thābit ﷺ to learn the script and language of the Jews, in order to be guarded from their plots and schemes.[80] This is why it is said, 'Learn a people's language and you will be safe from their plots.'

Before the battles of Badr and al-Aḥzāb, he ﷺ sent out scouts to find out how many troops the enemy had and how well armed they were. This indicates his complete vigilance, in which the perfection of his blessed intellect was manifested. On the day of al-Aḥzāb, he ﷺ sent Nuʿaym ibn Masʿūd al-Ashjaʿī to infiltrate the ranks of the enemy and spread dissent among them, saying to him: 'Sow dissent [amongst them] for us, if you can; for war is deception.'[81] Likewise, he ﷺ would conceal his military strategies from his enemies so that they could not discover them and prepare for them or gather more forces to meet them; and this saved many lives.

All of this shows his perfect vigilance in utilising the means for protection and caution, or the means for striking fear and dread into the hearts of enemies; and all this was due to his ﷺ perfect intellect.

80 Al-Ḥāfiẓ al-ʿAsqalānī, in *al-Iṣāba*, ascribed it to Bukhārī as a narration of *taʿlīq* (i.e. one in which he mentioned the chain of narration whilst not mentioning one or more narrators on his end of the chain), and to al-Baghawī and Abū Yaʿlā with unbroken chains of transmission.

81 Al-Ṭabarī, al-Munāwī.

His ﷺ Amiability in Social Settings

The perfection of his ﷺ intellect was further manifested in his friendliness and amiability when interacting with people, whatever their social status, in order to win their affection and draw them towards the truth which he had been sent to convey. He would be sociable with fools and simpletons in order to curb their mischief and evils, and to attract their hearts to righteousness and guidance. He would meet even the worst of people with a cheery face, in order to win their affection.

He ﷺ would say: 'Sociability towards others is charity.'[82] Sociability is a praiseworthy quality, and is not the same thing as sycophancy; for sociability means to sacrifice a worldly matter for the good of something else, whether worldly, religious, or both; sycophancy, on the other hand, means to sacrifice a religious matter for the sake of a worldly one.

[82] Ibn ʿUdayy, al-Ṭabarānī.

His ﷺ Wise Selection of Envoys

The perfection of his ﷺ intellect was further manifested in his selection of intelligent, sagacious envoys to be sent to rulers and kings to spread the message and advance wise and well-reasoned arguments. This is apparent from the skilful way they presented their case to these kings, and the powerful reasoning they employed.

An example: The Messenger of Allah ﷺ sent al-ʿAlāʾ ibn al-Ḥaḍramī to al-Mundhir ibn Sāwā with a written message inviting him to embrace Islam. When al-ʿAlāʾ reached al-Mundhir, he said: 'O Mundhir, you are a man of great sagacity, so do not allow yourself to be humiliated in the hereafter. This Zoroastrianism is an evil religion, which does not befit the nobility of the Arabs. It is not a characteristic of the people of true scripture that they marry those whom it is shameful to marry,[83] or that they eat that which it is dishonourable to eat, or that they worship in this world the same fire that will consume them on the Day of Resurrection. You are not a senseless man, nor a simpleton. Ask yourself, if a person never lies about this worldly life, is it appropriate to doubt him? If a person is never disloyal, is it appropriate to suspect him? If a person never fails to keep his word, is it appropriate to mistrust him?

'If all this is so, then here we have an unlettered prophet of whom, by Allah, no intelligent person can say: "If only he had prohibited that which he has enjoined, and enjoined that which he has permitted," or: "If only he would be more merciful, or less severe in requital." In all of these respects, he is in line with the expectations of those endowed with intelligence, and the thoughts of those endowed with discernment.'

Mundhir said to him: 'I have examined this Zoroastrian religion of mine, and have found it to be of use for this world, but not for the Hereafter. I have examined your religion, and found it to be of use both for the Hereafter and for this world. What is there to prevent me from accepting a religion in which there is contentment in life, and repose in death? Yesterday I was astounded by those who accepted it; today I am astounded by any who would refuse it. Part of extolling a message is to

83 This refers to the ancient Zoroastrian practice of adulterous marriage. [t]

extol the Messenger. I will consider the matter.'

Now the meaning of al-Mundhir's statement 'I will consider the matter' is that he would consider whether he would go and visit the Messenger of Allah ﷺ, or write to him, not that he would consider whether to embrace Islam or not; his words 'today I am astounded by any who would refuse it' show that he considered Islam to be the true religion.[84]

Another example: The Messenger of Allah ﷺ sent al-Muhājir ibn Abī Umayya al-Makhzūmī, the brother of Umm Salama the Mother of the Believers, to al-Ḥārith ibn ʿAbd Kulāl, one of the kings of Ḥumayr. When al-Muhājir met al-Ḥārith, he said: 'O Ḥārith, you were the first of those to whom the Prophet showed himself, and you neglected him. You are one of the most powerful kings; yet, when you consider the supremacy of kings, consider also the One who will conquer all kings. If today pleases you, fear tomorrow; for there were kings before you whose traces are gone but whose legends remain. They lived long, and their hopes were high but their preparations scant. Some of them were taken by death, and some of them were consumed by misfortune. I call you to the Lord who, if you desire guidance, will not withhold it from you; and if He desires anything for you, no one can keep it from you. I call you to the Unlettered Prophet: there is nothing finer than that which he enjoins, and nothing fouler than that which he prohibits. Know that you have a Lord who deals death to the living and gives life to the dead, and who knows the treachery of the eyes and what the heart conceals.'[85]

Another example: Ḥāṭib ibn Abī Baltaʿa said: 'The Messenger of Allah ﷺ sent me with a written message to al-Muqawqis, King of Alexandria. I took the Messenger of Allah's ﷺ message to him and he brought me into his home, where I spent several nights. He then sent for me, having assembled all his priests, and said: "I will now say things to you which I hope you will understand." I bade him go on, and he said: "Tell me about your companion: is he not a prophet?" "Indeed he is", I said, "he is the Messenger of Allah." "Why then", he said, "did he not pray against his people when they expelled him from his hometown?" I said to him: "Consider Jesus, son of Mary: do you testify that he was the Messenger of Allah?" He said that indeed this was so. "Then why", I said, "when his people seized him and wanted to crucify him, did he not pray to Allah

84 *Sharḥ al-Mawāhib.*

85 *Al-Rawḍ al-Unuf.*

to destroy them? [He did not], and in the end Allah raised him up into the heavens."

'"Well done", [Muqawqis] said. "You are wise, and have come from one who is wise. Here are some gifts for you to take back to Muḥammad, and I shall send guards with you to protect you on your homeward journey." He gave the Messenger of Allah ﷺ three maidservants: one of them later bore Ibrāhīm, the son of the Messenger of Allah ﷺ; another the Messenger of Allah ﷺ gave to Abū Jahm ibn Ḥudhayfa al-'Adawī; and another he gave to Ḥassān ibn Thābit al-Anṣārī. He also sent some robes made of their fine cloth.'[86]

86 *Al-Bidāya wal-Nihāya.*

His ﷺ Perfect Physical Strength

Allah combined in our master Muḥammad ﷺ both courage of heart and strength of body; and this constitutes perfect masculinity.

Our master Jābir ﷺ said: 'On the day of the Trench, we were digging when I came across a rock which could not be budged. They went to the Prophet ﷺ and said, "This rock is blocking us from digging the trench." He said, "I will go down", and then did so. When he stood, [I could see that] there was a stone tied to his stomach[87] – for we had not eaten in three days. The Prophet ﷺ took up the shovel and struck the rock, and it shattered into powder.'[88]

Some narrations of this story state that they did not go to the Messenger of Allah ﷺ until after they had proved unable to move the rock, and broken their spades on it; these narrations also state that the Messenger of Allah ﷺ only struck the rock three times before it broke. His ﷺ strength was such that the rock could only withstand three blows from him after having completely exhausted his Companions ﷺ despite their best efforts to budge it. This was how strong he ﷺ was after going three days without eating, so that he had to tie a stone to his stomach to abate his hunger. We all know how hunger weakens the body – so what do you imagine the hunger of going three days without food would be like? Had he ﷺ not been so hungry, there is no doubt that his strength would have been even greater still – and can you imagine this strength?

Isḥāq ibn Yassār reported that the Messenger of Allah ﷺ said to Rukāna ibn ʿAbd Yazīd: 'Enter Islam.' He replied, 'If I knew what you say to be true, I would do so.' Now Rukāna was one of the hardiest of people around, so the Messenger of Allah ﷺ said to him: 'Tell me – if I were to outwrestle you, would you know that it is the truth?' He said yes, so the Messenger of Allah ﷺ stood up and outwrestled him. 'Do it again, Muḥammad', he said, so the Messenger of Allah ﷺ repeated the feat, taking hold of him and throwing him to the ground a second time. Rukāna stormed away, saying: 'Such sorcery as this have I never seen in

87 To prevent it from distending through hunger. [t]

88 Al-Bukhārī, Ibn Saʿd, Ibn Jarīr, Ibn Abī Ḥātim, al-Bayhaqī, Abū Nuʿaym.

my life! By Allah, I was powerless to do anything when he pinned my side to the ground.'[89] Another narration of this story, reported by Rukāna himself, states that indeed he did enter Islam after this – may Allah be pleased with him!

Reflect on Rukāna's words 'I was powerless to do anything when he pinned my side to the ground'. From these words we can see that Rukāna ﷺ was easily overpowered by the Prophet's ﷺ hand as if he was nothing, even though Rukāna was in fact the strongest man of Quraysh, and had never been outwrestled by anyone before that day.

89 Abū Nuʿaym, al-Bayhaqī.

HIS ﷺ PERFECT KNOWLEDGE[90]

THE MESSENGER of Allah ﷺ was endowed with broad knowledge and deep understanding; Allah showered him with an abundance of beneficial knowledge and profound wisdom. Allah acknowledged the breadth of his ﷺ knowledge and announced the magnitude of his virtue by saying: [Allah has revealed unto you scripture and wisdom, and taught you what you knew not. The grace of Allah upon you has been great] [4:113].

He ﷺ is the most knowledgeable of Allah's creation, and the most well-acquainted of them with Allah; al-Bukhārī and Muslim narrate that he ﷺ said: 'The most god-fearing (atqā) of you, and the most knowledgeable (a'lam) of you concerning Allah, is I.' The narration of Aṣīlī has it: 'I am the most well-acquainted (a'raf)[91] of you with Allah.'

Whoever ponders Allah's instruction of His messengers and prophets (may Allah bless them and give them peace), as mentioned in the Holy Qur'ān, will plainly deduce that our master Muḥammad ﷺ was given by Allah knowledge of the greatest, amplest, broadest, and most extensive degree. This is because Allah ﷻ said: [And [He] taught you what you knew not], using the term [what], which implies comprehensiveness and encompassment, thus including all the knowledge that Allah ﷻ conveyed unto His messengers and prophets, as well as all the other things that Allah ﷻ conveyed unto him ﷺ alone.

Al-Bukhārī and Muslim narrate[92] that Anas ؓ said: 'The people would continuously put questions to the Prophet of Allah ﷺ, until they had asked him a copious amount of questions. One day, he ﷺ came out and climbed the pulpit and said: "Ask me: you will not ask anything except that I will answer it for you[93] ... Never have I seen good and evil such as I have seen this day: Paradise and Hell were shown to me, and I saw them

---

[90]   This chapter is largely drawn from Imam 'Abdullāh Sirājuddīn's study of the Prophet's ﷺ knowledge in Part III of *Our Master Muḥammad* ﷺ, vol. 1, and may be considered a summary of it. [t]

[91]   The difference between the Arabic terms 'ilm (knowledge) and ma'rifa (acquaintance) is subtle, and the two are often used interchangeably in ordinary speech. [t]

[92]   The wording here is that of Muslim.

[93]   One narration has it that he said: '...except that I will inform you concerning it, as long as I stand here.'

right in front of this wall.'"

One aspect of the breadth of his ﷺ knowledge is that Allah gave him the Qur'ān, with all the teachings and truths that are gathered therein. The Qur'ān is an ocean of knowledge and wisdom; and 'Alī ibn Abī Ṭālib ؓ said: 'If I spoke to you about *surat al-Fātiḥa*, it[94] would over-burden seventy camels.' What, then, of the knowledge of our master Muḥammad ﷺ, and the understanding that the Qur'ān imparted unto him?

Another aspect of the breadth of his ﷺ knowledge is the many aspects of the unseen (*al-ghayb*) that Allah imparted unto him. Allah says: [[He is] the Knower of the unseen, and He discloses His secret to none / save those Messengers whom He has chosen...) [72:26]. Allah divulged many aspects of the unseen to him ﷺ, including his ﷺ knowledge of everything from the beginning of creation until the people of Paradise enter Paradise and the people of Hell enter Hell. This is affirmed by the ḥadīth narrated by al-Bukhārī on the authority of 'Umar ibn al-Khaṭṭāb ؓ, in which he said: 'The Messenger of Allah ﷺ stood before us and informed us of everything from the beginning of creation until the people of Paradise enter Paradise, and the people of Hell enter Hell. Some of us remembered it, and some of us forgot it.'

Al-Bukhārī and Muslim also narrate that al-Hudhayfa said: 'The Messenger of Allah ﷺ stood before us and spoke, and did not leave anything [of all that will occur] until the Hour without making mention of it; some of us retained knowledge of it, and some of us did not. Thereafter I would see things I had forgotten and recognise them, just as one recognises a man one used to know when seeing him after a long absence.'

The Prophet ﷺ also gave information about that which would come to pass after him until the Day of Resurrection. Muslim narrates that 'Amr ibn Akhṭab al-Anṣārī ؓ said: 'The Messenger of Allah ﷺ led us in the dawn prayer one day, and then ascended the pulpit, and spoke to us until the midday prayer arrived. He came down, prayed, and then climbed the pulpit again, and spoke to us until the afternoon prayer. He came down, prayed, and then climbed the pulpit again, and spoke to us until sunset. He informed us of everything that would come to pass until the Day of Resurrection; the best informed of us are those who remember best.'

So he ﷺ did not leave a single matter that would come to pass until the Day of Resurrection without informing them of it.

---

94   That is, the books on which this would be written. [t]

Abū Dāwūd narrated that Ḥudhayfa ؓ said: 'By Allah, I do not know if my companions were made to forget, or if they simply forgot. By Allah, the Messenger of Allah ﷺ did not neglect to mention a single mischief-monger until the end of the world whose supporters numbered three hundred or more; he identified each one by his name, his father's name, and the name of his tribe.'

It is also reported that he ﷺ informed us about all the various tidings of the Hour, minor, medial and major; and the conditions of the Hereafter and its partitions; and the condition of the people of Paradise and the people of Hell, and details of all that is concerned with them. All of this is clearly shown in the books of the Sunnah. This is evidence of the breadth of the knowledge that Allah bestowed upon him ﷺ.

Another aspect of this was his ﷺ knowledge of the different realms (*al-ʿawālim*), as is attested to in the rigorously authenticated ḥadīths of the Miʿrāj, which tell how he ﷺ was taken up to the seven heavens, entering them all one by one, and seeing within them all that he saw; and how he met with the messengers (peace and blessings be upon them). It is also related that Allah showed the realm of the Throne to him ﷺ; for he ﷺ spoke about the Throne, saying that it is the vastest of all realms, and that it has a shadow, and has legs, and is encrusted with treasures. He ﷺ also spoke about the Throne-bearers and their strength and might. The *Musnad* narrates that the Prophet ﷺ said: 'I am Muḥammad, the Unlettered Prophet, and there shall be no prophet after me! [He repeated this three times.] I have been given the openings and the keys of speech, and I have been taught the number of the keepers of Hell, and the bearers of the Throne...'

It is also related that Allah showed him ﷺ the realms of Paradise and Hell, which were made manifest to him on numerous occasions, as in the ḥadīth of the Miʿrāj: '... Then I was entered into Paradise, wherein were domes of pearl, and whose dust was fragrant musk.'

It is also reported that Allah showed him ﷺ the realm of the Isthmus (*al-Barzakh*), and its states and affairs; and the realm of the Gathering and the state of mankind therein; and the realms of the Presentation (*al-ʿArḍ*), the Pool, the collection of the Records, the Reckoning, the Scale, and the Bridge; and the condition of the denizens of Paradise and the denizens of Hell; and he ﷺ spoke of all these realms, and described them in detail.

It is also reported that Allah showed him ﷺ the higher realms, and what takes place among the Supreme Assembly,[95] and their contention over atonements and ranks[96]; and all things were revealed to him, and he gained knowledge of them, as is related in the ḥadīth narrated by al-Tirmidhī, Aḥmad, and others in which he ﷺ said: 'I woke one night and prayed that which was destined for me; and I dozed in my prayer, until my sleep became heavy. I found myself with my Lord ﷻ, and He said to me: "O Muḥammad! For what does the Highest Gathering contend? I said: "I do not know."'

This ḥadīth shows that Allah granted the Prophet ﷺ such extensive knowledge that he said: 'And so all things were revealed to me, and I recognised them.[97] Then He said to me: "O Muḥammad! For what does the Highest Gathering contend?" I said: "For atonements, and ranks..."'

Another aspect of the breadth of his ﷺ knowledge is his ﷺ familiarity with the various species of creatures and the living things, the laws[98] that govern them, and their circumstances, and all other details concerning them.

Al-Ṭabarānī narrated, with a chain of narration the men of which are all rigorously authenticated, that Abū al-Dardāʾ ﷺ said: 'Before the Messenger of Allah ﷺ parted from us, there was not a single bird flying with its wings[99] save that he had taught us some knowledge pertaining to it.' In another narration, al-Ṭabarānī added that the Prophet ﷺ said: 'There is nothing that draws one close to Paradise, and distances one from Hell, save that I have made it clear to you all.'

Thus we see that he ﷺ imparted to the Companions a great deal of information about the world of birds, which is evidence that his ﷺ knowledge of the species of the entire world must have been vast. It is also evidence that he ﷺ clarified every important matter of creation that pertained to the benefit of the world and the happiness of mankind, in whatever way it might have been. For if he ﷺ took it upon himself to pass on information about the world of the birds, how could it be imagined that he neglected to clarify any detail concerning the betterment of

95 Of angels.

96 For mankind.

97 In one narration: 'and He taught me all things,' and in another: 'and He did not ask me anything save that I knew it.'

98 Whether natural or religious.

99 Imam Aḥmad's version has it: 'flapping its wings in the sky.'

mankind, failing to mention it and yet mentioning the world of the birds and its details? It cannot be imagined; rather, the Prophet ﷺ surely told us of all that is needed to achieve betterment and happiness for mankind.

This said, the fact remains that the oceans of his ﷺ knowledge cannot be encompassed by any but Allah, who showered them upon him. Al-Bukhārī and Muslim narrate[100] that Anas ؓ said: 'The Prophet ﷺ came out one day when the sun passed its zenith, and prayed the midday prayer. When the prayer ended, he ascended the pulpit, and mentioned the Hour, and said that before its arrival would come grave matters. He then said: "Whoever wishes to ask about anything, let him ask now, for by Allah, there is nothing you might ask me except that I will inform you of it, as long as I stand here." The Helpers began to weep copiously, and the Messenger of Allah repeated again and again: "Ask me!" A man stood up and said: "What is my fate, O Messenger of Allah?" He said: "Hell." ʿAbdullāh ibn Ḥudhāfa stood up and said: 'Who is my father, O Messenger of Allah?" He said: "Your father is Ḥudhāfa."

'He ﷺ then repeated many times: "Ask me! Ask me!" ʿUmar sank to his knees and said: "We are pleased with Allah as our Lord, and with Islam as our religion, and with Muḥammad ﷺ as our Messenger!" The Messenger of Allah ﷺ fell silent at ʿUmar's words, and then said: "By the One in whose hand is my soul, Paradise and Hell were shown to me, in the place of this wall, as I was praying presently. Never have I seen good and evil as I have seen them today.'

So we see that the Messenger of Allah ﷺ gave the Companions permission to ask about anything that occurred to them, for as long as he stood in that place.

100 Al-Bukhārī's wording is used here.

His ﷺ Perfect Eloquence

THE MESSENGER of Allah ﷺ was the most eloquent and well-spoken of Allah's creatures. He was given comprehensive and concise speech, astonishing wisdom, stern rebuke, decisive command, solid judgement, sound advice, profound counsel, irrefutable arguments, conclusive proofs, and manifest evidences. In this regard, he ﷺ said of himself: 'I am Muḥammad, the Unlettered Prophet, and there shall be no prophet after me! [He ﷺ repeated this three times.] I have been guided to the best ways of speech, and given its compendium[101]...'[102]

How could he not be the most eloquent of Allah's creation, when Allah gave him a way of speaking that expressed so much with such few words? He once said from the pulpit: 'O People! I have been given the compendium of speech and its keys, and for me it has been made as concise as can be.'[103] ʿUmar ؓ once asked him about the secret of his eloquence, saying: 'O Prophet of Allah, how can it be that you are the most eloquent of us, when you never left our sight?'[104] He ﷺ replied: 'The tongue of Ismāʿīl had vanished,[105] and so Jibrīl brought it to me and I retained it.'[106]

All were agreed that Muḥammad ﷺ, though unlettered, was given a miraculously concise mode of speech unrivalled by any teacher or student, however expert in Arabic they may have been. He possessed the compendium of speech and the marvels of wisdom, employing clear words, lucid turns of phrase and immortal expressions which were enlightening

101 *Jawāmiʿ*. The expression *jawāmiʿ al-kalim* does not translate easily into English; it means the skill of putting the most meaning into the least words; of being both comprehensive and concise. In order to retain something of the Arabic idiom, it is generally translated here in a near-literal way: 'the compendium of speech.' [t]

102 Aḥmad.

103 Abū Yaʿlā, Ibn Abī Ḥātim.

104 That is, you never went to live with any non-Qurayshi tribes, from whom you could have learned other dialects or languages (*Sharh al-Mawāhib*).

105 That is, eloquence had become exceedingly rare. Ismāʿīl ؑ is considered the father of the Arabs. [t]

106 Abū Nuʿaym.

without bearing the slightest hint of affectation. The great linguist and rhetorician al-Jāḥiẓ described the Prophet's ﷺ speech thus: 'Allah cast upon his speech love, and clothed it with acceptance, and made it both awesome and sweet. It needed no repetition, and the one who heard it never needed to decipher it. He spoke not even a single word idly, nor ever made a slip. No argument of his ever failed; no debater ever triumphed over him; no orator ever dumbfounded him. He would only silence debaters by using arguments they could understand and acknowledge. His arguments were drawn solely from truth. Indeed, no one ever heard words with more universal benefit, truth, justice and balance than his ﷺ.'

ʿAlī ؓ said: 'I never heard any rare expression of the Arabs save that I had already heard the Messenger of Allah ﷺ use it. Indeed, I heard him say *mātᵃ ḥatfᵃ anfhi*[107] before I heard any other Arab say it.'

His ﷺ speech was clear and to the point, with neither excess nor dearth, so that those who kept his company could memorise his words if they so wished. ʿĀʾisha ؓ said: 'The Messenger of Allah ﷺ would not draw out his words as you all do; he would speak so clearly and precisely that those in his company could memorise it.' It is also reported that she said: 'He would speak in such a way that one would be able to count his words if he wished to do so.'[108] Anas ؓ said: 'When he said something, he would repeat it three times.'[109]

His ﷺ Companions would say to him: 'We have seen no one more eloquent than you,' to which his reply was: 'Allah did not make me barbarous of tongue; He chose for me the best of speech: His Book, the Qurʾān.'

He ﷺ would also praise eloquence and condemn ungrammatical speech; when al-ʿAbbās ؓ asked him 'What is beauty?', he replied: 'The tongue.'[110] Another narration has it that he asked 'What makes a man beautiful?', and the Prophet ﷺ replied: 'The eloquence of his tongue.'[111] He also said: 'May Allah have mercy on him who rectifies his tongue!'[112]

Another aspect of his ﷺ perfect eloquence was that he would speak to every tribe with their own regional dialect and idioms, to the point where

107 This is an Arab idiom meaning 'to die of natural causes'. Literally it means 'to die through the nose'; that is, rather than through a wound. [t]

108 Al-Bukhārī, Muslim.

109 Al-Bukhārī, Muslim.

110 Al-Ḥākim.

111 Al-ʿAskarī.

112 Al-ʿAskarī.

many of his Companions would ask him to explain certain words and expressions he used. Whoever studies his words and his biography will clearly see this; the way he spoke to Quraysh, the Helpers, and the people of Hijaz and Najd in general was not the same as the way he spoke to the chieftains of Hadramaut and the kings of Yemen. The letter he ﷺ sent to Hamdān [of Yemen] was filled with words common to the Yemeni dialect.[113] The same is true of the way he ﷺ addressed the [Yemeni] tribe of Nahd, and the message he ﷺ gave Wā'il ibn Ḥajar to convey to the chieftains of Hadramaut, giving instructions on how the *zakāt* should be collected. Each of these was very different from the famous letter he ﷺ sent to Anas ﷺ on the same subject. Because the people in question spoke in this way and were accustomed to this rhetoric and this style, and used these words often, the Prophet ﷺ used the same style to explain the Revelation to them; he ﷺ spoke to the people in a way they could understand.

Another example of this is how he ﷺ said to ʿAṭiyya al-Saʿdī: 'The higher hand is the one that gives (*al-munṭiya*), and the lower hand is the one that takes (*al-munṭā*),'[114] to which ʿUṭiyya replied, 'The Messenger of Allah spoke to us in our own language!'[115] There was also the man of the ʿĀmirī tribe whom the Prophet ﷺ addressed in his dialect, saying to him *sal ʿanka*, 'ask of yourself', an idiom peculiar to the ʿĀmirī dialect meaning 'ask whatever you wish to ask'.

Let us return to his ﷺ usual way of speaking, his renowned eloquence, the comprehensiveness and conciseness of his words, and the aphorisms related from him. Many volumes have been written on these words and their meanings; and some of them are utterly unparalleled in their eloquence. In the hope of attaining blessing from his ﷺ words, we shall list a few of them here:[116]

113 Sheikh Muḥammad ibn ʿAlawī reproduces the letter here; it is filled with lexical items which were unknown to the Arabs of Hijaz at that time and would likely baffle most Arabs today as well. It suffices to say that virtually every single noun in the passage is either foreign to the Qurayshi dialect or used in a way unknown to Quraysh. [t]

114 The Quraysh would say *muʿṭiya* and *muʿṭā*; the tribe of Saʿd would replace the Arabic letter *ʿayn* with *nūn*. [t]

115 Abū Nuʿaym, *Maʿrifat al-Ṣaḥāba*, 4958; Ṭabarānī, *Musnad al-Shāmiyyīn*, 588.

116 The Sheikh has selected these ḥadīths from the large number quoted in al-Qasṭallānī's

'Actions are defined by intentions.' (Al-Bukhārī, Muslim)

'The doer gains no more from his deed than that which he intends thereby. The believer's intention is better than his deed.' (Al-Ṭabarānī)

'Knights of Allah, ride forth!' (Abū Dāwūd)

'All quarry is found in the belly of the wild donkey.'[117] (Al-Rāmahramzī)

'War is deception.' (Al-Bukhārī, Muslim)

'Beware of green dung: a beautiful woman with an evil background.' (Al-Rāmahramzī)

'The wrongdoer only wrongs himself.' (Aḥmad, Ibn Mājah)

'The mighty one is not he who defeats others, but he who defeats himself.' (Ibn Ḥibbān)

'The mighty one is not he who wrestles, but he who retains his self-control when angry.' (Al-Bukhārī, Muslim)

'To be told is not like to see for oneself.' (Aḥmad)

'Gatherings are bonds of trust.'[118] (Abū Dāwūd)

'Tribulation is called forth by the words [people speak].'[119] (Al-Bayhaqī, Ibn Abī Shayba)

al-Mawāhib al-Laduniyya in the section on the Prophet's ﷺ eloquence. [t]

117 This means that because of how much meat there is on a wild donkey, catching one is like catching all the quarry one could wish to hunt.

118 This either means that a host of a gathering must make sure he is trustworthy, or that those who attend gatherings must not divulge the secrets of others they may discover therein (*'Ayn al-Ma'būd*).

119 That is, 'Be careful what you wish for, and be careful what you predict, for your words may cause you problems later on.'

'Abstaining from evil is an act of charity.' (Al-Bukhārī[120])

'What disease is deadlier than miserliness?' (Al-Bukhārī, Muslim)

'Even goats would not dispute it.'[121] (Ibn ʿUdayy, Ibn Saʿd)

'Shyness begets naught but goodness.' (Al-Bukhārī, Muslim)

'False oaths turn households into wastelands.' (Al-Daylamī)

'He who serves the people leads the people.'[122] (Al-Sulamī, al-Khaṭīb, Abū Nuʿaym)

'The virtue of knowledge is greater than the virtue of devotional acts.' (Al-Ṭabarānī)

'Blessed be the manes of horses!'[123] (Al-Bukhārī, Muslim)

[Another narration has it: 'Horses have blessing fastened to their manes.']

'Of all good deeds, the quickest rewarded are kindness and the keeping of family ties; and of all evil deeds, the quickest to be punished are injustice and the cutting of family ties.' (Ibn Mājah)

'Some rhetoric is sorcery; some knowledge is ignorance; and some poetry is wisdom.' (Abū Dāwūd)

120 The exact wording of al-Bukhārī is: 'Abstain from doing evil to people, for it is an act of charity which you give to yourself.' The wording above is quoted in *al-Mawāhib* without a chain of transmission.

121 Literally, 'no two goats would butt one another over it'; said of something which is certain and indisputable. This was adopted by the Arabs as an idiom.

122 This translation is based on al-Zurqānī's convincing interpretation of the ḥadīth, which could also be rendered: 'He who leads the people serves the people'. Literal translation: 'The people's leader is their servant' (*sayyid al-qawm khādimᵘhum*). Al-Zurqānī asserts that there is an inversion here, and that the meaning is: 'The servant of the people is, as it were, their leader.' [t]

123 'Mane' here symbolises the whole horse in its noblest aspect; thus an adequate paraphrase of the ḥadīth might be: 'The noble horse is a source of great blessing.' [t]

'Two blessings which many people fritter away: health and free time.' (Al-Bukhārī)

'Deception and treachery are in hell.' (Al-Bayhaqī, al-Bazzār)

'To be asked for counsel is to be bound by a trust.'[124] (Aḥmad)

'Regret is repentance.' (Al-Ṭabarānī, Aḥmad)

'To direct another towards the good is akin to doing it.' (Al-ʿAskarī, al-Ṭabarānī)

'Love makes you blind and deaf.' (Aḥmad, Abū Dāwūd)

'Borrowed items must be given back, and borrowed livestock[125] must be returned, and debts must be repaid; and the guarantor is liable.' (Aḥmad, al-Tirmidhī)

''Ukkāsha beat you to it!'[126] (Al-Bukhārī, Muslim)

'The best of possessions is a flowing spring owned by a sleeping eye.'[127]

(This means that the best possession is that which continues to give

[124] Another ḥadīth explains this: 'If one of you asks his brother for counsel, he must advise him as best he can; for if he does not, he betrays him.' (Ibn Mājah)

[125] The word *manḥa* here means either livestock such as goats or cows which are lent to another for their milk, but must then be returned, or else land which is lent for sowing. (The borrower may keep the milk the animal gives him, and the crops the land gives him, but he does not actually own the animal or the land, and must give them back when their owner asks for them.)

[126] This was said to a man who asked if he was as virtuous as another named ʿUkkāsha, who, the Prophet ﷺ had said, would be one of the seventy thousand who will enter Paradise without having to face the Judgement. It has become an Arabic idiom: if one person beats another to something, the Arabs will say to the loser: ''Ukkāsha beat you to it!'

[127] The Arabic word *ʿayn* means both 'spring' and 'eye', which gives this phrase a very pleasant ring which is impossible to render in English: *ʿayn*[un] *sāhira li-ʿayn*[in] *nā'ima*. The word *sāhira* also means 'awake', which adds to the potency of the phrase: 'a waking eye for a sleeping eye' is another possible literal translation. This ḥadīth is given in *al-Mawāhib* without mention of any narrator or chain of transmission. [t]

benefit like a flowing spring which continues to flow even when its owner is asleep, bringing reward night and day.)

'The best a man can own is a productive mare and an avenue of date-palms.'[128] (Aḥmad, al-Ṭabarānī)

'If a man's deeds slow him down, his lineage will not speed him up.' (Muslim)

'Visit often – your love will grow.' (Al-Bazzār, al-Bayhaqī)

'You will never be able to share your wealth with everyone; instead, share your virtue with everyone.' (Abū Yaʿlā, al-Bazzār)

'This religion is firm; so enter into its depths gently.' (Aḥmad, al-Bazzār)

(The narration of al-Bazzār adds: 'For the isolated man traverses no land, nor preserves his mount.' This draws a metaphor from the one who is cut off from his travelling companions and tries to catch them up by spurring his mount and forcing it to go faster than it can, thereby wearing it out. In the end, he neither makes progress on his journey, nor spares the strength of his mount to bear him any further.)

'Religion is ease; those who try to make religion hard are always defeated by it.' (Al-Bukhārī)

'The wise one is he who judges himself and works for what comes after death; the fool is he who follows his soul's lusts, yet hopes for all kinds of things from his Lord.' (Aḥmad, al-Tirmidhī, al-Ḥākim)

'If something makes your heart uneasy, leave it.' (Al-Ṭabarānī)

(That is, if something makes you hesitant, then abstain from it, and do not listen to demonic whispers [*wasāwis*].)

[128] Again, there is a pleasant rhyme (*sajʿ*) to the words in Arabic: *mahra maʾmūra, wa sikka maʾbūra.* [t]

'A woman may be married for her beauty, her wealth, her religion or her lineage; choose the religious one, may your hand be covered in dust [if you do otherwise]!' (Al-Bukhārī, Muslim)

'Winter is spring for the believer: its days are short, that he might fast them; and its nights are long, that he might pass them in prayer.' (Al-Bayhaqī, al-ʿAskarī)

'Contentment is wealth which never runs out, and a treasure which never fades.' (Al-Tabarānī[129])

'He who defers to Allah's guidance[130] is never disappointed; he who seeks the counsel of others never regrets; he who is moderate never becomes destitute.' (Al-Ṭabarānī)

'Moderation in spending is half of all livelihood; treating people nicely is half of all wisdom; asking the right questions is half of all knowledge.' (Al-Bayhaqī, al-ʿAskarī)

'There is no intelligence like forethought, no scrupulousness like restraint, and no quality like good manners.' (Al-Tirmidhī, Ibn Ḥibbān)

['Restraint' here means to refrain from causing harm, or to restrain one's tongue.]

'The Muslim is he from whose tongue and hand the Muslims are safe; and the Emigrant is he who leaves aside all that Allah forbids.' (Al-Bukhārī, Muslim)

'Forethought is half of livelihood; amiability is half of all wisdom; grief is half of old age[131]; and one of the two conveniences of life is to have few dependents.[132]' (Al-Daylamī)

[129] The Sheikh points out here that there is some debate as to the authenticity of this ḥadīth, but that its meaning is nonetheless correct. [t]

[130] *Istakhāra*, literally 'to ask Allah to tell one what decision to make'. [t]

[131] That is, grief causes one to age and weaken.

[132] That is, to have few children is a blessing for those who would be too poor to raise many; the other of the 'two conveniences' (*al-yasārayn*) is to be wealthy and have many children (see

'He who cannot be trusted has no faith; he who has no covenant has no religion.' (Aḥmad, al-Bayhaqī)

'Honouring covenants is part of faith.' (Al-Ḥākim)

'The beauty of a man is in the eloquence of his tongue.' (Al-Qaḍāʿī, al-ʿAskarī)

'Two rapacious ones who are never satiated: the seeker of knowledge, and the seeker of worldly delights.' (Al-Ṭabarānī, al-Bayhaqī)

'There is no poverty worse than ignorance; no wealth finer than wisdom; and no loneliness worse than self-admiration.'[133] (Ibn Mājah)

'Sins will not be forgotten, kindnesses will never fade, and the Judge will never die; be, then, as you will.' (Al-Daylamī)

'There is no more beautiful combination than that of forbearance and knowledge.' (Al-ʿAskarī)

'Seek provision in the depths of the earth.' (Abū Sharīḥ, al-Ṭabarānī, al-Bayhaqī)

'Be in this world as though you were a stranger or a wayfarer, and count yourself among those who are in their graves.' (Al-Bukhārī, al-Tirmidhī, al-Bayhaqī)

'Righteous deeds guard against evil fates; secret charity appeases the wrath of the Lord; and keeping family ties increases life.' (Al-Ṭabarānī)

'Forgiving others increases one's dignity; humility increases one's rank; and giving charity never decreases one's wealth.' (Muslim and others, with minor variations)

Sharḥ al-Mawāhib).

133 This is because self-admiration leads one to despise others, and thus to be unable to form relationships with them. (*Sharḥ al-Mawāhib*)

There are countless other narrations which show us how he ﷺ spoke, addressed others, gave speeches, prayed and made covenants; they all show without any doubt how his ﷺ status in this regard was incomparable and unsurpassed.

His ﷺ Perfect Knowledge of Worldly Affairs

(Planning and organising matters of residence, trade, and so on)

The Prophet ﷺ would concern himself with the planning and directing of the construction of houses and residential areas, and he ﷺ knew much about the proper way to go about this and organise it according to sound principles that preserved the rights of the thoroughfare and those who used it, the rights of neighbours, and the rights of the mosque, and also took into account the necessary sanitary considerations. The Prophet ﷺ would state whether a certain place was appropriate for a certain building or not: residential areas had their place in his ﷺ plan, as did baths and marketplaces. And he ﷺ would carry out these plans himself, and provide the necessary guidance.

Ibn Saʿd narrates in his *Ṭabaqāt* that after the Prophet ﷺ had allocated the houses in Medina,[134] he designed the house of ʿUthmān ibn ʿAffān ﷺ.[135] Once while out walking, he ﷺ came to a spot and said, 'This would be a fine place for a bathhouse', so a bathhouse was built there. This shows his ﷺ knowledge of architecture, building and ventilation.[136]

Abū Dāwūd narrated in his *Sunan* that the Prophet ﷺ sent a message to his troops saying: 'Whosoever over-occupies an encampment,[137] or blocks a thoroughfare, is not a true *mujāhid*.' This is because the people had been over-occupying encampments and blocking thoroughfares. This shows how he ﷺ loved order even when it came to temporary campsites – how much more, then, must he have loved it for permanent settlements and buildings.

He ﷺ would also command that buildings be constructed according to sound principles. For example, when someone asked him ﷺ about the

134 That is, specified which Emigrants would be housed by which Helpers.

135 The house later passed on to the Maʿmar family line. It was demolished when the mosque of the Prophet ﷺ was extended in the mid-20th century.

136 See *al-Tarātīb al-Idāriyya*, vol. 1, p. 282.

137 That is, takes up too much space in the military encampment so that the other warriors are inconvenienced.

rights of the neighbour, he said: 'Do not make your building higher than his so that it prevents the wind from reaching it; and do not torment him with the aroma of your cooking-pot unless you are prepared to give him a share of it.'[138] Another narration has it: 'And do not prevent the wind from reaching him unless he gives you permission.'[139]

The Prophet ﷺ also designated a place for the market and directed its construction, and personally came to inspect it. Before this, he had gone to the old marketplace and said, 'This is no kind of market you have here!' When he saw the new market, it pleased him and he stamped his foot and said, 'What a wonderful market you have! Do not let it fail!', praising it and encouraging them to keep it busy.[140]

Another aspect of his ﷺ concern for the affairs of the marketplace is that he would inspect it and ask about how things were going, and ask to hear the latest news, paying complete attention to all this. When he found out that they were buying food directly from the caravans,[141] he sent a messenger to forbid them from doing so under pain of punishment. Al-Bukhārī narrates in his *Ṣaḥīḥ* that Ibn ʿUmar ﷺ said: 'They used to buy food from the caravans during the time of the Messenger of Allah ﷺ, so he sent someone to forbid them from selling it where they bought it, [directing them not to sell it] until they had brought it to the place where food was usually sold.' He ﷺ also forbade them from going out to meet the caravans early, as is reported in the *Ṣaḥīḥ*; and he forbade that a town-dweller sell on behalf of a desert-dweller.[142]

He ﷺ would go out to the marketplace himself to see what was going on there; a ḥadīth states that he ﷺ passed by a food seller, put his hand into the pile and felt some wetness there. 'What is this, food-seller?', he asked. The man replied, 'Rain fell on it, O Messenger of Allah.' 'Why, then', he said, 'did you not put it on the top of the pile so that the people could see it? He who cheats us is not one of us.'[143] After the conquest of Mecca, he ﷺ appointed Saʿīd ibn Saʿīd ibn al-ʿĀṣ inspector of the market in Mecca, and ʿUmar inspector of the market in Medina.[144]

138 Al-Bayhaqī.
139 Ibn ʿAdī.
140 Ibn Mājah, al-Ṭabarānī.
141 That is, before they reached market. [t]
142 I.e., that he act as a broker for him. [t]
143 Muslim, al-Tirmidhī.
144 *Al-Sīra al-Ḥalabiyya*, vol. 3, p. 354.

Another aspect of his ﷺ concern for the affairs of the marketplace is how he would observe the official weigher and command him to be just and virtuous. Abū Hurayra ؓ said: 'The market had an official weigher whose task it was to weigh things. The Prophet ﷺ once said to him: "Weigh, and add more."'[145] That is, weigh the dates and keep adding more until the scale tips over.

He ﷺ was also keen that the market always be amply stocked with wares so that they would be readily available and not get too expensive. In light of this principle, he ﷺ would say: 'The one who trades freely will gain provision; the one who hoards will be cursed.'[146] He ﷺ would also warn people about those craftsmen whom he knew to be duplicitous and dishonest, saying: 'The falsest people are dyers and jewellers.'[147]

He ﷺ would encourage people to go out to the market to buy, sell, and trade, and to engage in work and craft. When a man came to him complaining of poverty, he ﷺ encouraged him to gather firewood, saying: 'Go to [such-and-such] valley, and gather up every single twig and branch, and do not come back to me until ten days have passed,' encouraging him to gather firewood for a living.[148] Another time, Saʿd ibn ʿĀʾidh came to him ﷺ and complained of his meagre means, so he told him to go and engage in trade. He went out to the market and bought some acacia pods and sold them at a profit. He told the Prophet ﷺ of this, and he told him to carry on in that way, and so he made it his trade.[149] When he ﷺ saw young lads selling wares in the marketplace, he would pray for blessings for them, express his happiness with them, and encourage them. He ﷺ once passed by ʿAbdallāh ibn Jaʿfar selling wares along with some other boys, and said: 'Allah, give him blessing in his trade!'[150] Another narration, on the authority of al-ʿĀmirī, begins: 'We were boys working in the market…'[151]

Another aspect of his ﷺ concern for the affairs of the marketplace is

[145] Aḥmad.

[146] Ibn Mājah.

[147] Aḥmad, Ibn Mājah, al-Bayhaqī. Abū ʿUbayd al-Qāsim ibn Salām interpreted this ḥadīth symbolically, saying that 'dyers' are those who embellish their speech, and 'jewellers' are those who outright falsify it (al-Bayhaqī, *al-Sunan al-Kubrā*).

[148] Al-Tirmidhī.

[149] See *al-Iṣāba*. He thereafter became known as *Saʿd al-qarẓ*, 'Saʿd the acacia man'.

[150] *Al-Iṣāba*.

[151] Abū Dāwūd.

how he named those who bought and sold therein *tujjār*, when before they had been called *samāsira*.[152] Ibn Mājah narrates that Qays ibn Abī Gharaza said: 'We used to be called *samāsira* at the time of the Messenger of Allah ﷺ; and one day, the Messenger of Allah ﷺ passed us by and gave us a better name. He said: "O *tujjār*! Trade often involves oath-making and vain talk, so expiate this by giving charity."' The narration of al-Ṭabarānī adds: 'He was the first one to call us *tujjār*.' Al-Tirmidhī also narrates this ḥadīth in the chapter entitled: '*Tujjār*, and how the Prophet ﷺ gave them this name.'

The word *tājir* (the singular of *tujjār*) is more noble than *simsār* (the singular of *samāsira*) according to common custom; perhaps the reason for this is that *samāsira* is also used to mean 'tax collectors'; or perhaps the word had a negative connotation at the time of the Prophet ﷺ.

Another aspect of his ﷺ perfect knowledge of worldly matters was his knowledge of sewing. Our lady ʿĀʾisha ﷺ said: 'He ﷺ would do household chores, and would often sew.'[153]

Another aspect of his ﷺ perfect knowledge of worldly matters was how he instructed a man whose nose had been severed to get himself a golden nose to replace it. Abū Dāwūd narrates in his *Sunan* that ʿArfaja ibn Saʿd's nose was cut off at the Battle of al-Kulāb, so he made a false nose from silver, but it developed a foul stench. The Prophet ﷺ therefore instructed him to have a false nose made from gold. Al-Tirmidhī remarks in his *Sunan*: 'It is related that more than one scholar used gold fillings in their teeth, having learned from the Prophet's ﷺ instruction here that gold does not develop a foul stench [when used in this way].'[154]

When the Prophet ﷺ announced that Mecca was an inviolable space wherein no tree or plant may be cut, al-ʿAbbās ﷺ said: 'What about the sweet rushes (*al-idhkhir*), for our jewellers and for roofing our houses?' He

152 Both these words mean 'merchants' or 'traders', but *tujjār* is more dignified in Arabic; *samāsira* has the connotation of 'middleman', suggesting a kind of servitude. Al-Khaṭṭābī suggested that the word *samāsira* was a foreign word, given to the merchants because in times past the role had often been fulfilled by non-Arabs; *tujjār*, on the other hand, was a pure Arabic word (*Ḥāshiyat al-Sindī*). See also the author's explanation below. [t]

153 Ibn Saʿd.

154 See *Sunan al-Tirmidhī* and *al-Iṣāba*.

ﷺ replied: 'All except the sweet rushes,' and permitted them to be cut.[155]

If he ﷺ ever saw that a man had an aptitude for a certain craft, he would encourage him to do it until he became highly skilled at it. An example of this: he ﷺ once saw Ṭalq[156] ibn ʿAlī al-Ḥanafī joining in the building of the Holy Mosque in Medina, and noticed that he was adept at working clay, so he assigned him this task and said: 'Send the clay his way, for he knows how to work it.' Ṭalq ﷺ himself later told this story, saying: 'I came to the Prophet ﷺ in Medina whilst he was building his mosque, the Muslims working alongside him. I had experience in preparing and mixing clay, so I took the spade and mixed the clay. The Messenger of Allah ﷺ looked on, and said: "This Ḥanafite is skilled with clay!"' Another narration has it that he ﷺ said: 'He is the most skilled of you with clay.'[157]

Finally, Imām Mālik narrated that the Messenger of Allah ﷺ stood before a grave and saw a crack in one of the bricks, and so commanded that it be mended, saying: 'Allah loves that, when His servant does something, he does it well.'[158]

155 Al-Bukhārī.

156 The author names the Companion in question as Qays ibn Ṭalq; in fact it was Ṭalq, and his son Qays was the one who related the story from him. [t]

157 *Al-Iṣāba*, *Ṭabaqāt Ibn Saʿd*.

158 Ibn Rushd, *al-Bayān wal-Taḥṣīl*.

His ﷺ Perfect Oratory

The Prophet's ﷺ oratory was a perfect model which all those who call others to righteousness should emulate, basing their own speech on its principles and approaches, that they be better able to win others over with their words.

He ﷺ would always be careful to make sure that his counsel could be heard by his audience, word for word and letter for letter. He would give his sermons standing, with a raised voice, and speak from a high place; and in Medina, he had a pulpit set up in his mosque for this purpose. He would also be eager that his words touched the souls of those who heard them, and would employ familiar, carefully chosen words, and convey clear concepts with beautiful language. He would often repeat a sentence three times to show its importance, lest it pass by the ears of the listeners without penetrating their souls.

He ﷺ would not employ rhymed prose (*sajʿ*) in his speeches,[159] but would speak with natural prose, unless a rhyming expression happened to suggest itself naturally; for when rhymed prose is employed in a constant and deliberate way, it results in artifice and in a surrendering of substance to style. He ﷺ would not make his sermons long, lest people become uncomfortable and bored and thus fail to benefit from the counsel as they would if they were listening alertly. He would say, 'When a man lengthens his prayer and shortens his sermon, he shows his deep understanding.'[160] Although short, his sermons were endowed with wisdom and good counsel, filled with concise words and phrases which have since become famous proverbs and paragons of brevity and eloquence. Sometimes he would make the Friday sermon long if this were required; once he ﷺ began a sermon after the afternoon prayer, and was still speaking when the sun set.

He ﷺ would begin his sermons by praising and lauding Allah, and then follow this with the testimony of faith. He would then say *ammā baʿd*[161]

159 As was the custom of the Arabs.

160 Muslim.

161 An Arabic expression with no English equivalent, used to separate the formulaic

and turn to the subject of the sermon, whether related to wisdom or to counsel. During the course of the sermon, he might digress from the general theme in order to address a particular person in the audience, if a vital instruction needed to be given to him: a man once arrived as the Prophet ﷺ was giving the Friday sermon. The Prophet ﷺ said to him: 'Have you prayed?' He said no, so the Prophet ﷺ instructed him to stand and pray, and then carried on with the sermon.[162]

He ﷺ would sometimes give emphasis to a point by gesturing with his hand as was appropriate: in one of his sermons, he said: 'I was sent forth whilst the Hour and I are [as close] as these two,' putting his first and middle fingers together.[163] It is also related that he ﷺ would point with his first finger when speaking of Allah and beseeching Him. The signs of warning and wrath might show on him as he spoke, if the occasion and the words called for it; sometimes when he spoke his eyes would redden and he would become sorely wrathful, as though he were giving a warning to an army.

He would look to the condition of the people when he gave sermons, and tailor his words for it: if they were remiss in a certain area of righteousness, he would enjoin it, and if they were straying towards a certain sin, he would warn against it.

---

introduction of a speech from its given content. Literally it means: 'As for what follows...' [t]

162 Al-Bukhārī, Muslim.

163 Al-Bukhārī, Muslim.

The Perfect Wisdom of His ﷺ Way of Calling to Islam

TRUE PREACHING cannot have firm roots and long branches, nor bear any fruit, unless it is based on sound arguments, and unless the preacher acts with wisdom and beautiful conduct.

This was the way of his ﷺ call to Islam: it was presented in a way which inspired minds to accept it willingly and souls to hear it gladly. He ﷺ would endeavour to convey it in ways most likely to succeed, finding the right words for the right occasions and dressing each concept in the right garb. He would address different people in the way most suited to their minds, and treat them in the way most likely to win their acceptance and have the quickest success in guiding them away from their error.

He would call others to the truth, and follow this call with convincing arguments and the Holy Qur'ān. For every principle of the religion, he gave clear proofs and dispelled all doubts. He ﷺ supported his call with arguments, and countered any doubts which people may have had.

One aspect of his ﷺ call was the way he sent messages of wisdom; and the manifold beautiful wisdom of the Holy Book and the Noble Ḥadīth show those who examine them that the call of Islam is '...*a conclusive word, and no pleasantry*' [86:13-14]. One aspect of his wisdom is that he ﷺ would aid the spread of the call by the gifts of wealth he gave to the chieftains of tribes; for gifts dispel grudges and turn estrangement into accord. The purpose of these gifts was that they inspired hearts to consider the truth of the call objectively. He ﷺ would also do this when he saw that their faith was not completely firm and impervious to trials.

He ﷺ said about such people: 'I might give to one man though another is more beloved to me, because I fear that [otherwise] Allah might send him to Hell.'[164]

Another aspect of his ﷺ way of calling was that he would go about it with patience, delicacy, and forbearance. He would present it with gentle words, responding to those who treated him ignorantly by leaving them be, and

164 Al-Bukhārī, Muslim.

responding to those who wronged him by pardoning them and being kind to them. Much abuse was levelled at him ﷺ by the pagans and dolts of Quraysh, yet he endured this patiently, and did not allow it to detract from his resolve to continue the call in the slightest. Many a foul word was cast his way by certain of the hypocrites and the boorish Bedouins, and he met them with forgiveness, smiles and graces. When he ﷺ did give correction and rebuke for inappropriate behaviour, he would do so in a subtle way, not addressing the guilty person directly, but speaking generally, thus: 'What is wrong with people, that they disdain to do something I do? By Allah, I know Allah and fear Him more than any of you.'[165]

Another aspect of his ﷺ wise manner of calling to Islam was that he would not simply pile up advice on people, but would offer them counsel when they needed it or when they were eager to hear it. ʿAbdallāh ibn Masʿūd ﷺ said: 'The Prophet ﷺ would choose the best moments to counsel us, [not doing so constantly] for he hated to make us weary.'[166]

In the letters he ﷺ sent to kings and tribes, he would be concise, leaving it to the envoy who delivered the letter to explain the message and its arguments in detail, and to dispel any doubts that might be raised by the recipient; and he would choose as envoys those who were up to this task. The letter he ﷺ sent ʿAmr ibn al-ʿĀṣ ﷺ to deliver to the people of Najrān, Yemen, said:

> I call you to worship Allah instead of worshipping His slaves, and I call you to ally yourselves with Allah instead of with His slaves. If you decline, then [I will accept] the *jizya*[167]; if you decline, then I shall declare war upon you. Peace.

An aspect of his ﷺ brilliant way of answering questions was that he would give the answer in the form of a general principle, rather than simply saying yes or no. There was a man of the Muḥārib tribe who abused the Messenger of Allah ﷺ when he went to call the tribes to Islam. Some time later, this man came to Medina as part of a delegation from Muḥārib, having converted to Islam in the meantime. He reminded the Messenger of Allah ﷺ of how he had abused him, and said: 'Pray that I be forgiven.' He

165 Al-Bukhārī.

166 Al-Bukhārī, Muslim.

167 The poll tax paid by non-Muslims in a Muslim state to pay for the upkeep of the armies which protect them, and for exemption from military service. [t]

ﷺ said to him: 'Islam makes amends for the unbelief that came before it.'[168]

Another aspect of his method of calling to Islam was his brilliant use of similitude and parable, which each are very effective ways of making obscure and unfamiliar concepts seem familiar. One of the finest examples of this we have heard is his ﷺ saying: 'The believers, in their mutual love, mercy and affection, are like a body: if one part of it ails, the rest of the body responds to it with restlessness and fever.'[169]

A further aspect of his ﷺ strategy in calling to Islam was how he would speak to different people in a way they could understand, and took pains not to speak to anyone in a way his mind could not understand; he guided us to do the same when he said: 'Speak to people in a way they can understand: do you want Allah and His Messenger to be belied?'[170]

Sometimes he ﷺ would do something just to accommodate those who expected it to be done, as long as they were simple matters of custom, and not harmful in any way. He ﷺ once wanted to send letters to certain kings inviting them to Islam, when it was said to him: 'They only accept letters which are sealed.' Upon hearing this, he had a silver seal[171] made, engraved with the words *Muḥammad, the Messenger of Allah.*[172]

He ﷺ would also abstain from certain things in order to avoid strife, as long as there was no harm in abstaining from them. He abstained from demolishing the Kaʿba and rebuilding it according to the original foundations laid by Ibrāhīm ﷺ, so as not to cause strife for those new Muslims who had not long been free of paganism. He ﷺ said to ʿĀʾisha ﷺ: 'Were it not that your people are newly shed of paganism, I would order that the House[173] be demolished, return to it what was taken from it, and use it to enlarge the foundations of Ibrāhīm.'[174]

[168] Ibn Saʿd, Aḥmad, al-Ṭabarānī.

[169] Al-Bukhārī.

[170] Al-Daylamī narrates it as a saying of the Prophet ﷺ in a slightly different form; al-Bukhārī narrates it as a saying of Imam ʿAlī with the wording used above.

[171] *Khātam*, that is, a ring with a seal on it, as was the custom. [t]

[172] Al-Bukhārī, Muslim.

[173] Meaning the Kaʿba.

[174] Al-Bukhārī, al-Nasāʾī.

Part Two

How Allah Gave Him ﷺ Perfect Protection from all Flaws, and Guarded Him from Enemies, Demons and Sins

'Allah shall protect you from men.' [5:67]

Allah's Perfect Protection of Him ﷺ[175]

Allah says: *'Allah shall protect you from men'* [5:67], and: (Wait patiently for the fulfilment of your Lord's decree, for verily you are in Our sight) [52:48], and: *'Will Allah not suffice His servant?'* [39:36] – it is said that this means He will suffice Muḥammad ﷺ against his idolatrous enemies, and there have been other interpretations besides this.

He also says: *'Sufficient are We unto you against those who mock'* [15:95], and: *'Remember how the unbelievers plotted against you, to keep you in bonds, or slay you, or exile you. They plot and plan, and Allah too plans; but the best of planners is Allah'* [8:30].

ʿĀʾisha ﷺ said: 'The Prophet ﷺ used to be guarded [by sentries], until the verse was revealed: "*Allah shall protect you from men*" [5:67]. Upon this, he put his head through the opening in the tent and said to them, "Be gone, for my Lord ﷻ has protected me!"'[176]

It is related that when the Prophet ﷺ would rest in the middle of a journey, his Companions would choose a tree for him to nap under. Once while he was napping, a Bedouin man came along and unsheathed his sword, saying: 'Who now shall protect you from me?' The Prophet ﷺ said: 'Allah ﷻ', whereupon the Bedouin's hand trembled and he dropped his sword, and then struck his own head against the tree so violently that he drew blood; this verse was then revealed.[177] Ghawrath ibn al-Ḥārith, the Bedouin in question, related that the Prophet ﷺ then forgave him, and he went back to his people and said, 'I have just come to you from the best of all people.' A similar story is also said to have occurred at the Battle of Badr: the Prophet ﷺ is said to have separated from his Companions to answer a call of nature, when a hypocrite[178] followed him;

175 This chapter closely follows the *Shifā* of Qāḍī ʿIyāḍ, Volume 1, Part I, Chapter Four, section *fī ʿiṣmat Illāhi lahu…* [t]

176 Narrated by al-Tirmidhī with a slightly different wording.

177 Narrated by al-Bukhārī, Muslim, and others without mention of the Bedouin striking his own head against the tree.

178 *Munāfiq*, dissembler: one who pretends to be Muslim in order to infiltrate the Muslims

and events unfolded in the same way.

It is also related that the same thing happened at the Battle of Ghaṭafān at Dhū Amr to a man named Daʿthūr ibn al-Ḥārith[179]. He embraced Islam, and then went back to his people, who had charged him with the task of assassinating the Prophet ﷺ to begin with. The leader and most valiant of them said to him: 'Why didn't you do what you said you would, when you had the chance?' He replied: 'I saw a tall white man, who pushed my chest. I fell to the ground and dropped my sword. I realised that he was an angel, and so I entered Islam.' It is said that it was about this that the verse was revealed: '*O you who believe! Remember the favour of Allah unto you when certain men desired to stretch out their hands against you...*' [5:11].

Al-Khaṭṭābī's narration has it that Ghawrath ibn al-Ḥārith al-Muḥāribī wanted to ambush the Prophet ﷺ, who did not sense his presence until he was standing over him with his sword drawn. He said: 'O Allah, suffice me in whatever way You will!' Upon this, Ghawrath bent double and dropped his sword. This story has also been told in other ways, and it is said that it was about this that the verse was revealed: '*O you who believe! Remember the favour of Allah unto you when certain men desired to stretch out their hands against you...*' [5:11]. It is also said that the Messenger of Allah ﷺ used to be wary of Quraysh, but when this verse was revealed he relaxed and said, 'Whosoever wills, let him forsake me!'

ʿAbd ibn Ḥumayd related that the Wood-Carrier[180] used to lay smouldering thorns in the path of the Messenger of Allah ﷺ, and he would pass over it as though it were fine sand. Ibn Isḥāq related that when she heard about the revelation of '*Perish the hands of Abū Lahab...*' [111:1] and how Allah debased her and her husband therein, she went to find the Messenger of Allah ﷺ as he sat in the mosque with Abū Bakr, a stone pestle in her hand. When she came to them, she saw only Abū Bakr, and Allah veiled the Prophet ﷺ from her sight. 'Abū Bakr,' she said, 'where is your companion? I hear that he has been lampooning me; and by Allah, had I found him I would have shattered his mouth with this pestle!' The *Ḥamziyya*[181] says of this:

---

and cause them harm from within. [t]

179 It is likely that Daʿthūr here and Ghawrath in the aforementioned narration are the same person. See al-Shamanī's *Muzīl al-Khafā* and al-ʿAsqalānī's *al-Iṣāba*.

180 A derogatory name for the wife of Abū Lahab; see Qurʾān 111:4. [t]

181 Of Imam al-Buṣīrī.

The Wood-Carrier took her pestle
And came forth, swift as a hawk
On the day of her wrath: 'What,
Is one such as me to be mocked?'
She came, yet saw him not;
For can a blind eye see the sun?

Al-Ḥakam ibn Abī al-ʿĀṣ said: 'We agreed that we would assassinate the Prophet ﷺ, yet when we saw him we heard such a clamour behind us as made us think that no one in Tihāma[182] could have survived. We fell down and covered ourselves, and did not rise until he had finished praying and returned to his people. We then agreed to do it another night, yet when we had him in our sights, the mountains of Ṣafā and Marwa came and barred our way to him.'

ʿUmar ؓ said: 'Abū Jahm ibn Ḥudhayfa and I agreed on a night to kill the Messenger of Allah ﷺ. We went to his house and heard him begin to recite "*The Reality! What is the Reality?*" [69:1-2] until he reached "*Do you see, then, any remnant of them?*" [69:8].' Abū Jahm then struck ʿUmar's ؓ upper arm and said, 'Flee!', and they fled. This was the beginning of ʿUmar's journey to Islam.

There is also the famous story, which is sufficient to stand for all, of the time when Quraysh threatened him and lay in wait to kill him outside his house, yet he went out in the midst of them and stood right before them, Allah having hidden him from their sight, and threw dust over their heads and then evaded them. He was also hidden from their sight in the cave because of the wonders Allah worked for him, and the spider that spun its web over the entrance to the cave so that Umayya ibn Khalaf said, when the others wanted to go into the cave: 'He cannot be in there when there are so many spider-webs covering the entrance that they must have been here before Muḥammad was born!' And two doves sat at the entrance to the cave, so that the Qurayshis said, 'Were anyone in there, these doves would not have sat there.'

There is also the story of Surāqa ibn Mālik ibn Juʿsham. After the Emigration, Quraysh had put a bounty on the Prophet ﷺ and on Abū Bakr ؓ, and Juʿsham found out which way they had gone. He mounted his horse and followed them, and as he approached them the Prophet ﷺ

[182] Meaning here Mecca. [t]

made a prayer against him, and his horse's feet stuck fast to the ground, and he was thrown from it. He consulted his divining arrows,[183] which gave him an answer he did not like.[184] He mounted his horse again and approached until he could hear the sound of the Prophet ﷺ reciting, paying him no heed. Abū Bakr did pay him heed, however, saying to the Prophet ﷺ, 'We have been caught!' The Prophet ﷺ said, 'Fear not, Allah is with us.' Juʿsham's horse stopped in its tracks once again and threw him. He yelled at it, and it got up and bolted, kicking up a trail of dust like smoke. He called out to them for a truce, and the Prophet ﷺ agreed to write him a promise of truce, which Ibn Fuhayra[185] wrote (or it may have been Abū Bakr). He told them about what was going on.[186] The Prophet ﷺ commanded him not to let anyone else follow them. So Surāqa went back and told the others that there was no need to look that way. It is also said that Surāqa said to them: 'I know that you prayed against me – so pray now for me!' He got away safely, and began to think that the Prophet ﷺ was truly what he said he was.

Al-Būṣīrī says of the miracle of the cave, and the story of Surāqa:

Woe to a people who rejected a prophet
Beloved to even the lizards and gazelles of his land.
They forsook him, though a palm-trunk wept for him;[187]
They hated him, though strangers[188] loved him.
They drove him out, and a cave took him in,
And a white dove gave him her protection.
With its web, a spider gave him
The same aid as did the feathery dove.
He was hidden from them while right before their eyes:
His ascendancy was in the midst of his invisibility.[189]
The Chosen One headed for Medina,

183 The pagans would often carry divining arrows with them to consult when they had to make decisions. [t]

184 That is, they told him that his current course of action would bring him bad luck. [t]

185 Abū Bakr's servant.

186 That is, about the bounty Quraysh had put on them, and the others who were hunting them. [t]

187 A reference to certain miracles of the Prophet ﷺ. [t]

188 The Helpers.

189 A play on the word *ẓuhūr*, which means both 'visibility' and 'ascendancy' or 'triumph'. [t]

Though every direction from Mecca yearned for him.
The jinn sang his praises first, until
Mankind, too, exulted in that song.
Surāqa followed his traces in the sand,
Yet his fine steed flung him to the ground.
And he[190] called out to him[191] after his horse had shamed him;
For oft will a drowning man cry out!

Ibn Isḥāq and others relate that Abū Jahl, a boulder in his hands, approached the Messenger of Allah ﷺ as he prostrated in prayer, as Quraysh looked on. As he made as if to throw it, it remained in his hands, and his arms became fixed stiffly all the way up to his neck. He took a step back, and then asked the Prophet ﷺ to pray for him. He did so, and Abū Jahl's arms went back to normal. He had made a pact with Quraysh and sworn that if he saw him, he would smash the boulder down onto him. When they asked him what happened, he said: 'There came between me and him a stallion of which I had never seen the like, and it came towards me as if to devour me!' The Prophet ﷺ said: 'That was Jibrīl; had he come any closer, he would have seized him.'

Imam al-Būṣīrī says of this:

People tried to slay him, but the sword, being faithful,
Refused, and every boulder missed him;
Abū Jahl saw the stallion
Coming for him, as though it were a griffon!

The exegetes relate another version of this story on the authority of Abū Hurayra, as follows[192]: Abu Jahl promised Quraysh that if he saw Muḥammad ﷺ praying he would stamp on his neck. When the Messenger of Allah ﷺ began to pray, they let Abū Jahl know and he set off to him; but as he was approaching him, he suddenly turned his heels and fled, shielding himself with his arms. When he was asked about this, he said: 'As I approached him, I saw a moat filled with fire, into which I almost

190 Surāqa.

191 The Prophet ﷺ.

192 Sayyid Muḥammad ibn ʿAlawī follows the order of *al-Shifā* here, and includes this narration much further on in this chapter. I have moved it here so that the two versions of the same story can be presented side by side. [t]

fell; and I saw a great horror, and a beating of wings that filled the land.' The Messenger of Allah ❧ said: 'Those were the angels; had he come closer, they would have snatched him away, piece by piece.' Allah then revealed to the Prophet ❧: '*Nay! But man is ever given to insolence...*' [96:6], until the end of the chapter.

Al-Samarqandī related that a man of the Banū Mughīra tribe came to the Prophet ❧ to kill him, and Allah covered over his sight so he could not see the Prophet, though he heard his voice. He returned to his companions, and could not see them either, until they called him. It is said that it was about him that the verses were revealed: '*We have placed on their necks fetters, up to the chin, so their heads are raised; and We have put a barrier before them, and a barrier after them; and We have covered them, so they do not see*' [36:8-9].

Another case of this is the story related by Ibn Isḥāq, in which the Prophet ❧ went to Banū Qurayẓa with his companions, and sat under a wall of one of their high buildings. One of them, 'Amr ibn Jaḥḥāsh, went up to the roof to drop a boulder onto him; but the Prophet ❧ stood up and went back to Medina, and told them what had happened.

It is said that Allah's words '*O you who believe! Remember the favour of Allah unto you when certain men desired to stretch out their hands against you...*' [5:11] were revealed about this event.

Al-Samarqandī relates that the Prophet ❧ went to Banū al-Naḍīr to ask them to help in paying the blood indemnity for the two men of Kilāb who had been murdered by 'Amr ibn Umayya. Ḥuyay ibn Akhṭab said to him, 'Sit down, Muḥammad, so we can feed you and then give you what you seek.' The Messenger of Allah ❧ sat with Abū Bakr ❧ and 'Umar ❧ alongside him. Yet Ḥuyay was secretly plotting with the others to kill him, and Jibrīl ❧ told the Prophet ❧ of this. He got up and made as if he were going to answer a call of nature, and then went back to Medina.

It is related that Shayba ibn 'Uthmān al-Ḥajabī saw the Prophet ❧ at the Battle of Ḥunayn. Now both Shayba's father and uncle had been slain by Ḥamza ❧, so when he saw the Prophet ❧ he said, 'Today I shall settle my score with Muḥammad's kin!' When the two sides met, he approached the Prophet ❧ from behind and raised his sword to strike him. He later described what happened next: 'As I approached him, a flame of fire rose up before me, faster than lighting, and I fled from it. The Prophet ❧ sensed me there, and called me to him. He placed his hand on my chest, the man I hated more than any other – yet when he lifted it from me, he had become the man I loved more than any other. "Come and fight," he said to me, so I went before him and raised my sword, protecting his life with mine; and had I met my father at that moment, I would have killed him before letting him harm him ﷺ.'

Fuḍāla ibn ʿUmayr said: 'In the year of the Conquest,[193] I planned to kill the Prophet ﷺ as he circled the Kaʿba. When I approached him, he said, "O Fuḍāla!" "Yes?" I said. "What is it," he said, "that you are thinking of?" "Nothing," I said, and he smiled and prayed that I be forgiven, and then placed his hand on my chest. My heart became at peace, and by Allah, by the time he raised it there was nothing of Allah's creation more beloved to me than him. I went back to my family, on the way passing by a woman I used to chat with. She asked me to come and talk with her, but I said no.' Fuḍāla then went away, saying:

She said, 'Come hither', but I said: 'No,
Allah and Islam do not allow it.'
Had you seen Muḥammad and his folk,
At the Conquest, the day the idols were broken,
You would have seen Allah's religion rise like the sun,
And idolatry's face covered with shadows.

Another famous example of this is the story of ʿĀmir ibn al-Ṭufayl and Arbad ibn Qays, when they were sent in a delegation to the Prophet ﷺ. ʿĀmir had said to Arbad: 'I will distract Muḥammad's so that he turns his face from you – then, you strike him!' Yet he did not do it, and when he asked him afterwards what had gone wrong, he said: 'By Allah, every time I wanted to strike him I found you between me and him. What was I to do – strike you?'

Another manifestation of Allah's protection of him ﷺ was that many Jews and soothsayers warned of him, and pointed him out to Quraysh, and told them of how he would come to have power over them, and encouraged them to kill him [before he became powerful]; yet Allah protected him [from their plots] until his work was done.[194]

193 Of Mecca.

194 I am indebted to Mulla ʿAlī al-Qārī's explanation of this paragraph in his *Sharḥ al-Shifā*. [t]

This protection was also manifested in how the Prophet ﷺ was succoured by dread for a distance of a month's journey,[195] as the *Ṣaḥīḥ* collections report.

[195] That is, no one within a month's journey of the Prophet ﷺ dared to attack him because of the dread he instilled in their hearts. [t]

His ﷺ Perfect Protection from Satan

Qāḍī ʿIyāḍ says:[196] Know that the Muslim community is agreed that the Prophet ﷺ is protected from Satan and sufficed against him – not only in his physical person (against all that could harm it), nor only in his mind (against all misgivings that could be suggested to it), but in every way possible.

The *Ṣaḥīḥ* collections tell us that ʿAbdallāh ibn Masʿūd ﷺ said: 'The Messenger of Allah ﷺ said: "There is not one of you, but that there has been assigned to him a consort of the jinn and a consort of the angels." "Even you, O Messenger of Allah?", they said. "Even me," he said, "save that Allah aided me against him and he submitted."'

A narration on the authority of Manṣūr adds that he ﷺ said: '...so he enjoins upon me only that which is good.' ʿĀʾisha's ﷺ narration of it has, instead of *fa-aslama* ('he submitted'), *fa-aslamu*, meaning 'so I was freed of him'; some scholars say that this version is the more authentic one. The version which has *fa-aslama* ('he submitted') means that the demonic consort changed from a state of unbelief (*kufr*) to one of submission (*islām*), and thenceforth only enjoined what is good, just as angels do; this is the more obvious meaning of the ḥadīth. Another version has it *faʾstalama*, which also means 'he submitted'.

If this was the case with his demonic consort, the like of which was sent to all human beings, then what of those who were distant from him, and who were not in his company, and indeed were unable to come near him? There are reports of how demons were warded off him on many occasions, when they attempted to come near to him to extinguish his light, take his life, or pile distractions upon him, until they despaired of ever tempting him and went away disappointed. One such case was when a demon attempted to waylay him as he prayed, yet the Prophet ﷺ took hold of him and captured him.

[196] Much of what follows is drawn from *al-Shifā*, Volume 2, Part III, Chapter One, Section 4 (*waʿlam anna ʾl-umma mujmiʿa ʿalā ʿiṣmat al-Nabī* ﷺ...).

The *Ṣaḥīḥ* collections tell us, on the authority of Abū Hurayra ؓ, that the Prophet ﷺ said: 'Satan came to me[197] and tried his utmost to disturb me as I prayed. Allah gave me power over him, and I threw him down. I considered hanging him from a pillar so that you could all look upon him, but then I remembered what my brother Sulaymān said: '*Lord, forgive me, and give me a sovereignty that shall be given to none after me. Verily, You are the Giver*' [38:35]; so Allah sent him away, thwarted.'

Abū al-Dardā' ؓ reported that Allah's enemy Iblīs came to the Messenger of Allah ﷺ as he prayed with a tongue of fire, and made as if to strike him in the face with it. The Prophet ﷺ sought Allah's refuge from him and cursed him, and then wanted to catch hold of him to tie him up, so that the children of Medina could play with him... (the ḥadīth then follows the narration of Abū Hurayra ؓ above).[198]

The reports of the Miʿrāj also say that a demon made for the Prophet ﷺ with a tongue of fire, and so Jibrīl ؑ taught him the words to say to seek refuge from it. This is related in *al-Muwaṭṭa'*.

When Satan was unable to harm him ﷺ directly, he sought to come to him through his enemies, as was the case when he plotted with Quraysh to assassinate the Prophet ﷺ, appearing to them in the form of an old man from Najd, and another time (at the Battle of Badr) in the form of Surāqa ibn Mālik[199]; Allah alluded to this with His words: '*And when Satan made their deeds alluring to them...*' [8:48]. On another occasion, he appeared and gave warnings about the Prophet ﷺ at the occasion of the ʿAqaba Pledge.

Yet Allah sufficed the Prophet ﷺ against all of this, and protected him from Satan's harm and his evil intentions.

When, in his ﷺ final illness, a draught was administered to him and they said to him, 'We feared that you had pleurisy!',[200] he said: 'It[201] was from Satan, and Allah would never give him power over me.'

197 'Abd al-Razzāq's narration adds 'in the form of a cat'.

198 I have amended the original wording of this report for clarity's sake. [t]

199 That is, Satan possessed Surāqa in order to address the unbelievers and exhort them to fight.

200 This is the translation Lane gives for *dhāt al-janb*, an inflammatory tumour in the membrane within the ribs. [t]

201 I.e., the medicine they gave him ﷺ without his permission (*Sharḥ al-Qārī*).

It might be said, 'What, then, is the meaning of Allah's words "*And if a provocation from Satan should provoke you, seek refuge in Allah...*" [7:200]?'

The answer is that these words are meant to refer to the Prophet's ﷺ community, and is akin to many occasions in the Qur'ān when the Prophet ﷺ is addressed personally with words that apply to his whole community.

This is also true of Allah's words: '*Never We sent a messenger or prophet before you, save that, when he hoped (tamannā), Satan cast into his hope; but Allah annuls what Satan casts, and then Allah affirms His signs; and Allah is Knowing, Wise*' [22:52].

Many scholars have erred in their interpretation of this verse, and many readers have misunderstood it; they have understood the word *tamannā* to mean 'recited', thus inferring that when the messenger or prophet recited what was revealed to him, Satan meddled with his recitation and cast therein whatever he wished to, after which Allah annulled what Satan had cast.

To support this interpretation, they cite the story of the 'holy birds' (*al-gharānīq*), which says that when the Prophet ﷺ recited sūrat al-Najm, and reached '*Hast you seen, then, al-Lāt and 'Uzzā, and Manāt, the third of them?*' [53:19-20], he then said: 'They are the holy birds, and their intercession is much desired.'[202]

(The word *gharānīq* is the plural of *gharnūq*, which means a male sea-bird, and also a white-skinned boy (the birds are called this because of their whiteness). The idolaters claimed that their idols brought them nearer to Allah and interceded for them; thus they resembled birds, carrying their prayers up to the heavens.)

Now when the Prophet ﷺ finished reciting the sūra, so the story goes, the unbelievers prostrated alongside the Muslims, because of how they had heard their gods praised so.

The reports of this story state that Satan cast these words onto the tongue of the Prophet ﷺ, who had been hoping that something would be revealed to him that would bring him closer to his people. When Satan cast these words, the Prophet ﷺ was aggrieved, and so Allah consoled him by saying: '*Never We sent a messenger or prophet before you, save that, when he hoped (tamannā), Satan cast into his hope; but Allah annuls what Satan casts, and then Allah affirms His signs; and Allah is Knowing, Wise*'

[202] Various other wordings are also given here, all meaning essentially the same thing.

[22:52], and also saying: '*Indeed they were near to seducing you from that We revealed to you, that you might forge against Us another; and then they would surely have taken you as a friend*' [17:73].

The correct way to understand this verse, however, is the explanation given by the Imam and great Knower of Allah, Shaykh ʿAbd al-ʿAzīz al-Dabbāgh ﷺ, which is as follows:

Allah ﷻ never sent any messenger, nor any prophet, to any community, save that this messenger hoped that his community would have faith; every messenger would love for this to happen, and greatly desire and yearn for it, and would try his utmost to achieve it. This includes our Prophet ﷺ, to whom the Lord ﷻ said: '*Perchance you wilt consume yourself with grief, over their footsteps, if they believe not in this tiding*' [18:6], and said: '*And most people, though you may strive, will not believe*' [12:103], and said: '*Wilt thou, then, force the people to believe?*' [10:99], as well as many other verses besides that convey this same meaning. But then the community differs, as Allah says: '*But they fell into variance: some of them believed, and some disbelieved*' [2:253]. Now as for those who disbelieved, Satan cast slanderous misgivings into the message, which is what caused them to disbelieve. Even the believer is not immune to misgivings, because they are usually present wherever faith in the unseen is involved, although they afflict people in different degrees, and in accordance with their connections.

If this is acknowledged, then the meaning of *tamannā* is that [the prophet or messenger] hopes for faith for his community, and loves for them to have goodness, guidance, soundness, and salvation. This is the hope of every prophet and messenger. That Satan 'casts into it' means that he casts misgivings into the hearts of the community that hear the message, causing some of them to disbelieve. Allah then has mercy on the disbelievers and annuls this from their hearts and affirms therein His signs which point to His Oneness and the truth of His message; and He ﷻ causes it to remain in the hearts of the hypocrites and disbelievers, who fall prey to it. This implies that these misgivings are at first cast into the hearts of both factions, but do not remain with the believers as they do with the disbelievers.[203]

[203] *Al-Ibrīz*, pp. 215-216.

This explains to us what this holy verse means; and as for the story of the 'holy birds', it is utterly false, both textually and rationally.

As far as its textual authority goes, this story was not collected by any of the compilers of the authentic collections, nor narrated by any trustworthy narrators with a sound and unbroken chain. It is but one of those reports collected by those exegetes and historians who collect every unusual story, and make use of everything they read, whether it be sound or spurious.

Qāḍī Abū Bakr ibn al-ʿAlāʾ al-Mālikī spoke the truth when he said[204]: Strife has been caused by certain folk who seek out every capricious tale and exegesis, and people bent on unbelief have attached themselves to [this tale] despite its weak narration, its conflicting versions, its lack of complete transmission, and the many differing wordings of it. Some say it happened during prayer, others that he ﷺ said it while asleep, others that he said it accidentally, others that Satan said it using his ﷺ tongue; others say that when the Prophet ﷺ presented it to Jibrīl ﷺ, he said, 'This is not how I transmitted it to you'; and still others say that Satan told the people that the Prophet ﷺ had read it this way, and when the Prophet ﷺ heard of this he said, 'By Allah, it was not revealed this way'; and there are other versions besides these. None of the exegetes or people of the Second Generation who told this tale gave any chain of transmission for it, nor said who they heard it from; and most of the chains of transmission that link it to them, in turn, are weak and spurious.

As for the rational side, it has been proven (and the Muslim community has agreed) that the Messenger of Allah ﷺ is divinely protected and absolved from such base things. It is unimaginable that he would hope for such words of praise for false gods to be revealed to him (which would be unbelief), or that Satan would overcome him and cause him to insert anything into the Qurʾān that was alien to it, and that the Prophet ﷺ would imagine that something alien to the Qurʾān were really from it, so that Jibrīl would need to correct him ﷺ. Such a thing is impossible for him ﷺ. It is equally unimaginable that the Prophet ﷺ would invent such a thing himself, whether deliberately (which would be unbelief) or accidentally; for he was protected from anything like that.

204 This paragraph is from the *Shifā*; it is not clear, either here or in the original, where Qāḍī Abū al-Mālikī's words come to an end and Qāḍī ʿIyāḍ's words are resumed. [t]

It has been clearly established, by proofs and by Muslim consensus, that the Prophet ﷺ was protected from any trace of unbelief ever crossing his heart or his tongue, whether deliberately or accidentally, and from the possibility that he could confuse an angelic revelation with a satanic one, or that Satan could ever get to him, or that he could ever attribute any words to Allah (whether deliberately or accidentally) that Allah did not reveal to him. Allah Himself says: '*Had he invented against Us any sayings, We would have seized him by the right hand...*' [69:44-45], and says: '*Then would We have let you taste the double of life and the double of death; and then you wouldst have found none to help you against Us*' [17:75].

Were this tale truly as it has been suggested, then it would have been completely inconsistent because of the contradictions it would have entailed, and the mixture between praise and condemnation [of false gods] it would have involved,[205] and the utter lack of harmony in the discourse; and the Prophet, the Muslims and the pagans (including their chieftains) would all have had to be completely oblivious to this. Yet no one who gives it even a moment's thought could be oblivious to such a thing – so how could it escape the attention of one whose forbearance was immense, and had vast knowledge of what constitutes clear and eloquent speech?

Moreover, it is well-known that the hypocrites, idolaters, and those Muslims who were weak-hearted and ignorant would leap at the slightest chance to attack the Prophet ﷺ for the least of things, and to criticise and insult the Muslims whenever possible; and those weak-hearted people who professed Islam would leave the religion because of the least doubt that arose. Yet this story has never been told by anyone, save for these few weak narrations; if it were really true, then Quraysh would have used it to attack the Muslims, and the Jews would have seized it as an argument against them, just as they did – in their arrogance – with the story of the Miʿrāj, causing some weak-hearted believers to apostatise.

Yet when it comes to this story, there are no reports that any opponent of Islam used it as an argument, nor that any Muslim ever raised an objection about it. This shows that it is false and utterly without foundation. There is no doubt that certain demons, whether human

205 Because the rest of the chapter, and indeed the whole Qurʾān, does nothing but condemn these false gods.

beings or jinn, invented this story and spread it by means of certain careless ḥadīth narrators, in order to cause confusion for those Muslims whose faith is weak.

Allah's Perfect Protection of Him ﷺ from all Flaws and Doubts

THERE ARE many reports and narrations showing how our Prophet ﷺ was free of all flaws from the moment he was born, and grew up not only possessing faith in the Oneness of Allah, but illumined by the lights of divine knowledge and the breezes of spiritual felicity.

Because of this, his ﷺ recognition of Allah's Oneness, knowledge of His Qualities, and faith in Him and in all that He revealed to him, were based on a foundation of the deepest knowledge and certitude, completely free of any trace of ignorance, doubt or uncertainty, and divinely protected against anything that might impair that knowledge and certitude.

Now if there are any texts which, on the surface, might seem to suggest otherwise, we shall briefly clarify the truth about them here, according to what the great scholars of Islam have said about them; and then we shall give our own opinion on the matter.

Qāḍī ʿIyāḍ says, of Allah's words '*So, if you are in doubt regarding what We have sent down to you, ask those who recite the Book before you. The truth has come to you from your Lord; so be not of the doubters*' [10:94]:[206]

Beware (may Allah strengthen you) of imagining that there is any truth to what some of the exegetes have said (supposedly on the authority of Ibn ʿAbbās, or others) about the Prophet ﷺ ever having had doubts about what was revealed to him. It is simply impossible for this to be the case; and indeed, Ibn ʿAbbās said[207]: 'The Prophet ﷺ never doubted, and never asked'; and both Ibn Jubayr and Ḥasan [al-Baṣrī] are reported to have said the same thing; and Qatāda reported that the Prophet ﷺ himself said: 'I do not doubt, and I will not ask.' The majority of exegetes are of this opinion; they differ, however, as to what the verse actually does mean.

206 What follows is taken from *al-Shifā*, Volume 2, Part III, Chapter One, Section 1 (*Fī ḥukm ʿaqd qalb al-Nabī* ﷺ...).

207 As Ibn Ḥātim reported, with an authentic chain of transmission (*Sharḥ al-Qārī*).

Some say that it means: 'Say, Muḥammad, to those who doubt: "*So, if you are in doubt regarding what We have sent down to you…*".' They say that the context in which this verse occurs is proof of this interpretation, since it is closely followed by: '*Say: O people, if you are in doubt regarding my religion…*' [10:104].

It is also said to be addressed to the Arabs, not the Prophet ﷺ, as is the case for Allah's words: '*If you ascribe a partner to Allah, your work shall surely fail*' [39:65], wherein he is addressed in the second person but it is really others who are meant. Another example of this is: '*So be you not in any doubt concerning what these people worship*' [11:109]; and there are many similar instances.

Do you not see that He says: '*Nor be of those who belie Allah's signs*' [10:95], when it was the Prophet ﷺ who was belied by others concerning the message he brought? How could he, then, be one of those who belied it? This all indicates that it is others, not the Prophet ﷺ, who are being addressed here.

Another verse which is similar to this one is: '*The Most Merciful: ask one who is informed of Him!*' [25:59]. These words are telling other people to ask the Prophet ﷺ; for the Prophet ﷺ is better informed, and more fitting to be asked, than any other.

It is also said that the 'doubt', which Allah commanded people other than the Prophet ﷺ to ask 'those who recite the Book' about, means only those stories that Allah has told us of the communities of old, and not the matters of Divine Oneness and Sacred Law unto which the Prophet ﷺ was calling.

Another example of this is Allah's words '*Ask those of Our messengers We sent before you…*' [43:45], which are actually addressed to the idolaters, though worded as though addressed to the Prophet ﷺ. It is also said that this means 'Ask [Us about] those of Our messengers We sent before you', with the elision of 'Us about', and that these words are a complete sentence, after which a new sentence begins: '*Have We appointed, apart from the Most Merciful, gods to be served?*' [43:45], a rhetorical question meant to express strong denial. It is also said that Allah commanded the Prophet ﷺ to ask this of the prophets on the Miʿrāj. Yet his certitude was far too great for him to have any need to ask this; and it is reported that he ﷺ said: 'I shall not ask, for I am sufficed.'

It is also said that it means 'Ask the communities of those messengers We sent if they conveyed to them any doctrine other than the Divine Oneness'; this was the position of Mujāhid, al-Suddī, al-Ḍaḥḥāk, and Qatāda. The purpose of both the verses in question was to inform the Prophet ﷺ of what the messengers had been sent to convey, and that Allah did not ever allow anyone to worship anything other than Him. This was a rebuttal to any idolaters, whether Arab or otherwise, who said: '*We worship them only that they may bring us nigh in nearness to Allah*' [39:3].

Another verse of this sort is: 'Those whom We have given the Book know it is sent down from your *Lord with the truth; so be not of the doubters*' [6:114]. That is, 'Do not doubt that they know you are the Messenger of Allah, though they have not acknowledged this.' So this does not mean that he ﷺ could have had any doubt in what is stated at the beginning of the verse.[208]

Another possibility is to interpret the verse in the same way as the aforementioned others; that is: 'Say, O Muḥammad, to those who doubt this: Be not of the doubters.' This is supported by what Allah says at the beginning of the verse: '*What, shall I seek any judge but Allah?*', which is clearly something the Prophet ﷺ is supposed to say to others.

It is also said that these words were meant to evoke an acknowledgement [from Quraysh],[209] as is the case with His words: '*O Jesus son of Mary, did you say unto men, "Take me and my mother as gods, apart from Allah"?*' [5:116], when He knew that Christ said no such thing.

It is also said that *wa in kunta fī shakk*[210] here [in 10:94] means 'So you are in no doubt', the word *in* meaning *mā*,[211] and the verse continuing: '*Then ask…*,' in order to add further assurance and knowledge to the knowledge and certitude you already have.

It is also said it means: 'If you are in doubt concerning the honours and graces We have given you, then ask them about the descriptions of you in their scriptures, and the virtues ascribed to you therein.'

Abū ʿUbayda is said to have explained it thus: 'If you are in doubt about anyone else, concerning what We have sent down...'

208 The whole verse reads: '*What, shall I seek any judge but Allah? For it is He who sent down to you the Book well-distinguished; and those whom We have given the Book know it is sent down from your Lord with the truth; so be not of the doubters*' [6:114].

209 *Sharḥ al-Qārī.*

210 'So, if you are in doubt' according to the usual understanding.

211 I am following Qārī's understanding of the word *mā* here as 'no', rather than 'in so far as', as others commentators on the *Shifā* have it. [t]

One might ask: 'What, then, does '*Till, when the messengers despaired and thought that they had been lied to...*' [12:110] mean, according to the canonical reading *kudhibū*?'[212] Well, the meaning of this has been explained to us by our lady ʿĀʾisha ﷺ, who said: 'Allah forbid that the messengers could ever think such a thing of their Lord! This only means that when the messengers despaired, they thought that those of their followers who had promised to help them had lied to them.' Most exegetes understand it this way.

It is also said that 'they thought' here does not refer to the messengers but to their followers; this was the opinion of Ibn ʿAbbās, al-Nakhaʿī, Ibn Jubayr, and several scholars. Along these lines, Mujāhid read the verse as *kadhabū*, 'they [the followers] thought that they [the messengers] had lied.'

Do not, then, pay any heed to minority interpretations that say anything else about this; for such a suggestion would be unworthy of the scholars, never mind the prophets.

Another example of this is found in Allah's words to our master Muḥammad ﷺ: '*Had Allah willed, He would have gathered them all in guidance. So be not of the ignorant*' [6:35]. Some interpret this as meaning 'Do not be of those who are ignorant of the fact that had Allah willed, He would have gathered them all in guidance.' But this is ridiculous, because even those with the least of faith are not ignorant of this fact, so how could the master of the faithful ﷺ not know it? This would imply that he were ignorant of one of Allah's Qualities; and this is impossible for any prophet.

Rather, the intention of these words is to advise him ﷺ not act in a way that resembles the attributes of those who are ignorant. It is also said that these words are addressed to the whole Muḥammadan community, telling them not to be among the ignorant.

Other examples of this are His words: '*If you ascribe a partner to Allah, your work shall surely fail*' [39:65], '*Do not call, apart from Allah, on that which neither profits you nor harms you*) [10:106], '*Then would We have let you taste the double of life...*' [17:75], '*We would have seized him by the right hand...*' [69:45], '*If you obeyest the most part of those on earth they will lead you astray from the path of Allah*' [6:116], '*If Allah willed, He would set a seal on your heart*' [42:24], '*If you do not, you wilt not have delivered His*

[212] The primary meaning of *kudhibū* is 'they were lied to'; this verse is usually translated into English as '...thought that they had been denied', or the like.

message' [5:67], and '*O Prophet, fear Allah, and obey not the unbelievers and the hypocrites*' [33:1].

Know, then, may Allah give success to us all, that it is not possible for him ﷺ to fail to deliver his message, or to disobey his Lord's commandments, or to associate partners with Him, or to invent something about Him that He does not approve, or to lie about Him, or to go astray, or to have his heart sealed, or to obey the disbelievers; for Allah made his affair easy for him by giving him unveilings and clarifications in the course of his preaching to those who opposed him, and made it clear to him that if he had delivered the message any other way it would not have been accepted,[213] and gave ease to his soul and strength to his heart by saying: '*Allah shall protect you from men*' [5:67].

As for His words '*Had he invented against Us any sayings, We would have seized him by the right hand...*' [69:44-45], and His words '*Then would We have let you taste the double of life...*' [17:75], they mean: 'This would be the requital for one who acted in that way, and would be your requital if you acted in that way'; they do not mean that he ﷺ actually did act that way.

As for His words '*If you obeyest the most part of those on earth they will lead you astray from the path of Allah*' [6:116], this is implicitly addressed to other than the Prophet ﷺ, as Allah says elsewhere: '*If you obey*[214] *those who disbelieve...*' [3:139] The same is true of His words '*If Allah willed, He would set a seal on your heart*' [42:24] and '*If you ascribe a partner to Allah, your work shall surely fail*' [39:65]: they are implicitly addressed to other than the Prophet ﷺ, for they speak of the condition of one who commits idolatry, which is impossible for the Prophet ﷺ.

Finally, His words '*O Prophet, fear Allah, and obey not the unbelievers and the hypocrites*' [33:1] do not say that he ﷺ actually obeyed them; Allah may forbid the Prophet ﷺ whatever He will, and command him whatever He will. Likewise, He says: '*And do not drive away those who call upon their Lord at morning and evening desiring His countenance*' [6:52], although the Prophet ﷺ never did drive them away, nor do them any wrong.

213 That is, Allah made it clear to the Prophet ﷺ that he had delivered the message in exactly the right way.

214 *Tuṭīʿū*, in the third person plural (addressing the believers).

The Author's Own Opinion

Another opinion concerning these verses occurred to me, which may be correct (Allah willing), which is that we can divide these verses into two categories: those which prohibit him ﷺ from things that he could never possibly do; and those which hypothetically posit his doing things that are well beneath his ﷺ station.

THE FIRST CATEGORY

This category contains those verses that prohibit him ﷺ from doing things that he of all people would never do – things that one cannot imagine him ﷺ doing, or even someone of a lesser rank than him doing. It includes also those verses that command him ﷺ to do something he was already doing – things which the clear proofs and authentic narrations of his ﷺ biography tell us that he had already attained and perfectly mastered even before his prophethood began, being as they are the natural manifestations of his tremendous character and noble attributes.

My opinion on this category of verses is that their purpose was to exhort him ﷺ to continue to hold firm to what he was already doing, whether in the form of prohibitions of those actions that opposed his own, or commandments of actions that conformed to his own.

Examples of this are Allah's words '*O Prophet, fear Allah*' [33:1], '*Have clemency, enjoin what is right, and turn away from the ignorant*' [7:199], and '*O Prophet! Strive against the unbelievers and the hypocrites*' [66:9]. It should not be understood from these verses that the Prophet ﷺ did not have clemency, enjoin what is right or fear Allah before they were revealed – Allah forbid! Rather, these verses did not command the Prophet ﷺ to begin an action or form it, but rather to continue doing what he was already doing, and to remain as he was. It is as though Allah were saying: 'O Prophet, keep on fearing Allah as you do, and maintain your refined character by continuing to have clemency, enjoin what is right, turn away from the ignorant, and strive against the unbelievers.'

This is the case because he ﷺ was already endowed with these qualities and had complete mastery of them; and indeed some of them had been part of his character, for which he was well-known, before his prophetic mission had yet begun: he was forbearing, generous, clement, and ever enjoining what was right and turning away from the ignorant.

Another example of this is found in Allah's words: '*We have sent down to you the Book with the truth, so that you mayest judge between the people by that which Allah has shown you. Be not, then, an advocate for traitors*' [4:105]. This verse was revealed in connection with Qatāda ibn al-Nuʿmān, who, when his belongings were stolen from him, accused Banū Ubayriq (who were hypocrites) as well as a group of believers, of the crime. The Messenger of Allah ﷺ scolded him for this, saying: 'You have spoken of a household known for their piety and righteousness, and accused them of theft without any proof or evidence!' Qatāda took back his accusation, and then this verse was revealed. The word 'advocate' seems to imply that the Prophet ﷺ wanted to side with the traitors and advocate for them – yet far be it that this be the case, for he ﷺ was the Trustworthy One, and was known for this even before his prophetic mission began; and he was always known for his purity and incorruptibility.

I submit that the meaning of these words is: 'Continue, O Muḥammad, with your praiseworthy conduct and lofty ethics by maintaining your refusal of aid, cooperation or defence to traitors.'

Likewise, Allah's words '*be not of the ignorant*' [6:35] mean: 'Maintain your knowledge and wisdom, and continue to distance yourself from the ignorant'; and His words '*be not of the doubters*' [10:94] mean: 'Maintain your certitude and faith, and continue to distance yourself from the doubters and the irresolute'; and His words '*Do not call, apart from Allah, on that which neither profits you nor harms you*' [10:106] mean: 'Continue to call on Allah alone, and turn to Him alone, and hold fast to Him alone.'

I do not think that even an ignorant person would suggest that the Prophet ﷺ ever did otherwise, or that it even crossed his mind to do otherwise.

The greatest evidence for this is found in Allah's words '*Nor be of those who belie Allah's signs*' [10:95]; for it is obvious and indisputable, and beyond any doubt, that he ﷺ was the one who was belied by others concerning the message he brought; how, then, could he be among those who belied it?

I submit that the meaning of this verse is: 'Continue, O Muḥammad, to hold to the strength of your conviction, the perfection of your belief, and the immensity of your faith.'

All of this is akin to what a teacher would say to a hardworking, bright pupil: 'Work hard, do not be lazy or slack, and do not play around', although he is already working hard, and not playing around at all.

Thus all of this is well within the scope of the Arabic language, and the believer's heart is at ease with it.

THE SECOND CATEGORY

This category contains those verses that hypothetically posit his ﷺ doing things that under no circumstances could one imagine him doing; and it is unacceptable to understand from these verses that he could ever do such things, or that such things could be attributed to him. The exegetes have spoken much about these verses and posited different explanations for them, many of which have strayed into the realms of affectation and absurdity.

My view is that these verses, some of which we shall mention presently, do not necessitate the interpretations suggested by certain exegetes, who came up with arguments and theories which they then – because of their faith – had to explain away with feeble interpretations and weak theories. The reason all this is not needed is that these verses are meant to posit hypothetical situations, and not to suggest that these situations could actually come to pass. Rather, we believe that it is impossible they could come to pass; and the fact that they are hypothetically posited does not mean it is right to attribute them to the Prophet ﷺ.

It is possible, after all, to speak hypothetically about the occurrence of something impossible, and to do so does not in any way suggest that this thing could ever happen. This is borne out by Allah's words: '*Say: "If the Most Merciful had a son, I would be the first one to worship!"*' [43:81]. Could we say, then, that this verse implies that such a thing could happen? Only an ignorant idolater would say that. It is but a hypothetical; that is: 'Assuming, for argument's sake, that the Most Merciful had a son', though in fact this is impossible without any doubt.

The same response can be given to any questions raised by Allah's words: '*So, if you are in doubt regarding what We have sent down to you, ask those who recite the Book before you*' [10:94]. The meaning is: 'If, for argument's sake, any doubt were to enter your mind, then ask those who recite the Book'; but this is impossible, and will never happen.

Other examples of this are the Almighty's words: '*If you obeyest the most part of those on earth they will lead you astray from the path of Allah)* [6:116], '*If Allah willed, He would set a seal on your heart*' [42:24], and '*If you ascribe a partner to Allah, your work shall surely fail*' [39:65]. Each one of these is a hypothetical situation that could never happen, and must not be attributed to him ﷺ. No intelligent believer, after all, could imagine that the Prophet ﷺ would obey anyone on earth, when Allah commanded everyone on earth to obey him ﷺ, saying: '*O you who believe! Obey Allah, and obey the Messenger*' [4:59]. No intelligent believer could imagine that Allah would set a seal of the heart of Muḥammad ﷺ, when Allah sets a seal on the hearts of any who do not believe in him ﷺ: '*Allah has set a seal on their hearts and on their hearing, and over their eyes is a veil*' [2:7].

Concerning the Story of Zayd ibn Ḥāritha

Another instance of this is the story of Zayd ibn Ḥāritha: '*When you said to him whom Allah had favoured and you had favoured, 'Keep your wife to yourself, and fear Allah,' and you were concealing within yourself what Allah would reveal, and you did fear men, though Allah has a better right that you should fear Him. So when Zayd had performed that necessary formality [of divorce] from her, then We gave her in marriage to you, so that there should not be any sin for believers in respect of the wives of their adopted sons, when the latter have performed that necessary formality [of divorce] from them; and Allah's commandment must be fulfilled*' [33:37].

Some exegetes have erred in their exegesis of this, saying that it means that when the Prophet ﷺ saw Zaynab she aroused his admiration, and he hoped that Zayd would divorce her, yet kept this hope a secret and commanded Zayd to keep her, out of civility.

Were this true, it would be extremely problematic, and would suggest that he ﷺ turned his eyes to those adornments of the life of this world that were forbidden to him.[215] This would be the very blameworthy envy which Allah does not accept, and which even ordinary pious people are above, never mind the Master of the Prophets ﷺ. Al-Qushayrī said of this:

> This shows a great temerity and a scanty knowledge of the Prophet's ﷺ rights and virtues. How can anyone maintain that he ﷺ saw her and that she then suddenly aroused his admiration? She was, after all, his cousin, whom he had seen regularly since she was born; and women would not veil themselves from him; and he ﷺ was the one who arranged her marriage to Zayd in the first place![216]

Had he ﷺ wanted, he could have married her himself before Zayd did,

[215] Allusion to Qur'ān 18:28: '*Let not your eyes turn away from them, desiring the adornment of the present life*'.

[216] *Al-Shifā*.

and she would have been as happy as can be about this, especially given that she only married Zayd out of obedience to the Messenger of Allah ﷺ.

The truth in which we are confident before Allah is that Allah informed His Prophet ﷺ that Zaynab would be his wife after Zayd for a legislative purpose, to which the aforementioned verse alludes at its end.[217] Zayd often complained to the Messenger of Allah ﷺ that he felt unsettled and ill at ease with being married to her, because of several differences that existed between them, making it difficult for them to achieve mutual comfort and harmony. Whenever Zayd conveyed these complaints to the Messenger of Allah ﷺ, he would tell him: 'Keep your wife to yourself, and fear Allah,' and would conceal from him what Allah had told him, which was that he was destined to marry her; yet Allah brought this all out into the open when Zayd brought the marriage to an end and divorced her.

This was, then, an act of manners and taste on his ﷺ part, and perfect sensitivity to the feelings of others, even though it would not have been blameworthy on his part to simply say 'Allah has told me that Zaynab shall be my wife after you.' This verse was Allah's way of praising the Prophet ﷺ for behaving this way and taking this stance.

This is the meaning of Allah's words '*thou were concealing within yourself what Allah would reveal*' [33:37].

This is supported by what al-Zuhrī is reported to have said: 'Jibrīl came to the Prophet ﷺ to inform him that Allah had married him to Zaynab bint Jaḥsh; and this is what he concealed within himself.'[218]

This is further corroborated by what the exegetes say about Allah's words in the same verse: '*and Allah's commandment must be fulfilled*'; that is, 'You must marry her.' It is further clarified by the fact that Allah did not 'reveal' anything connected with the Prophet ﷺ and Zaynab other than his marriage to her; this indicates that this was what he ﷺ 'concealed', and what Allah had informed him of.

The wisdom behind the Prophet's ﷺ marriage to her was to put an end to the notion that adoption constitutes a permanent family tie, and to annul the practice of it; for the Prophet ﷺ had adopted Zayd, who had thereafter become known as 'Zayd, son of Muḥammad'. Allah annulled this custom with His words '*Muḥammad is not the father of any man among*

217 The author is referring to Allah's words: '*...So that there should not be any sin for believers in respect of the wives of their adopted sons, when the latter have performed that necessary formality [of divorce] from them; and Allah's commandment must be fulfilled*' [33:37]. [t]

218 *Al-Shifā*.

you' [33:40], and annulled it practically by commanding the Prophet ﷺ to marry Zaynab.[219] Allah alludes to this when He says at the end of the verse: '*...So that there should not be any sin for believers in respect of the wives of their adopted sons, when the latter have performed that necessary formality [of divorce] from them; and Allah's commandment must be fulfilled*'.

One might ask: 'In that case, what was the point of the Prophet ﷺ telling Zayd to keep his wife to himself?' Well, although Allah had informed His Prophet ﷺ that she would be his wife, Allah had not yet given leave for the divorce to take place; and therefore he continued to advise him to retain her until the time came when Allah willed the divorce to take place.

One might say: 'What, then, is the meaning of His words "*and you did fear men, though Allah has a better right that you should fear Him*"?' Well, the word 'fear' here means shyness, and not fright; that is, 'You felt shy of them lest they say, "he has married his son's wife!".' What he feared of men was the calumny of the hypocrites and Jews, and the mischief they could cause for the Muslims by saying, 'He has married his son's ex-wife, after having forbidden marriage to the former wives of one's sons!' Therefore Allah corrected him for this, and instructed him to rise above paying any attention to them when it came to what He had made lawful for him, just as He corrected him for being too eager to please his wives by saying: '*Why do you forbid something that Allah has made lawful unto you?*' [66:1]. In the same way, He says here: '*and you did fear men, though Allah has a better right that you should fear Him*'.

It is reported that both al-Ḥasan[220] and ʿĀʾisha said: 'Were the Messenger of Allah ﷺ to have concealed anything, he would have concealed this verse, because of how it corrected him and revealed what he had concealed.'[221]

219 Fostering is allowed in Islam, but the child must retain its father's name and not be named after the foster-family. [t]

220 Al-Baṣrī.

221 *Al-Shifā*, Tirmidhī, Ibn Jarīr.

"And He Found You Wandering, and Guided You", and another Contentious Issue[222]

Another example of this is found in Allah's words '*And He found you wandering (ḍāllan), and guided you*' [93:7]. It is said that this means 'He found you wandering from prophethood, so He guided you to it', or 'He found you amid a people of error (*ḍalāl*)[223] and so protected you from it, and led you to faith and made you their guide', or 'He found you without knowledge of your Shariah, and so guided you to it'. In this case, *ḍalāl* means 'bewilderment' (*taḥayyur*). Thus the Prophet ﷺ would keep solitary vigils in the cave of Ḥirā᾿, seeking a way to approach his Lord and a law to follow, until Allah guided him to Islam. It is also said to mean 'You did not know the truth, so He guided you to it'; this is akin to Allah's words: '*He taught you what you knew not*' [4:113].

Jaʿfar ibn Muḥammad[224] is reported to have said: 'I found you unaware of My pre-eternal love for you (that is, you did not know of it), so I blessed you with knowledge of Me.'

Al-Ḥasan ibn ʿAlī recited this verse as 'And the stray one found you, and was guided'[225]; though this is an uncommon way to recite it.

The meaning that seems best to me is: 'He found you uncertain about how to proclaim what was revealed unto you, and how to guide people and convey the message to them, and so guided you in that.' This is suggested by what He says elsewhere: '*We have sent down to you the Remembrance that you mayest make clear to mankind what was sent down to them; and so haply they will reflect*' [16:44]. It has come to my

222 This chapter draws from *al-Shifā*, Volume 2, Part III, Chapter One, Section 2 (*wa ammā ʿiṣmatuhum...*).

223 The active participle *ḍāll* (gerund *ḍalāl*) can mean 'errant', 'wandering', 'confused', 'astray', 'misguided', 'foolishly in love', and so on. [t]

224 Jaʿfar al-Ṣādiq.

225 *Wa wajadaka ḍāllun fa-hadā.*

attention that this was also the opinion of al-Junayd.

Ibn ʿAṭāʾ said that *ḍāll* here means 'loving', that is, 'loving to gain knowledge of Me'; for *ḍāll* can mean 'one who loves', as was the case when [Yaʿqūb's sons] said [to their father]: '*Thou holdest still to your ancient love [ḍalāl]!*' [12:95]; they were not speaking about their father's religion here, for had they said such a thing about a prophet they would have been guilty of unbelief. Another example of this usage is: '*Certain women that were in the city said, "The Governor's wife has been soliciting her page; he has smitten her heart with love. Indeed, we see her in manifest error [ḍalāl]!"*'[226]

Al-Junayd said that it means: 'He found you confused about how to convey what He had sent down to you, and so showed you how to convey it', due to His words: '*We have sent down to you the Remembrance...*' [16:44].[227] It is also said to mean 'He found you in a state where your prophethood was known to no one, and then He made you known, so that the felicitous were guided by you.'

A similar instance is found in Allah's words '*Thou knewest not what the Book was, nor faith...*' [42:52]. The correct understanding of this is: 'Before the Revelation came, you did not know how to read the Qurʾān, nor how to call mankind unto faith.' Others say that 'faith' here means the obligations and laws of Islam. For even before the Revelation, he ﷺ was a believer in Allah's Oneness; and then the laws of Islam were revealed, which had been unknown to him before, and thus his faith increased because of the addition to it of religious responsibility. This is the best way to understand these words.

Another similar instance is found in His words: '... *though before it you were one of the unaware [al-ghāfilīn]*' [12:3].[228] Al-Azharī says that *al-ghāfilīn* here means 'those who forgot', which is akin to His words elsewhere: '*lest one of them forget [tuḍill]*' [2:282][229]. One must be aware that the meaning here is not the same as in '*those who are heedless (ghāfilūn) of Our signs*' [10:7]. Abū ʿAbdallāh al-Harawī said that *ghāfilīn*

226 The author only quotes the final part of this verse, since the Arab readership would immediately recognise it; I have included the whole verse, to show the context and how the word *ḍalāl* here again is connected with love. [t]

227 See the author's explanation of this above, where the verse is fully cited.

228 *Ghāfil* (the singular form of *ghāfilīn*) can also mean 'heedless'.

229 This verse is cited here because *ḍalāl* is something of a synonym for *ghafla* ('heedlessness' or 'obliviousness'); thus if *tuḍill* can mean 'forget', *ghāfil* could mean 'one who forgets'.

in verse 12:3 means 'those who were unaware of the story of Yūsuf, for you could only know it by means of Our revelation.'[230]

---

[230]   This verse occurs directly before the story of Yūsuf ✤ is told.

Ascribing Sin to His Blessed Person ﷺ[231]

Another issue of contention concerns Allah's words '*That Allah may forgive you your sins of the past and those to follow*' [48:2]. This verse seems on the surface to suggest that it is possible for the Prophet ﷺ to commit sins deliberately, since forgiveness only follows sin. Some scholars have asserted this view and supported it, saying that it is possible that he might commit minor sins [*ṣaghā'ir*], backing this up by adducing certain Qur'ānic verses and ḥadīths which on the surface seem to suggest this.

These include His words: '*And ask forgiveness for your sin, and for the believers, men and women*' [47:19], '*And [did We not] lift from you your burden,*[232] *which weighed down your back?*' [94:2-3], '*Allah pardon you! Why did you give them leave?*' [9:43], '*Had it not been for a prior prescription from Allah, there would have afflicted you, for what you took, a mighty chastisement*' [8:68], and '*He frowned and turned away, that the blind man came to him*' [80:1-2]. As for the ḥadīths, they include the Prophet's words: 'O Allah, forgive me for what I have done, and what I will do, and what I have hidden, and what I have revealed,'[233] and other similar prayers. They also include his ﷺ words: 'Indeed my heart becomes veiled, and I ask forgiveness of my Lord'[234], and the ḥadīth reported by Abū Hurayra ؓ: 'I ask forgiveness of Allah and repent to Him more than seventy times a day.'[235]

The Shaykh and Imam Qāḍī ʿIyāḍ (may Allah have mercy on him) gave many answers to the questions raised by '*That Allah may forgive you your sins of the past and those to follow*' [48:2]. One was that this refers to the sins of his ﷺ community; another was that it means those things that were done accidentally, forgetfully or with some other valid explanation;

231 This chapter is partially drawn from *al-Shifā*, Volume 2, Part III, Chapter One, Section *fil-radd ʿalā man ajāza ʿalayhim al-ṣaghā'ir.*

232 The reason this is relevant is that the word *wizr* ('burden') can also mean 'sin'. [t]

233 Al-Bukhārī, Muslim.

234 Muslim.

235 Al-Bukhārī.

another was that 'forgiveness' here means 'protection from the occurrence of sin'; another was that when the Prophet ﷺ was commanded to say '*and I know not what shall be done with me or with you. I only follow what is revealed to me; I am only a clear warner*' [46:9], the disbelievers were pleased to hear this, and so Allah revealed His words '*That Allah may forgive you your sins of the past and those to follow*'. Thus, the meaning of the verse is: 'You are forgiven, and would not be punished for a sin even if you were to commit one.'

The Imam and Knower of Allah ʿAbd al-ʿAzīz al-Dabbāgh also gave a fine answer to this issue, the essence of which is that the meaning of 'victory' in the verse that precedes this one, '*Surely We have given you a manifest victory*' [48:1], is 'vision', that is, a vision of the Almighty. In His mercy to the Prophet ﷺ, He removed the veil from him and blessed him with direct vision of Himself, so that he thereafter saw only that which is from the Real, or leads to the Real. This is what the 'manifest victory' was, and it was given to the Prophet ﷺ even in his youth, for he was never veiled from Allah. Yet this victory is given to every prophet, and indeed to every knower of Allah; what distinguished the vision of the Prophet ﷺ was the perfection therein of his power and strength, and the aptitude of his mind, spirit, soul, being, and inner secret, far beyond that of anyone else.

As for the word 'sin' in His words '*That Allah may forgive you your sins of the past and those to follow*', it means the obliviousness and darkness of the veil, which is part of man's origin, being as he is created from dust. In turn, 'of the past and those to follow' is an allusion to the obliteration of this veil; the meaning of 'forgiveness' here is 'obliteration'.

It is as though He were saying, then: 'We have given you a manifest victory by completely removing from you the veil, and fulfilling Our favour unto you, and ensuring your guidance and succour.' There is no greater favour, after all, than the removal of the veil, and no greater guidance than direct and experimental knowledge of Allah, and no better succour than to be granted such a state. This is the essence of what Shaykh al-Dabbāgh says on the matter.

I say, moreover, that when it comes to Allah's commandment to the Prophet ﷺ to ask forgiveness of Him, and his ﷺ obedience to this, and the occasions when he called upon Allah and asked forgiveness of him, this is all a manifestation of his ﷺ perfect humility and his perfect willingness to be a servant of Allah, and his need for his Lord, and his unwillingness to do without His grace, and his refusal to allow himself to be deluded by what his Lord had already given him. It is as though his spiritual state were saying: 'Despite the grace, reward, and lofty states and high ranks with which my Lord has blessed me, I have not ceased to desire His grace, and seek His favour, and stand supplicant at His door, and strive to attain all that is good and righteous.' Indeed, he ﷺ stated this openly when he said: 'I have more fear, consciousness and knowledge of Allah than any of you.'[236] This was also a way of teaching the Muslim community, so that they would follow his example. It was, moreover, an expression of gratitude to Allah in the form of perpetual service to Him. Why should this not be the case, when he ﷺ said: 'Should I not, then, be a grateful servant?'[237]

Imam al-Shādhilī (Allah have mercy on him) said: 'I heard related to me the words of the Messenger of Allah ﷺ, "Indeed my heart becomes veiled, and I ask forgiveness of my Lord seventy times a day," and could not understand what it meant. Then I saw the Messenger of Allah ﷺ, and he said to me: "O blessed one! That is the veil of light, not the veil of contingent things!"'

As for Allah's words '*And [did We not] lift from you your burden, which weighed down your back?*' [94:2-3], it is said that this means that he ﷺ was protected from sin before his prophethood began, for otherwise the burden of it would have weighed down his back.

It is also said that the 'burden' refers to the responsibilities of delivering the message, which weighed down his back until he had conveyed it.

It is also said to mean: 'You were weighed down by your innermost heart's concern and confusion, and your desire for your Shariah, until We gave it to you.'

It is also said to mean: 'We eased the burden of all that you had to bear by giving protection to all that [Revelation] which you asked to be protected.'

It is also said to mean 'We relieved you of the heavy burden of the pagan

236 Narrated in different version by al-Bukhārī, Muslim, Mālik, al-Nasā'ī, etc.
237 Al-Bukhārī, Muslim.

ignorance [that had afflicted your people].'

The meaning of 'weighed down your back' is that it almost weighed it down; or it means that Allah protected him ﷺ from sins which, had they occurred, would have weighed down his back; or it refers to the burden of the message, or the way his ﷺ heart was burdened and troubled by the pagan ignorance which had afflicted his people; or it was Allah's way of telling him that the revelation would be preserved for him, as he had requested.

As for His words *'Allah pardon you! Why did you give them leave?'* [9:43][238], this did not concern something that Allah had forbidden to the Prophet ﷺ before, that it might be deemed a sin[239]; and Allah did not deem it a sin. The people of knowledge do not even consider this to be a rebuke, and they made it clear that anyone who did think so is mistaken.

The truth of the matter is that the Prophet ﷺ had the right to do whatever he willed as long as nothing specific had been revealed about it; this is clearly shown by Allah's words '*Give leave to whom you wilt of them*' [24:62]. When he ﷺ did give them leave, Allah divulged to him information about them which he had not had, which was that even if he had not given them leave they would have stayed behind anyway. He could not be blamed for what he did, and the word 'pardon' (*'afā*) here does not mean 'forgive'. The Prophet ﷺ once said 'Allah has pardoned you from giving charity[240] for horses and slaves', though it had never been obligatory for them to give it in the first place and He had never asked it of them. This is also the way al-Qushayrī explains it, saying that only those who have no knowledge of Arabic say that *'afā* only means 'pardon for sin', when in fact saying 'May Allah pardon you' does not necessarily imply that you have sinned. Al-Dāwūdī and Makkī said that the expression is a kind of opening phrase of respect, similar to 'May Allah be good to you!', or 'May Allah ennoble you!', used to begin a dialogue or address. Al-Samarqandī said that it means 'May Allah give you health.'[241]

238 This verse refers to the occasion when the Prophet ﷺ gave leave to certain people to stay behind in Medina rather than go out to the expedition of Tabūk. [t]

239 That is, Allah had not forbidden the Prophet ﷺ from giving them leave. [t]

240 Meaning the *zakāt*. [t]

241 The verbs *'afā* ('to pardon') and *'āfā* ('to give good health') share the same lexical root. [t]

As for His words '*He frowned and turned away, that the blind man came to him. What could inform you but that he might grow in purity, or yet remember, and the Reminder profit him? But as for him who thinks himself independent, unto him you pay regard; though it is not your concern if he grow not in purity*' [80:1-7], they do not affirm that the Prophet ﷺ committed any sin; rather, they are meant to inform us that the one to whom he paid regard was one of those who refused to grow in purity. So the words are addressed to us. They also affirm that it would have been better – had the Prophet ﷺ been informed of the inner states of the two men – to give preference to the blind man, rather than the other.

Yet the Prophet's ﷺ action, in paying regard to that unbeliever, was an act of obedience to Allah and an attempt to deliver His message and draw people to His guidance, as He had commanded him to do. It was not in any way an act of disobedience or sin. The reason Allah conveyed this story unto the Prophet ﷺ here was to divulge to him the inner state of these two men, and to make clear to him that the other man was the worse of the two, and to instruct him to turn away from that disbeliever thenceforth, which is what He meant by '*though it is not your concern if he grow not in purity*' [80:7].

My view is that it is also possible that it is a rebuke from the Real for what he ﷺ did, thinking it the best course of action and deeming it likely to succeed, though Allah ﷻ had willed otherwise. Rebuke [*itāb*] does not at all entail that there must have been a sin or contravention, and this is true even of people in their ordinary affairs: a man might rebuke his brother, and a lover might rebuke his beloved, simply for doing the lesser of two good things, or the least perfect of them; and on the other hand, a father might rebuke his son for being remiss or doing something wrong. Thus the act of rebuke is too broad to have only one single form.

It is also said that the subject of the words '*He frowned and turned away*' are actually the unbeliever with whom the Prophet ﷺ was speaking; this was the opinion of Abū Tamām.

Another issue of contention concerns what the Prophet ✽ is narrated to have said to Khadīja ✽ when the Revelation first came to him: 'Verily, I feared for myself.'[242]

This does not mean that he ✽ had any doubt about what Allah had sent him, having seen the angel; rather, perhaps he feared that his strength would not be able to bear contact with the angel and the great burdens of the Revelation, and that his heart would give out or his soul give itself up. This applies to those authentic narrations which state that he ✽ said this after seeing the angel. It is also possible that he ✽ said this before he met the angel; for Allah had already informed him of his prophethood by means of the miraculous things that happened to him, such as the greetings given to him by stones and trees, and the visions and tidings that came to him.

Certain versions of this ḥadīth state that these visions would first come while the Prophet ✽ was asleep, and then the same thing would be shown to him when he was awake, in order to make him ✽ comfortable, lest he be surprised in a waking state by a vision of something completely new to him that his human form could not bear.

The authentic collections narrate that 'Ā'isha ✽ said: 'The Revelation came first to the Messenger of Allah ✽ in the form of true visions; and then he began to love keeping solitary vigils, until the truth came to him as he was in the cave of Ḥirā'.'[243]

Ibn 'Abbās ✽ is related to have said: 'The Prophet ✽ spent fifteen years in Mecca: for seven years he heard a voice and saw a light but nothing else, and then for eight years the Revelation came to him.'[244]

Ibn Isḥāq relates that the Prophet ✽ spoke about the time he spent in the cave of Ḥirā', and then said: 'As I was sleeping, he came to me and said: "Recite!", so I said "What should I recite?"[245] He then told, as 'Ā'isha's report includes, of how the angel whelmed him in his embrace and dictated to him: *Recite: In the Name of your Lord...* [96:1], and then said: 'He then left me, and I awoke from my sleep with the events, as it were, inscribed in my heart. I detested nothing so much as a poet or madman, and I said to myself: "Quraysh will never speak of me as such!

---

242 Al-Bukhārī, Muslim.
243 Al-Bukhārī, Muslim.
244 Muslim.
245 Or 'I do not recite' (*mā aqra'*). [t]

I shall go to a high place in the mountain and throw myself from it and kill myself." As I was going to do so, I heard a call from the heavens: "O Muḥammad! You are the Messenger of Allah, and I am Jibrīl!" I raised my head, and there was Jibrīl, in the form of a man...'

This makes it clear that what he ﷺ said, and the intention that he had, were only before he had met Jibrīl ﷺ face to face, and before Allah had informed him of his prophethood.[246]

Another such point of contention is his ﷺ words 'Indeed my heart becomes veiled, and I ask forgiveness of my Lord one hundred times a day' (one narration has it 'more than seventy times a day'). Qāḍī ʿIyāḍ said:

Beware of imagining that this 'veil' [*ghayn*] means that misgivings or doubts entered his ﷺ heart; rather, the basic meaning of *ghayn* here is something that covers the heart and enfolds it, as Abū ʿUbayd affirmed. Originally, the word *ghayn* describes the way in which clouds cover the sky. Others say that *ghayn* is something that covers the heart without enfolding it entirely, like the thin clouds that hang in the sky without blocking out the light of the sun.

What is meant by this 'veil' is an allusion to the times when his heart would be outwardly occupied, and the times when his soul would not keep up constant invocation and witnessing of the Real; this would be forced upon him ﷺ by the necessities of human nature, the direction of Muslim affairs, family responsibilities, dealing with friends and foes, seeing to personal needs, and the great burdens he had to bear of conveying the message and fulfilling his trusts. In all of these things he was obeying his Lord, and worshipping his Creator; but since he ﷺ had the loftiest place with Allah of all creation, and the highest rank,

246 Publisher's note: It is worthy of note that the hadith scholars do not consider this portion of the hadith to be authentic. Ibn Hajar says, 'It is one of al-Zuhrī's *balāghāt* [unattributed narrations] and has no complete chain of transmission' (*Fatḥ al-Bārī* vol. 19, p 449). Al-Zuhrī said '*fee ma balaghana* – according to what we have heard', and then mentions these words about going to the mountain. None of the other narrations of this hadith found in Muslim's *Ṣaḥīḥ*, the *Musnad* of Imam Aḥmad, the *Mustadrak* of Imam Ḥākim, Bayhaqī's *Dalāʾil al-Nubuwwa*, nor indeed the other two versions that are found in the *Ṣaḥīḥ* of al-Bukhari, contain these words.

and had the most perfect [divine] knowledge of all of them, and since his state when his heart and aspiration were purely concentrated on his Lord, and his entire being was turned to Him, was the greater of the two states he ever occupied – [since all this was the case,] he ﷺ viewed the times when he was temporarily out of this state [while distracted by something else] as lapses in his higher state, and a fall back to a lower station; so he asked his Lord's forgiveness for that. This is the best and most well-supported interpretation of these words, and many people incline towards this view and find it fitting; now it should be pointed out that this view is based on the opinion that it was possible for the Prophet ﷺ to go through temporary moments of forgetfulness and distraction in those matters not directly connected to the delivery of the Message.[247]

There are others, though, among those endowed with enlightened hearts, and the masters of Sufism, who affirm that all this is impossible for the Prophet ﷺ, and that he is far above being susceptible to forgetfulness or heedlessness. They say that the meaning of this ḥadīth is that he ﷺ would become concerned and worried for the affairs of his community because of his deep care and compassion for them, and so would ask Allah's forgiveness for them.

They also say that this 'veil' on his heart may mean the inner peace [*sakīna*] that enfolded it, according to Allah's words: '*Then Allah sent down on him His inner peace*' [9:40]; and the prayers for forgiveness he ﷺ made at these times were an expression of worship and neediness.

Ibn ʿAṭāʾ said that his ﷺ prayers for forgiveness were meant to encourage the Muslims to seek forgiveness and show them how to do it; and others say that it was meant to inspire caution in them, that they not be too sure of their safety.[248]

It could also be explained that this 'veiling' was a moment of fear and awe that enveloped the heart, whereupon he ﷺ would ask forgiveness of Allah by way of expressing gratitude and servitude to Him, as he said of his constant worship: 'Shall I not be, then, a grateful servant?'[249]

247 It is not possible that these moments of forgetfulness could apply to the delivery of the Message because it is impossible that any messenger of Allah could fail to deliver his message as Allah intended.

248 That is, to make them think: 'If even the Messenger of Allah ﷺ asks Allah's forgiveness, how should we not do so?'

249 *Al-Shifā*, Volume 2, Part III, Chapter One, Section One.

We have already seen, moreover, what Imam Abū al-Ḥasan al-Shādhilī said about this ḥadīth, and how he saw the Prophet ﷺ in a dream saying to him: 'That is the veil of light, not the veil of contingent things!'

His ﷺ Moments of Forgetfulness did not Negate His Perfection

Another issue of contention concerns the 'ḥadīth of forgetting' [*ḥadīth al-sahw*],[250] which tells of the occasion when the Prophet ﷺ prayed the afternoon prayer and made the final *salām* after only two cycles. Dhul-Yadayn stood up and said, 'O Messenger of Allah, did you shorten the prayer or did you forget?' The Messenger of Allah replied: 'Neither one nor the other.' (One narration has it that he ﷺ said 'I neither shortened nor forgot.') Dhul-Yadayn replied, 'It must have been one of them, O Messenger of Allah.' The Messenger of Allah ﷺ asked the people if Dhul-Yadayn was right, and they said he was; so the Messenger of Allah ﷺ completed the rest of the prayer and then added two extra prostrations after the final *salām*. Now this ḥadīth seems on the surface to suggest that he ﷺ denied that either was the case, and affirmed that there was no shortening nor any forgetting, even though one of them must have occurred, as Dhul-Yadayn pointed out.

The scholars have responded to this in several ways; one such response is that the Prophet ﷺ was speaking about what he believed to be the case: when he denied that he had shortened the prayer, this was true and correct in every way; and when he ﷺ denied that he had forgotten, he was expressing what he believed to be the case, namely that he did not think that he had forgotten at the time. His intention, then, was to express what he surmised to be the case, even if he did not phrase it in that way; thus he was speaking the truth in this case, as well.

What makes most sense to me is that his ﷺ words 'I did not forget' were meant to deny this particular way of phrasing it only, and that he ﷺ was alluding to the fact that he had been *made to forget* rather than that he had simply forgotten. This is akin to the way he ﷺ would discourage people from saying 'I forgot such-and-such verse [of Qurʾān]'. It is related that he ﷺ said: 'How wrong it is for one of you to say "I forgot"; rather,

[250] The author (following ʿIyāḍ in *al-Shifā*) does not relate the whole story here; I have translated Muslim's version for clarity's sake. [t]

he was made to forget.' Thus, when the questioner said to him 'Did you shorten the prayer, or did you forget?', he denied that he shortened it (as was the case) and then denied that he had forgotten it of his own volition, and that if such a thing had occurred, it had been sent upon him so that others could ask him about it. Thus we see that he was made to forget, and that this was sent upon him, so that it could be an example for others.[251]

So when he ﷺ said 'I did not forget', 'I did not shorten', and 'I did neither one nor the other', this was true: he did not shorten, and he did not really forget, but he was made to forget. This is supported by the ḥadīth narrated by Mālik in the *Muwaṭṭā'*: 'I forget, or I am made to forget, in order that I may give [you] an example to follow.' Another narration has it that he ﷺ said: 'I do not forget, but I am made to forget.'

Now, this does not contradict the ḥadīth 'I am but a human being like you: I forget, just as you forget'[252], because this ḥadīth affirms the act of forgetting, whilst the aforementioned ḥadīth negated the word itself and the title when used in a particular way, but not the concept of forgetting in a general sense; thus there is no contradiction.

This explains his ﷺ words 'I neither shortened nor forgot'; there still remains the question of the very ascription of forgetting to him ﷺ, and what it means.

There are three authentic ḥadīths wherein it is stated that the Prophet ﷺ forgot something. The first is the aforementioned ḥadīth of Dhul-Yadayn, when the Prophet ﷺ ended the prayer after two cycles; the second is the ḥadīth of Ibn Buḥayna, when the Prophet ﷺ stood after two cycles (without pausing to sit for the *tashahhud*); the third is the ḥadīth of Ibn Masʿūd ﷺ, when the Prophet ﷺ prayed five cycles for the midday prayer. This is what is established by authentic narrations.

Now, these ḥadīths all detail *acts* of forgetfulness, and in every case they were filled by Allah in order to give to the Muslims an example of how to act in these situations: for actions speak louder than words. This is the

251 That is, so that people would know the correct *sunna* way to amend a prayer when the wrong amount of cycles are offered. [t]

252 Al-Bukhārī, Muslim.

case as long as the mistake is not left unobserved, but rather is pointed out so that there is no confusion, and the lesson is clearly imparted. No instance of forgetting or mistakes in his ﷺ actions, then, contradicts any miracle of his, or casts doubt on his integrity.

This is so because there is a difference between those teachings which take the form of actions, and those which take the form of words. Apparent mistakes or acts of forgetfulness could occur in the deeds he ﷺ did; and this is possible, as the aforementioned ḥadīths of forgetfulness in prayer show. What was not possible, however, was that there could be any forgetfulness or error in the lessons he ﷺ imparted by speech; for an aspect of his miraculous prophetic nature was that he always spoke the truth, and forgetfulness in speech would contradict this.

As for forgetfulness in deeds, it does not contradict the truthfulness of speech, nor cast doubt on prophethood; indeed, error in action is a defining human characteristic, as he ﷺ said: 'I am but a human being; I forget, as you forget. If I forget, remind me.' Moreover, any apparent errors or acts of forgetfulness on his ﷺ part were actually a means of imparting knowledge and affirming points of Shariah, as he ﷺ said: 'I forget, or I am made to forget, in order that I may give [you] an example to follow', or in another narration: 'It is not that I forget, but that I am made to forget in order that I may give [you] an example to follow.'

This matter was, then, a way to increase the clarity and efficacy of his ﷺ teachings, and a blessing for him; it was not in the least any kind of flaw, or a valid object of criticism.

As for those of his ﷺ actions which were not in any way concerned with teaching or legislation, meaning those affairs of this worldly life or interior concerns which he did not do in order to be emulated by others, most of the Muslims scholars are of the opinion that it was possible for him ﷺ to err occasionally in such worldly matters. This was due to the great burdens he had to bear, such as the necessities of human life, directing Muslim affairs, fulfilling family responsibilities, and dealing with friends and foes. But none of these could ever be continued or repeated, but would always come and go in an instant. Others say that all errors, mistakes, and instances of forgetfulness and heedlessness are completely impossible for him ﷺ; this is the opinion of many of those with firm knowledge, enlightened hearts and spiritual stations – may Allah be well pleased with them!

The Issue of the Captives of Badr

THOSE WHO are of the opinion that it was possible for the Prophet ﷺ to make a temporary mistake without persisting in it adduce, as evidence for this opinion, the story of the captives of Badr:

Aḥmad narrated in his *Musnad* that Anas ﷺ said: 'The Prophet ﷺ asked the people's opinion about the captives taken at Badr, saying, "Allah Almighty has left it to you to decide their fate." ʿUmar ibn al-Khaṭṭāb stood up and said, "O Messenger of Allah, strike their necks!", but the Prophet ﷺ turned away from him. Then the Messenger of Allah ﷺ repeated: "O people, Allah has given you to decide their fate – and just yesterday they were your brethren." ʿUmar again stood and said, "O Messenger of Allah, strike their necks!" But the Prophet ﷺ turned away from him, and repeated his words to the people. Abū Bakr al-Ṣiddīq ﷺ then stood up and said, "Messenger of Allah, we think you should be lenient to them, and accept ransoms for them." Upon this, the concern left the face of the Messenger of Allah ﷺ, and so he relented towards them, and accepted ransoms for them. Then Allah Almighty revealed: "*Were it not for a prior decree of Allah, you would surely have been visited by an awful torment on account of what you took*" [8:68].'

Now anyone who reflects deeply on this story will see without doubt that the Prophet ﷺ was completely right to do as he did. Several observations can be made about these events:[253]

1 – The Prophet ﷺ came to this decision because of taking counsel as he was commanded to do by Allah ﷻ when He said: '*Consult them about their affairs; and once you are resolved, put your trust in Allah*' [3:159].

2 – The Prophet ﷺ inclined to the opinion of those who preferred to take the ransom because it was the way of mercy and leniency, which reflects the station in which Allah placed him, according to His word:

[253] See Shaykh ʿAbdallāh Sirājuddīn al-Ḥusayni, *Our Master Muḥammad ﷺ The Messenger of Allah* (Sunni Publications, 2011), vol. 2, pp. 194-200.

'And we have not sent you save as a mercy to the worlds' [21:107].

3 – His ﷺ action was in agreement with what had already been predestined in the Primordial Decree, in which Allah ﷻ made the taking of battles-spoils lawful for him ﷺ alone, having forbidden this to all who came before him. Ibn ʿAbbās ﷺ explained the verse thus: '*Were it not for a prior decree of Allah*', that is, in the Primordial Decree, stating that taking battle-spoils and captives is lawful for you (the Muslims), '*you would surely have been visited by an awful torment on account of what you took*'.

4 – Just as the Prophet's ﷺ acceptance of the ransoms was in accordance with Allah's Primordial Decree, it was also in accordance with the Sacred Ordinance that would presently be revealed in the Qurʾān,[254] namely Allah's word: '*Yet enjoy the spoils ye have won as lawful and good*' [8:69]. How could something that was in accordance with both the Primordial Decree and the Shariah which was about to be affirmed, ever be deemed a mistake?

5 – The revelation of the lawfulness of taking battle-spoils, namely Allah's word '*Yet enjoy the spoils ye have won as lawful and good*', was an endorsement of the Messenger of Allah's ﷺ actions, and an affirmation of his sound judgement. Had he ﷺ been mistaken in doing what he did, how could Allah ﷻ give it sanction by making it part of the permanent Divine Law? Even according to the opinion of those who believe that the Prophet ﷺ could make a mistake momentarily before being corrected by Allah, it could not be said what he ﷺ did with the captives of Badr was a mistake, since Allah ﷻ endorsed his action. Where, then, is the error? Al-Ḥāfiẓ Ibn Kathīr said in his *Tafsīr*:

The ruling established here concerning captives remains applicable according to the majority of scholars, namely that the ruler is free to choose from the following options:

(1) He can execute them, as was the case with the Banī Qurayẓa, or (2) he can ransom them for money, as was done with the captives of Badr; or exchange them for Muslim captives, as the Messenger of Allah ﷺ

[254] In the very next verse.

did with the slave-girl and her daughter who were captured by Salama ibn al-Akwaʿ, exchanging them for an equal number of Muslim captives held by the idolaters, or (3) he can keep the captives as bondsmen. This is the opinion of Imam Shāfiʿī and other scholars; the details of the scholarly difference of opinion on this matter can be found in the books of jurisprudence.

6 – If what the Prophet ﷺ did with the captives at Badr had been an error, Allah ﷻ would have commanded him to return the ransoms, and seek forgiveness from Him for the wrong he had done by taking them; yet Allah endorsed his action and sanctioned it with His words '*Yet enjoy the spoils ye have won as lawful and good...*'. If it had been a mistake, Allah ﷻ would not have endorsed it for him, nor would He have sanctioned it in this way.

7 – How could it be judged that the Prophet ﷺ was wrong in his dealings with the captives of Badr, when he ﷺ was commanded to give the decision to his Companions, and then acted in accordance with this decision? Al-Tirmidhī, al-Nasāʾī, Ibn Ḥibbān and al-Ḥākim all narrate with a rigorously authenticated chain of transmission that ʿAlī ﷺ said: 'Jibrīl ﷺ came to the Messenger of Allah ﷺ on the day of Badr and said, "Give your Companions the decision regarding the captives: if they wish they may execute them, and if they wish they may ransom them, on the understanding that a similar number of them (i.e. the Companions) shall be slain next year." And so they said, "We choose the ransom, and that we be slain."' (That is, that seventy of them be slain in turn, and thus be martyred in Allah's cause.)

Ibn Saʿd also narrates with a *mursal*[255] chain from Qatāda that their reply was: 'We shall ransom them, and thus gain strength over them by their means; and next year seventy of us shall enter Paradise,' and then they ransomed them.

Al-Ḥāfiẓ al-Qasṭallānī said: 'This shows that they only did what they had been permitted to do.'

As for Allah's words '*It is not for a Prophet to hold captives until he has made great slaughter in the land. You would have for yourselves the gains of*

255 A *mursal* narration is one where the Companion who reported the ḥadīth is not mentioned by name in the chain of transmission. [t]

this world, whilst Allah would have for you the Hereafter...' [8:67], the verse does not in any way constitute a rebuke of the Prophet ﷺ, but is rather a rebuke of those who advised the Prophet ﷺ to accept the ransoms out of desire for (the gains of this world) (namely, the wealth that would be given for the ransom) when he sought the advice of the people in general before seeking it in private from Abū Bakr, ʿUmar, and ʿAlī, as is mentioned above. Thus by His words '*You would have for yourselves the gains of this world*', Allah meant the people who desired to gain wealth.

As for our master the Messenger of Allah ﷺ, he did not accept the ransoms out of desire for the gains of this world – far be it for him to do any such thing! The life of this world in its entirety had no value for him whatsoever, and he ﷺ himself said: 'What have I to do with this world? My place in this world is no more than that of a traveller who seeks rest beneath a tree and, then moves on and leaves it.'[256] The mountain of Tihāma's weight in gold was offered to him and he refused it: what did he have to do with the gains of this world?

Similarly, Allah's words '*Were it not for a prior decree of Allah, you would surely have been visited by an awful torment on account of what you took; yet enjoy the spoils ye have won as lawful and good*' is a declaration from Him of the favour and blessing He bestowed upon this community by the grace of their Prophet ﷺ, and an announcement that it was already decreed in pre-eternity that battle-spoils were lawful for this community alone, as a blessing and favour from Him by the grace of their Prophet ﷺ and his noble status in the sight of Allah. Therefore the Prophet ﷺ would later celebrate this honour and make mention of this blessing as one of the great honours with which Allah singled him out, saying: 'I have been given five that none before me were given: Every Prophet was sent to his people alone, whilst I have been sent to all men, the red and the black; and battle-spoils were made lawful for me, having been lawful for none before me...'[257]

A FURTHER CLARIFICATION

256 Aḥmad.

257 Al-Bukhārī, Muslim.

In another narration of these events, it is reported that ʿUmar ؓ said: 'The next day, I returned to the Prophet ﷺ and Abū Bakr and found them weeping. "Why do you and your companion weep?" I asked, "for if I am moved to weep, I shall weep, and if not, I shall make myself weep that I might weep with you." The Messenger of Allah ﷺ said: "I weep for what I have been informed of your companions' punishment for accepting the ransoms; for their punishment has been shown to me more clearly than this tree (he pointed to a nearby tree)." Allah then revealed: '*It is not for a Prophet to hold captives until he has made great slaughter in the land. You would have for yourselves the gains of this world, whilst Allah would have for you the Hereafter; and Allah is Mighty, Wise. Were it not for a prior decree of Allah, you would surely have been visited by an awful torment on account of what you took; yet enjoy the spoils ye have won as lawful and good, and be mindful of Allah. Allah is forgiving, Merciful*' [8:67-69]. With that, Allah made battle-spoils lawful to them.'[258]

I say that the correct understanding of this is that this vision of their punishment was shown to him ﷺ before these verses were revealed, endorsing his actions and supporting the position he took, after his heart inclined to the view of Abū Bakr ؓ. The reason this vision of their punishment was shown to him ﷺ was to increase the great blessing Allah bestowed upon them by allowing them that which had been forbidden to those who came before them; and this, by making clear the penalty that these captives would have deserved had things been done in the same way they had always been done before. The vision of their punishment that the Prophet ﷺ saw was a vision of what they would have deserved had it not been that Allah's decreed law was the very thing to which His Truthful Messenger ﷺ had been guided – namely, to accept the ransoms and take the battle-spoils. When this was shown to the Chosen Prophet ﷺ, he wept, because he thought that this was Allah's decree for them, and imagined that he had been wrong to choose the course he chose; but Allah Almighty let him know that in fact he had been right, sending down verses that affirmed that he had done the right thing, supported his words and deeds, and turned the course he had chosen into an official position of the Shariah and a foundation of prisoner-of-war policy that would last until the end of time.

As for His words '*It is not for a Prophet to hold captives until he has*

258 Muslim, Abū Dāwūd, al-Tirmidhī.

made great slaughter in the land...', the correct understanding is that Allah revealed this verse to inform His Prophet Muḥammad ﷺ of what the position of the previous revealed laws had been on this matter, as though saying to him: 'O Muḥammad, none of the prophets who came before you were allowed to take captives until they had dealt much slaughter and damage to the enemy. This was the case in the past; but as for you, We have allowed you to do so, and given you a special rank and position which makes you distinct from all the others.'

This verse gives us, then, a clear indication of the great blessing that was bestowed upon Muḥammad ﷺ, showing us as it does how his Lord favoured him and singled him out by permitting him that which had been forbidden to those who came before him. Reflect on this. There was neither any rebuke nor any objection; and praise be to Allah for that. This is what I have to say on the matter; and we ask Him I to give us a sound understanding of His Holy Book.

The Incident of the Date-Palms[259]

Those who say it was possible for the Prophet ﷺ to make temporary errors also cite the story of the cross-pollination of the date-palms. The story goes that the Prophet ﷺ passed by some people cross-pollinating date-palms, and said to them: 'Were you not to do so, it would be well.' The trees then produced poor yields. The Prophet ﷺ passed by them again, and said, 'What has befallen your date-palms?' They replied, 'You said such-and-such.' He ﷺ replied, 'You know best the affairs of your world.'[260] From this ḥadīth, some people have understood that the Prophet ﷺ could be wrong about worldly matters, and have gone as far as to list the things they believe the Messenger of Allah ﷺ was wrong about.

But the truth has more right to be followed, and the truth is that the words and deeds of the Prophet ﷺ explain one another, and resemble one another; and Allah ﷻ protected him ﷺ from error just as He protected him from sin. So we say, and all success comes from Allah:

First of all, the Prophet ﷺ grew up in those blessed lands in which date-palms are grown, and was raised amongst people who knew well the art of cultivating them, and the careful processes that it required. How could it be imagined that he ﷺ would be unaware of the unchanging customs of date-palm cultivation, and the necessity of cross-pollination as a basic agricultural principle? It is not as though this was a secret of date-palm cultivation, or some kind of hidden inside knowledge pertaining to it. He must, then, have known about it just as well as they did; but he wanted to teach them something which they could not have learned by themselves.

Secondly, the Noble Messenger ﷺ was possessed of great knowledge, and Allah ﷻ bestowed much information upon him, to the extent that he could speak in detail with the Companions about any subject. Al-Ṭabarānī narrates that Abū Dharr ؓ said: 'When the Messenger of Allah left us, there was not a single bird flapping its wings in the sky save that he had taught us something about it.' How could it be imagined, then,

259 See also Imam ʿAbdullah Sirajuddīn, *Our Master Muḥammad* ﷺ, Volume 2, pp 203-209. [t]

260 Muslim.

that the Prophet ﷺ was not aware that date-palms need to be cross-pollinated, as is the normal agricultural practice? It must therefore be that the Messenger of Allah ﷺ had something else in mind.

Thirdly, there occurred other incidents similar to this one from which we can deduce what the Prophet ﷺ had in mind, one of which is the ḥadīth of the sheep's leg:

Aḥmad relates in his *Musnad* that Abū Rāfiʿ said: 'A sheep was roasted for the Messenger of Allah ﷺ and brought to him. He said, "Abū Rāfiʿ, pass me the foreleg," and so I passed it to him. After a time he said, "Pass me the [other] foreleg," so I passed it to him. He then said again, "Pass me the foreleg." I said, "Messenger of Allah, has a sheep more than two forelegs?" He ﷺ replied, "Had you only been silent, you would have passed me as many forelegs as I asked for." The Messenger of Allah ﷺ used to favour the foreleg.'[261]

It is also narrated that Abū ʿUbayd said: 'I cooked a plate of meat for the Messenger of Allah ﷺ, who said: "Pass me its foreleg," so I passed it to him, and then he said, "Pass me its foreleg," so I passed it so him, and then he ﷺ said, "Pass me its foreleg," so I said, "Prophet of Allah, how many forelegs does a sheep have?" He ﷺ replied, "By He in whose hand is my soul, had you been silent, you would have given me as many forelegs as I asked for."' This incident was not the same one as the previous narration, as al-Ḥāfiẓ al-Zurqānī and others have pointed out.

It is narrated in Majmaʿ al-Zawāʾid, on the authority on Ibn Isḥāq, who heard from a man of the tribe of Ghifār at a gathering of Sālim ibn ʿAbdallāh, that the Messenger of Allah ﷺ was presented with a meal of bread and meat. He ﷺ said, 'Pass me the foreleg,' and so it was passed to him, and he ate it. Then he said, 'Pass me the foreleg,' so the other was passed to him, and he ate it. Then he said, 'Pass me the foreleg.' They said to him, 'Messenger of Allah, there are only two forelegs!' He replied, 'By your father, had you been silent, I would have continued taking as many forelegs as I asked for.'[262]

So when the Prophet ﷺ said 'Pass me the foreleg' the third time, despite knowing well that a sheep has only two forelegs, he did so out

[261] Al-Haythamī says in *Majmaʿ al-Zawāʾid*: 'This ḥadīth was narrated by Aḥmad and al-Ṭabarānī with several chains of transmission, one of which has it that Abū Rāfiʿ said: "The Messenger of Allah ﷺ asked me to roast a sheep for him, so I did so..." Al-Ṭabarānī narrated it in *al-Awsaṭ* in a shorter form, and one of the narrations of Aḥmad is sound.'

[262] Narrated by Aḥmad; its chain contains one narrator whose name is not mentioned.

of a wish to display a miracle of divine generosity, and a clear proof of his prophethood; but since he did not find a suitable occasion for it, the miracle did not take place. Al-Ḥāfiẓ al-Zurqānī therefore said:

The meaning of the Prophet's ﷺ words "Had you only been silent, you would have passed me foreleg after foreleg for as long as you were silent" is that this would have gone on as long as he was silent, because Allah would have created foreleg after foreleg as a miracle for him ﷺ; yet the attendant's human instinct for haste made him say, 'A sheep has only two forelegs', and so the divine outpourings were cut off. For such a thing could only come from the divine outpourings of the Beneficent [*al-Karīm*], as a generous gift to the Finest of His Creation ﷺ. If the attendant had only responded with proper manners, and remained silent and alert to this miraculous wonder, this would have been an expression of gratitude on his part sufficient to merit the blessing of this divine outpouring being channelled though his own hands; but he responded with incredulity, and so the grace went back whence it came, finding no suitable place to manifest itself; for no one deserves to witness such a miracle – for the mere witnessing of it is a great honour for the witness – save one whose submission is absolute, and who is without the slightest trace of independent desire or will.

The same was true of the incident of the date-palms. When the Prophet ﷺ passed by the men cross-pollinating the palms, he wanted to honour them by showing them a miracle that went against the usual custom of tending palms by cross-pollination, and so ennoble them by making the trees bear fruit without any pollination; for he ﷺ was as well aware of the usual need to pollinate date palms as they were, because he ﷺ lived amongst them and knew their ways. But when some of the hearts of these men did not accept this, and did not completely submit to his ﷺ words 'Were you not to do so, it would be well', but instead clung to their worldly knowledge of the art of date-palm cultivation, which is that their prosperity depends on pollination; and so the divine plenitude found no place to manifest, and returned whence it came.

This is why the Prophet ﷺ then bade them return to their ordinary way of doing things, to which they clung and been unable to leave behind, saying: 'You know best the affairs of your world'; that is, 'return to working as your own knowledge of your worldly matters dictates.'

The truth of what we have just stated, and our understanding that he ﷺ did not make a mistake in this matter, is attested to by what the great Shaykh and Knower of Allah, the author of al-Ibrīz, may Allah benefit us with his knowledge,[263] said when asked about the incident of the date-palms:

His ﷺ statement 'Were you not to do so, it would be well' was a statement of absolute truth, and these words issued from him because of the certitude he possessed that Allah is the true Doer. This certitude was based on his witnessing of the diffusion of Allah's actions in all existence without intermediary or means, so that not a seed settles, nor a hair moves, nor a heart beats, nor a vein pulses, nor an eye glimpses, nor an eyelid blinks, except that He is the direct Agent of these actions without any intermediary.

This is a matter that the Prophet ﷺ witnessed for himself just as plainly as he saw or sensed anything else, and it never escaped his attention for a moment, neither when he woke nor when he slept; for his ﷺ heart, in which this witnessing took place, never slept. There is no doubt that if anyone were to witness such a thing, all causality would fall away from their sight, and they would advance from faith in the Unseen to direct and firsthand witnessing; and they would witness firsthand the words of Allah '*And Allah created you, and all that you do*' [37:96], and be endowed with an absolute certitude that befits such a witnessing, which means to affirm the meaning of the verse with such an affirmation that the notion that any action could be the work of any but Allah would never cross their mind for the slightest moment.

There is no doubt that a certitude of this nature would be enough to break the natural order, and influence the run of things; and it is the secret of Allah ﷻ, alongside whom there can remain no other cause or intermediary. Therefore if someone who occupied this station were to indicate the nonexistence of causality, and were to ascribe an action directly to the Lord of lords, his words would be the absolute truth.

As for those who occupy the station of faith in the Unseen, they do not directly witness Allah's words '*And Allah created you, and all that you do*', but rather they witness the ascription of actions to those at whose

263 Meaning ʿAbd al-ʿAzīz Dabbāgh ؓ. [t]

hands they occur, and are only pulled towards the meaning of the verse and the ascription of all actions to Allah by means of the faith that He has granted them. So they are pulled in two directions by two things: the first is their Lord, in the form of faith, which pulls them towards the truth; the second is their nature, and how their eyes see that actions are performed by others, which pulls them towards falsehood.

So they are always caught between these two things, but sometimes the side of faith is stronger, and so they are able to taste the meaning of the aforementioned verse for a moment or two; and sometimes the side of their nature is stronger, and so they forget the meaning of the verse for a day or two – and at these times of forgetfulness, the certitude which can break the natural order is absent.

Therefore that to which the Prophet ﷺ alluded did not come to pass, because there were those among the Companions (i.e. among the farmers) who at the time were not attuned to this overwhelming certitude, which filled his ﷺ entire inner being, and caused these words to leave his mouth; and he ﷺ spoke the truth.

So when he ﷺ realised why what he had mentioned had not come to pass, and saw that the surpassing of this obstacle was not within their capabilities at the time, he left them as they were, and said: 'You know best the affairs of your world.'[264]

In any case, it cannot be said that the Prophet ﷺ was wrong in the case of the date-palms any more than it could be said he ﷺ was wrong when he said to Abū 'Ubayd, 'Pass me the foreleg' the third time. It was not a mistake, but was rather correct, and expressed a wish to honour the men with a miraculous act of blessing and increase; but it did not come to pass because of the presence of an obstacle to it.

The equivalent of this is the cutting of the blessed increase from the skin of butter which the Prophet ﷺ had blessed, when Umm Mālik squeezed it. Muslim narrates in his *Saḥīḥ* on the authority of Jābir ﷺ that Umm Mālik al-Anṣāriyya owned a skin containing butter which she would reserve for the Prophet ﷺ; and when her children would come to her asking for butter and she found they had none, she would go to the skin she reserved for him ﷺ and find that there was still butter in it. The skin continued to provide butter for her whole family until she squeezed

264 *Al-Ibrīz*, as quoted in *Our Master Muḥammad* ﷺ.

it, whereupon it ran out. She went to the Prophet ﷺ to ask about this. 'Did you squeeze it?' he asked. She said yes. 'Had you left it,' he said, it would have remained.'

Muslim also narrates on the authority of Jābir ﷺ that a man from the countryside came to the Prophet ﷺ and asked him for food, so the Prophet ﷺ gave him a half *wasq*[265] of barley. He, his wife, and any guests they had continued to eat from it until he weighed it, whereupon it began to decrease. He went to the Prophet ﷺ and told him of this. 'Had you not weighed it,' said the Prophet ﷺ, 'You would have eaten from it [evermore], and it would have remained for you.' That is, it would have remained as long as they lived without ever decreasing. So the weighing of the barley spelled the end of the blessing. Imām Nawawī explained the wisdom behind this, saying:

> The scholars have said that wisdom behind this is that the squeezing [of the skin] and weighing [of the barley] were contrary to the principle of submission and absolute trust in Allah's provision, and were signs of planning and the use of one's own power, and an attempt to encompass the secrets of the decree and bounty of Allah Almighty; and the penalty for anyone who does such a thing is to have the blessing taken from him.

Al-Ḥāfiẓ al-Zurqānī said:

> This does not contradict the words of the Prophet ﷺ: 'Weigh your food, and you will find blessed increase therein,' because this refers to those who fear foul play; or it means 'weigh that which you intend to spend in charity, lest you spend more or less than you can afford, but do not weigh what remains'; or it means one should weigh when buying, or when entering the house [after buying].

[265] This is equivalent to just over 60 kilograms (*Reliance of the Traveller*, w15.1).

That Sorcery Was Worked on Him ﷺ Does Not Negate His Perfection

Another issue of contention concerns the authentic reports stating that the Prophet ﷺ fell victim to sorcery. ʿĀʾisha ﷺ is reported to have said: 'The Messenger of Allah ﷺ was bewitched, so that it would seem to him that he had done something when actually he had not.'[266] Another narration has it: 'So that it would seem to him that he had gone to his wives, when actually he had not.'[267]

People differ greatly over this ḥadīth; some reject it and suggest it is inauthentic, while others become confused by it and find cause in it to doubt the prophetic infallibility. Yet the truth of the matter is that this ḥadīth is rigorously authentic, and agreed upon by the greatest scholars of ḥadīth; and it in no way gives us cause to doubt the Prophet's ﷺ infallibility.

Allah protected His Law and His Prophet ﷺ from anything that could taint them; sorcery is only an illness and a passing impairment that could afflict him ﷺ just as any illness could; and such a thing does not cast any doubt on his prophethood.

As for the words 'it would seem to him that he had done something when actually he had not', they do not refer to those things connected to his teachings or his legislation, or undermine his veracity, since it is proven and accepted by consensus that he was divinely protected from this. Rather, these words only refer to those private matters of his worldly life which were neither the purpose of his mission nor the cause of his greatness. In such things, he was susceptible to ailments just like any other human being, and thus it is not impossible that something pertaining to them might seem to him to be the case when in fact it was not; yet the truth of the matter would become clear to him in no short time.

266 Al-Bukhārī, Muslim.

267 *Al-Shifā.*

The clearest evidence I can see that his ﷺ heart and intellect were protected from the sorcery is that during that time, his speech was consistent with its usual form, without any impairment, contradiction or corruption of any kind whatsoever. It remained perfect, complete and harmonised. This, despite the fact that his enemies were always watching him and hanging on his every word, hoping to find something to use against him and slake their rage. Had they found any opportunity to do so, they would have grasped it and made the most of it; yet there is nothing to suggest that this happened. Allah protected His Prophet ﷺ, and left the disbelievers to wallow in their rage: *'And Allah repulsed the unbelievers in their rage, and they attained no good; and Allah spared the believers of fighting'* [33:25].

Indeed, I see that the opposite was the case: the fact that he ﷺ was subjected to sorcery, which affected his outward state, and yet his heart, intellect, belief, and speech remained unaffected by it, is the greatest proof of the perfect protection Allah gave to him, and proof that his prophethood was divinely protected and impervious to human vicissitudes, however powerful they might have been. Though his human nature may have been affected by such things, his prophetic nature was divinely protected from them, although the soul which bore these human and prophetic natures was one single soul: the soul of Muḥammad ﷺ.

Imagine if a thief were to manage to break into a house filled with pearls and jewels and the most precious objects, but then found himself unable to take any of these treasures because of an irresistible power which overcame him, despite the apparent absence of any guards or sentries, and sent him packing empty-handed. Thus, the sorcery had effect on a certain elect of his ﷺ human nature, yet had no effect whatsoever on his heart or his intellect.

This indicates that the Prophet ﷺ is protected with a special kind of protection, and guarded with a special kind of guard, so that no one can have any power over him: he is protected by Allah, the One, the Ruler: Master of truths, Keeper of mysteries, Giver of lights, and Revealer of secrets.

Did He ﷺ Ever Curse Anyone?[268]

Another issue of contention concerns the Prophet's ﷺ words: 'O Allah, Muḥammad is only a human being who becomes angry as human beings do. I have made a covenant with You which You will not break: if I ever harm a believer, or revile him, or scourge him, then make it an expiation for his sins, and a means of his being drawn nearer to You on the Day of Resurrection.' Another narration has it 'So if I ever make a supplication against someone…'; another adds '…who does not deserve it…'; and another adds 'So if I revile, curse or scourge a man of the Muslims, make it for him a source of purification, connection [to You] and mercy.'[269]

Now someone might say: 'How could the Prophet ﷺ curse someone who did not deserve to be cursed, revile someone who did not deserve to be reviled, scourge someone who did not deserve to be scourged, or do any such thing as this in a state of anger, when he was divinely protected from all of that?'

You should know – may Allah expand your breast – that the Prophet's ﷺ words 'who does not deserve it' means 'in Your view, Lord, of the inner reality of the situation'; for the Prophet ﷺ would judge such things according to their outward appearance, as he said.[270]

And for the reason we have mentioned,[271] the Prophet ﷺ would judge that someone be scourged or chastised by words of reviling or cursing based on the judgement suggested by the outer appearance of the matter. After this, he ﷺ prayed for them, because of the compassion and tenderness he felt for his community, and the mercy he felt for the believers (as Allah Himself said of him[272]), and his worry that Allah would accept the

268 This chapter is drawn from *al-Shifā*, Volume 2, Part III, Chapter Two, Section *Fa in qīl^a mā wajh^u ḥadīthih….*

269 This translation is based on al-Qārī's interpretation. [t]

270 The Prophet ﷺ is related to have said: 'We judge according to the outward appearance of things, and Allah takes care of what is hidden' (*Sharḥ al-Shifā*).

271 Namely, that the Prophet's ﷺ judgements were based on the outer appearances of things, so that his community could follow this example (*Sharḥ al-Shifā*).

272 *'Now there has come to you a messenger from among yourselves; grievous to him is your suffering;*

supplications he made against such people – he prayed that his prayers against them, and his actions towards them, would bring them nothing but mercy. This is the meaning of his words 'who does not deserve it', not that his ﷺ anger and fury drove him to do these things to Muslims who did not deserve it.

This is the correct way to understand it. Nor should his ﷺ words 'I get angry as human beings do' be taken to mean that anger drove him to do something he shouldn't have done; rather, this could mean that anger for Allah's sake drove him to punish the people involved by cursing or reviling them, while he could instead have held back and pardoned them; or, it may refer to those offences for which he ﷺ was allowed to choose whether to punish or pardon. Or it may be that the intention of his supplication [against these offenders] was to inspire dread in them, and teach his community to be fearful of violating Allah's boundaries.

It may also be that this supplication of his ﷺ was meant as a retraction of the times when, without meaning anything by them, he uttered certain phrases which the Arabs were accustomed to using in their conversations and which took the form of curses, such as 'May Allah fight him', 'woe betide his mother', 'no father has he', all of which were used when speaking well of someone and praising his actions; this was a well-known convention of Arab speech, and by no means were these words meant to be taken seriously.

One example of this is his words 'may your right hand be covered in dust!', as al-Bukhārī and Muslim narrate. Another was his words 'May Allah not fill your belly!', which he ﷺ said to Muʿāwiya ؓ, as Muslim narrates on the authority of Ibn ʿAbbās, as follows: 'Once I was with the other boys when the Messenger of Allah ﷺ came along. I hid behind the door, and he said: "Go and call Muʿāwiya for me." I went and said to him, "He is eating." He said a second time, "Go and call him." I went and said, "He is eating." He told me to go again, so I went again and said, "He is eating." He ﷺ said: "May Allah not fill his belly!"'

Another such instance was when the Prophet ﷺ said *ʿaqrā ḥalqā* to Ṣafiyya bint Ḥuyayy, the Mother of the Believers ؓ during the Farewell Pilgrimage. Al-Bukhārī narrates that ʿĀ'isha ؓ said: 'We set off with the Messenger of Allah ﷺ for the pilgrimage, and on the night of departure

anxious is he over you, full of tenderness and mercy for the believers' [9:128].

Ṣafiyya got her menses. The Prophet ﷺ said: "*ʿAqrā ḥalqā*! She will surely hold you all up."'

The word *ʿaqrā* is an exclamation of disapproval in the feminine form, derived from a word meaning either 'hamstring (of an animal)' or 'loud voice'; and *ḥalqā* is also an exclamation of disapproval, meaning 'sore throat'.[273]

Now more than one person described the Prophet ﷺ by saying 'He ﷺ was not vulgar'; and Anas said: 'He was given to neither scornful speech, nor vulgarity, nor cursing; and he would say of one of use, by way of rebuke, "What is wrong with him, may his brow be covered in dust!"'[274] This ḥadīth may also be counted as one of these.

So the Prophet ﷺ then worried that these sorts of (innocent) phrases would actually be answered by Allah, and so made a covenant with his Lord – as he said in the aforementioned ḥadīth – to make them a source of purification, mercy, and divine nearness for all those to whom he said them. He did this out of his compassion for them, and to set their minds at ease so that they would not feel dread and panic at having been actually cursed by the Prophet ﷺ, which would otherwise have led them into despair and misery.

These words of the Prophet ﷺ could also have been an entreaty to his Lord on behalf of those whom he scourged or reviled for a good reason, and who deserved it, asking Him to make it an expiation for them and an effacement of their sins, so that their punishment in this world would bring them pardon and forgiveness. This is suggested by another ḥadīth: 'And if someone commits any of these things and is punished for it in this world, it is an expiation for him.'[275]

[273] So the Arabic expression would mean something like 'may she be hamstrung and pained in her throat.' It was a customary expression of the Arabs. [t]

[274] Al-Bukhārī.

[275] Al-Bukhārī, Muslim.

Conclusion

In conclusion, the Muslim must not rush to say that it was possible for the Prophet ﷺ to commit sin simply because he sees a few texts in which he ﷺ expresses repentance, seeks forgiveness of Allah, turns to Him, and expresses his fear of Him. In doing so, one risks falling into erroneous doctrine and corrupt belief, which is a deadly disease – we seek Allah's refuge from it!

The Muslim should know that the rank occupied by the prophets in sanctity and knowledge of Allah, and His ways with His servants, and the glory of His sovereignty and the power of His grasp, is what makes them fear Him and dread that He will take them to task for things which He would excuse of others. There are things which they were neither forbidden from doing nor commanded to do, yet they were taken to task and rebuked for doing them, or warned of being taken to task on account of them, even if they did them excusably, accidentally, or as merely a means of living their ordinary lives; and they feel great fear and dread on account of them, considering them to be sins for those of their status, and acts of disobedience when compared to their perfect obedience. They are in no way akin to the sins and acts of disobedience committed by others.

The word *dhanb* ('sin') literally means something low or base; the *dhanb* of something is the final part of it, and people's *adhnāb* are the basest parts of their nature. Therefore these trifling matters are, for the prophets, the lowest of their actions and the worst of their states, because of how pure and unblemished they are, and because of how their inner and outer states are saturated with righteous deeds, good words, outward and inward invocation, and fear and awe of Allah in public and in private.

Other people are so polluted by sins and evil acts that the very same trifling deeds for them would seem like good deeds. Someone said, 'Allah takes the Prophets to task for atom-weights', because of how high their rank is in His sight; and He forgives the rest of humanity for the manifold evil deeds they commit because He is less concerned about them.

The prophets are taken to account for these things in this world, as a means of raising their ranks; they are tested by this so that their recognition of it causes their status to rise, as Allah says: '*Then his Lord chose him, and turned to him, and guided*' [20:122]. And He said of Dāwūd: '*We forgave him for that...*' [38:25]; and after Mūsā said '*I repent unto You*' [7:143], He said: '*I have chosen you above all mankind*' [7:144]; and after speaking of the trial of Sulaymān, He said: '*So We subdued for him the wind, which ran at his commandment, softly, wherever he might light on; and the demons, every builder and diver, and others also, coupled in fetters: 'This is Our gift; bestow or withhold without reckoning.' And he had a near place in Our presence and a fair resort*' [38:36-40].

One of the theologians said: 'The errors of the prophets look like errors on the surface, but in reality they are divine gifts and means of drawing nigh unto Allah.' These events also have the function of alerting the rest of mankind that if the prophets were taken to task for such things, then this is all the more reason for them to be cautious, and to hold themselves to account, and to maintain an attitude of gratitude for blessings and patience in the face of trials. This is easier to do when we contemplate what happened to those who had such lofty ranks, and who indeed were divinely protected – what, then, of those who are lower than them?

It occurred to me, when reading the Qur'ānic verses directed to the Prophet ﷺ which contain words of rebuke or threat, or may seem to put the prophetic infallibility into question, that all of this does not even really need a response, since there is no real problem: this is Allah speaking to the prophets, and He is their Lord and Master, and may address them however He wills, and rebuke them, threaten them, censure them, correct them, and warn them. This does not give anyone else the right to speak to them in the same way, or use these words as support for whatever understanding he might like to derive from these words: for example, to infer from words of rebuke that it is possible that they could sin, or to infer from the words (*Allah pardon you*) that it is possible that they could err. Nay, this is insolent presumption and intrusion on the part of one who makes such claims; for a father may beat, rebuke, or scorn his child, yet he would not like anyone else to do the same, proffering the excuse that 'his father does the same to him'! No father would accept this. Allah ﷻ may deal with His prophets as He pleases, and address them how He chooses; but He does not accept for us to deal with them as He does. Attention must be paid to this.

Part Three

The Perfection of His Magnificent Character and Noble Attributes

"*Verily, you are of a tremendous nature*" [4:68]

His ﷺ Perfect Mercy[276]

His ﷺ Mercy to the World

Allah says: *'And we have not sent you except as a mercy to the worlds'* [21:107]. He ﷺ is the Messenger of mercy, whom Allah ﷻ sent as a mercy to all created beings: a mercy to the believers, and a mercy to the disbelievers, and a mercy to the hypocrites; a mercy to all humanity, men, women and children, and a mercy to the birds and the animals. He is an all-embracing mercy to all of Allah's creation. As for his compassion, tenderness, and mercy for all mankind, Allah says of him: *'Grievous to him is your suffering; anxious is he over you, full of tenderness and mercy for the believers)* [9:128]. It has been said that it is a mark of the Prophet's ﷺ virtue that Allah gave two of His Names to him when He said 'full of tenderness and mercy (*ra'ūf*ᵘⁿ *raḥīm*) for the believers'.[277]

It is related that a Bedouin came to the Messenger of Allah ﷺ asking for something. The Messenger of Allah ﷺ gave him something, and said to him: 'Have I been good to you?'The Bedouin man said: 'No, and you have not acted decently!' Some of the Muslims became angry, and made as if to stand up to him. The Messenger of Allah ﷺ indicated to them that they should stand down. He ﷺ then went home, and sent the man something else, and said to him: 'Have I been good to you?' The Bedouin replied: 'Yes, may Allah reward you with goodness of family and kinsfolk!' The Prophet ﷺ said: "You said what you said, and this has provoked something in the souls of my companions; so if you like, say before them what you just said before me, so that their ill feelings towards you leave their hearts.' He agreed to do this.

The next day, the man came back, and the Prophet ﷺ said: 'This Bedouin said what he said, and then we gave him more, and he declared himself satisfied. Is that right?' The Bedouin said: 'Yes, may Allah reward you with goodness of family and kinsfolk!' The Prophet ﷺ then said: 'The likeness of myself and this Bedouin is as that of a man who had

276 This chapter draws from sections of *Our Master Muḥammad* ﷺ, Volume 1, Part V.

277 *Al-Ra'ūf* and *al-Raḥīm* are Names of Allah ('the Tender, the Merciful').

a camel that ran away, and the people gave chase but only succeeded in making it run further still. The owner of the camel said to them: "Get from between me and my camel, for I am gentler than you with it, and I know it better." He then went to it, and picked some grass for it, and called it, until it came to him and knelt. Then he secured to it its saddle, and mounted it. Had I left you when the man said what he said, and had you killed him, he would have gone to Hell.'[278]

It is related that the Prophet ﷺ said: 'Let none of you tell me anything about any of my Companions; for I love to come out to you with a heart at peace.'[279]

Another manifestation of his ﷺ compassion for his community was the way he would seek to make things easier for them, and express dislike for certain things out of fear that they would become obligatory for them. Examples of this are his ﷺ words 'Were it not for my concern for my community, I would have commanded them to use the tooth-stick with every ablution'; the ḥadīth about the night prayer and how he ﷺ forbade them from fasting night and day; how he disliked entering the Kaʿba lest his community take it as a burden upon themselves to do so; how he entreated his Lord to make his expression of reviling and curse a means of mercy for their objects; and how hearing the sound of a child crying would cause him to speed up the prayer.[280]

Another manifestation of his ﷺ compassion was that he called upon his Lord and made a covenant with Him, saying: 'If I ever revile or curse a man, then make for him a source of purification, mercy, and connection [to You], and a means of his being drawn nearer to You on the Day of Resurrection.'

When his ﷺ people belied him,[281] Jibrīl ﷺ came to him and said: 'Allah Almighty has heard the words of your people to you, and how they have rejected you; and He has commanded the angel of the mountain to obey your command to do with them as you will.' The angel of the mountain then called to him and greeted him, and said: 'Command me as you will. If you desire it, I will cause the Akhshabayn[282] to tumble down upon them!' The Prophet ﷺ replied: 'Nay, for I have hope that from their progeny will

278 Aḥmad.

279 Abū Dāwūd.

280 All these incidents can be found in the *Ṣaḥīḥ* collection.

281 In the early stages of the prophetic mission in Mecca. [t]

282 The two mountains of Mecca, Abū Qabīs and Qaʿīqaʿān.

come forth those who worship Allah, and associate nothing with Him.' Ibn al-Munkadir also narrated that Jibrīl ﷺ said to the Prophet ﷺ: 'Allah Almighty has commanded the heavens, the earth, and the mountains to obey you,' and he ﷺ replied: 'I shall give my community respite, that perchance Allah might relent to them.'

ʿĀʾisha ؓ said: 'the Messenger of Allah ﷺ was never given to choose between two things save that he chose the easier of them.'[283] Ibn Masūd ؓ said: 'The Messenger of Allah ﷺ would give us counsel at choice moments, fearing lest we became bored.'[284] ʿĀʾisha also related that she once mounted a camel which gave her difficulty. She began to pull it here and there, when the Messenger of Allah ﷺ said to her: 'Be gentle.'[285]

Another example of his ﷺ universal mercy was his mercy to the hypocrites, in that he gave them security from being fought and captured, out of deference to their outward profession of Islam in this world.

Another example of his ﷺ universal mercy was his mercy to the unbelievers, in that they were spared annihilation in this world; for the previous communities, when Allah sent to them messengers in whom they disbelieved, were visited by punishment that encompassed them all. Allah informed us about the people of Nūḥ, ʿĀd, Thamūd, Lūṭ, and others, and how punishment enveloped them, and how the very thing they had scorned before came to overwhelm them.

As for the unbelievers of this Muḥammadan community,[286] Allah spared them the encompassing punishment that would have annihilated them, just as the unbelievers of the previous communities were totally annihilated. This was a tribute to this noble Messenger ﷺ, whom Allah sent as a mercy to the worlds.

283 Al-Bukhārī, Muslim.

284 Al-Bukhārī, Muslim.

285 Muslim.

286 Meaning all those to whom the Messenger of Allah ﷺ was sent, who constitute the 'community of the message' (*ummat al-daʿwa*). [t]

HIS ﷺ MERCY WITH HIS FAMILY AND
HOUSEHOLD

MUSLIM NARRATED in his *Ṣaḥīḥ*, on the authority of ʿAmr ibn Saʿīd, that Anas ؓ said: 'I never saw anyone more merciful with their household than the Messenger of Allah ﷺ. Ibrāhīm[287] used to be nursed in a house in the elevated area of Medina. He ﷺ used to go, and we would go with him, and enter the house, from which smoke was rising (for his wet-nurse's husband was a blacksmith), and pick up his son and kiss him, and then go back out. When Ibrāhīm died, the Messenger of Allah ﷺ said: "Ibrāhīm is my son, and he died whilst still at the breast.[288] He has two wet-nurses, who will complete his nursing in Paradise."'[289]

An example of his mercy ﷺ with his family is that he would help them with the household chores, as was mentioned in the ḥadīth of al-Aswad, who said: 'I asked ʿĀʾisha ؓ what the Prophet ﷺ used to do around the house. She replied: "He was at the service of his family; and when the time for the prayer came, he would go to pray."' He ﷺ was not one of the oppressive men; rather, he would often serve himself ﷺ: It is narrated in the *Musnad* of Aḥmad, and elsewhere, that ʿĀʾisha ؓ said: 'The Prophet ﷺ would sew his clothes, and cobble his shoes, and do all the work that men do in their houses.'

---

[287] The Prophet's ﷺ son ؓ.

[288] I.e., at the breastfeeding age.

[289] I.e., they will complete his two years of suckling, for he died at the age of sixteen months, or seventeen months (*Sharḥ al-Nawawī*).

HIS ﷺ MERCY WITH CHILDREN, ORPHANS, WIDOWS, SICK PEOPLE, AND OTHERS

AL-BUKHĀRĪ, MUSLIM, and others narrate, on the authority of Anas ﷺ, that the Prophet ﷺ said: 'I sometimes begin to pray,[290] intending to lengthen it, and then hear the cries of a child, and so lighten the prayer, because I know the severity of his mother's angst.'

Another manifestation of his mercy with children is that he would pat their heads, and kiss them: It is narrated in the *Ṣaḥīḥ* collections of al-Bukhārī and Muslim that ʿĀʾisha ﷺ said: 'The Messenger of Allah ﷺ kissed al-Ḥasan and al-Ḥusayn, the sons of ʿAlī, whilst in the company of al-Aqraʿ ibn Ḥābis al-Tamīmī. Al-Aqraʿ said: "I have children, not one of whom I have ever kissed!" The Messenger of Allah ﷺ looked at him, and then said: "Those who show no mercy will be shown no mercy."'

It is also narrated in the *Ṣaḥīḥ* collections of al-Bukhārī and Muslim that ʿĀʾisha ﷺ said: 'A Bedouin man came to the Messenger of Allah ﷺ and said: "You kiss children, but we do not kiss them!" The Messenger of Allah ﷺ replied: "Can I avail you aught if Allah has removed mercy from your heart?"' This means that those who have mercy in their hearts for children are driven by that to kiss them; and those whose hearts are bereft of mercy refuse to kiss them.

Al-Bukhārī, Muslim, and al-Tirmidhī narrate that al-Barrāʾ ﷺ said: 'I saw the Messenger of Allah ﷺ with al-Ḥasan on his shoulder. He ﷺ was saying: "O Allah, I love him, so love him!"' Al-Tirmidhī narrated, on the authority of Anas ﷺ, that the Prophet ﷺ was asked who from amongst his household was the most beloved to him. He ﷺ replied: 'Al-Ḥasan and al-Ḥusayn.' And he ﷺ used to say to Fāṭima (upon whom be peace): 'Call my sons to me!', and embrace them ﷺ.

Another manifestation of his mercy ﷺ with children, and his love for spreading joy amongst them, is that when the first crop of fruits were

[290] I.e., the communal prayer in the mosque.

brought to him he would give them to any children who were present. Al-Ṭabarānī narrated, on the authority of Ibn ʿAbbās ☙, that when the Prophet ☙ was brought the first harvest of a fruit, he would place them on his eyes, and then on his lips, and say: 'O Allah, as you have shown us the first of it, show us the last of it!' Then, he would give it to any children that were present.[291]

Another manifestation of his mercy ☙ was when his eyes shed tears for the loss of his son Ibrāhīm ☙. Anas ☙ reported that the Messenger of Allah ☙ went to see his son Ibrāhīm ☙ when he was close to passing away. The Messenger of Allah's ☙ eyes began to shed tears. ʿAbd al-Raḥmān ibn ʿAwf said to him: 'Is this you, O Messenger of Allah?' The Prophet ☙ replied: 'O Ibn ʿAwf, it is mercy!' Then, another tear fell, and he said: 'The eyes shed tears, and the heart grieves; yet we say not except that which pleases our Lord. O Ibrāhīm, for your loss we are deeply saddened!'[292]

Usāma ibn Zayd ☙ reported that one of the nephews of the Messenger of Allah ☙ was close to death. As the baby was handed to him ☙, his eyes welled with tears. Saʿd said to him: 'What is this, O Messenger of Allah?' He ☙ replied: 'It is mercy, which Allah placed in the hearts of His servants; and Allah only shows mercy to those of His servants who are merciful.'[293]

Another manifestation of his mercy was that he ☙ would not disdain to walk with widows and poor people, and fulfil for them their needs[294]; and he would visit weak and sick Muslims, and attend their funerals.'[295] He ☙ would treat orphans well, and be kind to them, and enjoin their fostering and good treatment; and he clearly elucidated the merits of these actions when he ☙ said: 'I and the one who fosters the orphan will be like this in Paradise,' twisting his fingers together,[296] and 'The best of the houses of the Muslims is the one in which there resides an orphan who is well treated.'[297]

---

[291]   Ibn al-Sinnī also narrated it on the authority of Abū Hurayra. Al-Ḥāfiẓ al-Haythamī said: 'It was narrated by al-Ṭabarānī in al-Kabīr and al-Ṣaghīr, and the men of the chain of transmission in al-Ṣaghīr are rigorously authenticated.'

[292]   Narrated by al-Bukhārī; parts of it are narrated by Muslim.

[293]   Al-Bukhārī, Muslim.

[294]   Al-Nasāʾī.

[295]   Abū Yaʿlā, al-Ṭabarānī.

[296]   Al-Bukhārī.

[297]   Ibn Mājah.

Another aspect of his mercy was that if he saw any of his Companions in a state of difficulty or misfortune, he would be overcome with grief and his heart would be filled with compassion, and he would weep on account of it. He went with ʿAbd al-Raḥmān ibn ʿAwf and some others to visit Saʿd ibn ʿUbāda, and when he saw him he began to weep, and the others wept with him.[298] And he ﷺ kissed ʿUthmān ibn Maẓʿūn as he lay dying, and wept; ʿĀʾisha said: 'I saw the Prophet's ﷺ tears run down ʿUthmān's cheek.'[299] Another narration says that he ﷺ kissed him between the eyes, and then wept a long while.[300]

298 Al-Bukhārī, Muslim.

299 Al-Tirmidhī.

300 Ibn al-Jawzī.

HIS ﷺ MERCY WITH ANIMALS

THE PROPHET ﷺ would enjoin mercy to animals, and forbid their owners from starving them, wearing them out, making them carry loads constantly, overburdening them, or treating them in any way that caused them suffering.

The Messenger of Allah ﷺ once passed by a donkey that was severely emaciated. He ﷺ said: 'Be mindful of Allah where these beasts are concerned: take care of them when you ride them; and take care of them when you eat them.'[301]

He ﷺ once entered an orchard belonging to a man of the Helpers, in which there was a camel. When it saw the Prophet ﷺ, it cried out, and its eyes shed tears. The Messenger of Allah ﷺ went to it, and patted its head, and it became quiet. He ﷺ said: 'Who owns this camel? Whose camel is this?' A young man from the Helpers approached, and so he ﷺ said to him: 'Do you not fear Allah for the sake of this beast, which Allah has given you? He complained to me that you starve him, and wear him out!'[302]

He ﷺ also forbade the overburdening of animals by stopping and sitting on them without any need. He once came upon a group of people sitting on their stationary mounts. He said to them: 'Mount properly, and dismount properly, and do not take them as chairs upon which to chat in the streets and marketplaces. Many a mount is better than he who mounted it, and more abundant in remembering Allah.'[303]

The Messenger of Allah ﷺ also forbade the killing of frogs, saying: 'Their croaking is glorification [of Allah].'[304]

He ﷺ also said: 'A woman entered Hell because of a cat that she tied up. She neither fed it, nor let it eat beasts from the floor.'[305]

He ﷺ also forbade the abuse of animals by setting them upon one another for blood sport, and provoking them into violence.[306]

301 Abū Dāwūd, Ibn Khuzayma.

302 Aḥmad, Abū Dāwūd, al-Ḥākim.

303 Aḥmad, Abū Yaʿlā, al-Ṭabarānī.

304 Al-Nasāʾī.

305 Al-Bukhārī.

306 Abū Dāwūd, al-Tirmidhī.

The Messenger of Allah ﷺ also forbade people from frightening a bird by threatening its young. When someone took some chicks from a lark's nest, and she began to panic, he ﷺ said: 'Who has caused her to fret about her brood? Give her offspring back to her.' He also saw a hive of bees that someone had burned. 'Who burned this?', he asked. They answered that they had done it, and he said: 'It is not for anyone to punish with fire but the Lord of the Fire.'[307]

He ﷺ also forbade the killing of birds for sport, without any beneficial reason such as eating them, saying: 'If anyone kills a sparrow, it will declaim before Allah on the Day of Resurrection, saying: "O my Lord! So-and-so killed me for mere sport, and did not kill me for any good reason!"'[308]

He ﷺ also enjoined gentleness and kindness when slaughtering animals, saying to a man who had lain a sheep down on its side [to slaughter it] whilst still sharpening his knife: 'Do you wish to kill it twice? Would that you had sharpened your knife before laying it down!'[309]

He ﷺ also forbade the use of any animal, or anything with a spirit, as a target for archery.[310]

307 Abū Dāwūd.

308 Al-Nasā'ī.

309 Al-Ṭabarānī.

310 Al-Bukhārī, Muslim.

His ﷺ Perfect Shyness[311]

Shyness is a characteristic that leads to the avoidance of shameful matters, and prevents any negligence in allotting people their rights. For this reason, the Prophet ﷺ said: 'Be shy before Allah, as He deserves.' The people said: 'We indeed are shy before Allah, praise be to Him!' He ﷺ replied: 'This is not the case; rather, shyness before Allah entails that you protect the head and that which it contains, and protect the stomach, and that which it contains...'[312] This makes it clear that shyness inspires the one who possesses it to strive for perfection, and keeps him from settling for less. The Prophet ﷺ also said: 'Shyness brings nothing but good.'[313]

The Messenger of Allah ﷺ was the shyest of people because he was the greatest of them in faith, and He ﷺ said: 'Shyness is born of faith.'[314] Al-Bukhārī and Muslim narrate that Abū Saʿīd al-Khudrī ﷺ said: 'The Messenger of Allah ﷺ was shyer than a maiden in her chamber.' The narration of al-Bukhārī adds: 'If he disliked something, it would be seen in his face.' It is well-known that a maiden (a virgin girl) who is hidden away in her chamber (her room in the house or encampment) is especially shy; yet the Messenger of Allah ﷺ was shyer even than she.

His ﷺ shyness was such that he would never confront a person with something they would dislike. Rather, he ﷺ would hint at the problem, or tell one of his companions to address the person directly. Abū Dāwūd, al-Tirmidhī and others narrate that Anas ﷺ said: 'The Messenger of Allah ﷺ would never directly confront a person with something they would dislike. Once, there visited him a man with a yellow stain on his clothes. When he stood to leave, the Prophet ﷺ said to his companions: "You might tell this fellow to wash off this yellow stain."'

Abū Dāwūd narrated that ʿĀ'isha ﷺ said: : 'If the Messenger of Allah ﷺ heard something about a man, he would not say: "What is wrong with

311 See also *Our Master Muḥammad* ﷺ, Volume 2, pp 21-25.

312 Al-Ṭabarī.

313 Al-Bukhārī.

314 Aḥmad, al-Tirmidhī, Ibn Ḥibbān.

so-and-so", but would say: "What is wrong with people, that they say such-and-such?"'

Another example of his ﷺ shyness was when the people sat with him too long after eating, and he was too shy to ask them to leave, until a verse of the Quran was revealed specifically regarding this: Al-Bukhārī narrated in his *Ṣaḥīḥ* collection that Anas ﷺ said: 'When the Messenger of Allah ﷺ was to marry Zaynab, Umm Sulaym said to me: "We should give the Messenger of Allah ﷺ a gift." I agreed. She took some dates, butter and cheese, and made a stew in a pot, which I took to him ﷺ. He ﷺ told me to put it down, and then told me to invite certain men, whom he named, and to invite whomever else I met. I did as he bade me. When I returned, the house was crowded with his relatives, and I saw the Messenger of Allah ﷺ place his hand in the stew and speak as long as Allah intended, and then call people ten at a time to eat from it, saying to them: "Mention Allah's Name, and let each man eat what is nearest to him." This continued until they had all dispersed.'

Muslim's narration continues: 'The Prophet ﷺ was too shy [to ask them to leave]. Then, he ﷺ went out and made for the bed-chambers, and I went out after him, and said: "They have gone." The Prophet ﷺ returned, and entered the house, and let down the curtains. I was in the room, and he ﷺ recited: [O you who believe! Do not enter the houses of the Prophet unless permission is granted to you for a meal; and wait not for its preparation. But if you are invited, enter, and when you have eaten, disperse, lingering not for conversation. This would trouble the Prophet, yet he is shy from you; and Allah does not shy from the truth] [33:53].'

This means that because of his generosity, he ﷺ was too shy to tell them to leave whilst they were sitting with him; yet Allah does not shy away from proclaiming the truth that must be honoured. This does not contradict that He ﷻ is characterised by a generous shyness in a way befitting His Divinity, as the Prophet ﷺ said: 'Your Lord is shy, and generous; when His servant raises his hands to Him, He is shy to refuse him.'[315]

Because they were sitting in his house, the Prophet ﷺ was too shy to be direct with them, out of his generosity. However, the situation was in dire need of clarification, and so the Qur'ān brought clarification from the Almighty Sovereign Himself ﷻ.

[315] Al-Tirmidhī and others.

Another aspect of his ✤ shyness was that when he needed to answer a call of nature, he would go far away to an isolated place, as was narrated by Ibn Mājah on the authority of Bilāl ibn Ḥarth, and indicated to be authentic in *al-Jāmiʿ al-Ṣaghīr*. Another aspect of his ✤ shyness was that when he wanted to answer a call of nature, he would not lift his robe until he was close to the earth, as al-Tirmidhī and Abū Dāwūd narrate. Another aspect of his ✤ shyness was that when he entered the place where he would relieve himself, he would wear his shoes and cover his head, as Ibn Saʿd narrates.

Another aspect of his ✤ shyness is revealed in what Imam al-Tirmidhī narrates in his *Shamāʾil*, on the authority of ʿĀʾisha, who said: 'I never looked at [or 'I never saw'[316]] the private parts of the Messenger of Allah ✤.' This was due to his shyness, and his perfect dignity ✤, and his desire to cover himself perpetually. Shaykh al-Qārī and Shaykh Muḥammad ibn Qāsim Jasūs state in their commentaries of the *Shamāʾil* that Abū Ṣāliḥ narrated, on the authority of Ibn ʿAbbās ✤, that ʿĀʾisha ✤ said: 'The Messenger of Allah ✤ never approached any of his wives except that he was covered, with a cloth draped over his head; and I never saw his [private parts], nor he mine.'[317]

Al-Bazzār narrated that Ibn ʿAbbās ✤ said: 'The Messenger of Allah ✤ would bathe behind the chambers; and no one ever saw him naked.' In *Sharḥ al-Shamāʾil*, al-Qārī declared this to be a sound transmission.

---

[316] There are two different narrations.
[317] Shaykh ʿAbdallāh Sirājuddīn states that this was also narrated by Ibn al-Jawzī in *al-Wafā*.

His ﷺ Perfect Generosity[318]

Generosity or munificence means to spend willingly on that which causes great benefit or fulfils a vital need, or to donate money to a good and righteous cause.

Generosity was an innate, divinely-invested quality of the Prophet ﷺ, and a directive from the Qur'ān; and therefore he ﷺ would encourage others to be generous, saying: 'The generous person is near to Allah, near to the people and near to Paradise; and the miser is far from Allah, far from the people and far from Paradise.'[319] He ﷺ also said: 'Every day when [Allah's] servants rise, two angels descend. One of them says, "O Allah, give recompense to him who spends"; the other says: "O Allah, give ruin to him who withholds."'[320] He ﷺ also said: 'Beware of miserliness, for it destroyed those who came before you.'[321]

His ﷺ generosity was not for the sake of earning praise or avoiding criticism, nor was it for the sake of boasting, exploitation or attracting admirers; rather, it was all in Allah's cause, and to seek Allah's goodly acceptance. It was for the protection of the religion, the spread of the call, and the struggle against those who stand in the way of Allah's cause. It was for the material support of those poor Muslims who had lost their wealth in Allah's cause, or were unable to earn. It was for the care of orphans and widows, and the freeing of slaves whose owners were contracted to free them for a price. It was for the attracting of those non-Muslims whose hearts he ﷺ deemed could be won over to Islam.

The Prophet's ﷺ generosity meant that he would put others ahead of himself and his household; he would give away those things he needed most, and give a lot when he needed a little.

He ﷺ would give all to Allah's cause that he was able to give, and would deem whatever he gave to be a little. He would give a huge amount, but not view it as a lot. He was never asked for anything for the sake of Islam save that he gave it; indeed, he never said no to any request.

He ﷺ was so generous that he would be shy to send a petitioner away empty-handed, with the excuse that he did not have anything to give. A

318 This chapter is partially drawn from *Our Master Muḥammad*, Volume 1, pp 221-224.

319 Al-Tirmidhī.

320 Muslim.

321 Abū Dāwūd, al-Ḥākim.

man came to him and asked him to give him something. The Prophet ﷺ said: 'I have nothing, but buy something in my name, and when I get something, I will pay for it.' 'O Messenger of Allah,' said ʿUmar, 'you gave to him! Allah did not make you responsible for what you have not the means to do!' The Prophet ﷺ did not like what ʿUmar said, and so a man of the Helpers said: 'O Messenger of Allah, spend, and do not fear any decrease from the Possessor of the Throne!' The Messenger of Allah ﷺ smiled, and his face showed delight in what the Helper had said. Then he ﷺ said: 'This is what I was commanded to do.'[322]

Muslim narrates that Anas ﷺ said: 'The Messenger of Allah was never asked for anything except that he gave it. A man (Ṣafwān ibn Umayya) came, and he ﷺ gave him all the sheep between two mountains. The man returned to his people, and said: "O my people, embrace Islam, for Muḥammad gives like one who does not fear poverty!"'

On the day of Ḥunayn, in order to open their hearts to Islam, the Prophet ﷺ gave each of the freed captives one thousand camels. One of those who were freed was Mālik ibn 'Awf, who composed a poem of praise in his honour ﷺ.

Al-Tirmidhī narrated, on the authority of Saʿīd ibn al-Musayyib, that Ṣafwān ibn Umayya said: 'The Messenger of Allah ﷺ gave me what he gave me at a time when he was the most hateful of people to me. He did not cease giving to me until he was the most beloved of people to me.'

Al-Wāqidī narrated in his *Maghāzī* that Ṣafwān went around with the Prophet ﷺ examining the battle-spoils on the day of Ḥunayn, when they came upon a ravine filled with camels and sheep. Ṣafwān was impressed by it, and began to stare at it. The Prophet ﷺ said to him: 'Does this ravine please you, O Abū Wahb?' He replied: 'Yes.' The Prophet ﷺ said: 'It is yours, along with all that it contains.' Ṣafwān said: 'I testify that you are the Messenger of Allah, for none but a prophet could be willing to do such a thing!'

Al-Tirmidhī narrates that the Prophet ﷺ was brought ninety thousand dirhams, which were laid out on a mat. He then began to divide it, and did not refuse anyone who asked for it until he had gone through it all.

It is narrated that Abū Saʿīd ﷺ said: 'Some people from the Helpers asked something of the Messenger of Allah ﷺ, and he gave them what they asked. Then they asked him again, so he gave them what they

322 Al-Tirmidhī.

asked. Then they asked him again, so he gave them what they asked, until all he had was spent, whereupon he said: 'Whatever good I possess, I would not keep it from you. Whosoever seeks modesty will be granted modesty by Allah, and whosoever is satisfied with his lot will be sufficed by Allah, and whosoever acts patiently will be granted patience by Allah; and no one was ever given any gift finer and more abundant for him than patience.'[323]

Ibn Mājah narrated that ʿĀʾisha ﷺ said: 'I never saw the Messenger of Allah ﷺ entrust the delivery of his charity to another person: he ﷺ would be the one to put it in the beggar's hand.'

Ibn Saʿd narrated that Ziyād, the freed slave of ʿAyyāsh ibn Rabīʿa said: 'There were two things that the Messenger of Allah ﷺ would never appoint anyone else to see to: his water for ablutions when he rose at night; and the beggar, to whom he ﷺ would give in person.'

Al-Bayhaqī and Abū Dāwūd narrate in their *Sunan* collections that ʿAbdallāh al-Hawzanī said: 'I met Bilāl, and said to him: "O Bilāl, tell me how the Messenger of Allah ﷺ used to spend." He replied: "He had nothing, and I was the one who would arrange his financial affairs, from the time Allah ﷻ sent him until he passed away. If anyone ever came to him as a [new] Muslim, and he ﷺ saw them to be without clothing, he would have me go and borrow some money to clothe and feed them."' Al-Bukhārī and Muslim narrate in their *Ṣaḥīḥ* collections that Ibn ʿAbbās ﷺ said: 'The Messenger of Allah ﷺ was the most generous of people, and he would be at his most generous during Ramaḍān, when he met with Jibrīl to study the Qurʾān with him. Indeed, the Messenger of Allah ﷺ was more generous in bestowing goodness than the very wind.'

323 Narrated in all of the six major collections.

His ﷺ Perfect Loyalty

Loyalty is a lofty quality only possessed by those who live good lives and have clear consciences. The Prophet ﷺ called us and encouraged us to attain this quality.

Perhaps the finest example of loyalty to a covenant occurred during the events of the Truce of Ḥudaybiyya, when the Prophet ﷺ and the idolaters made a truce with the following stipulations: that if anyone from the idolaters went to him ﷺ, he would return him to them; yet if any Muslim went to them, they would not have to send him back. As the truce was being written, Abū Jandal came to him, walking in his fetters. The Prophet ﷺ returned him to them, out of loyalty to the treaty which had not yet been signed. Abū Jandal began to scream at the top of his voice, 'O Muslims! Am I to be returned to the idolaters, that they may persecute me because of my religion?' The people were all the more aggrieved because of this. But the Messenger of Allah ﷺ said: 'Abū Jandal! Have patience, and expect the best; for Allah will give you, and the other persecuted folk alongside you, a release and a way out.'[324]

The Prophet ﷺ then returned to Medina, where a man of Quraysh named Abū Baṣīr came to him, having embraced Islam. Quraysh sent two men to demand his return, saying 'Honour the treaty you made with us.' The Prophet ﷺ gave him over to the two men, and they set off with him. When they reached Dhul-Ḥalīfa, they stopped to eat some dates. Abū Baṣīr said to one of them: 'By Allah, that is a fine sword you have there!' The man unsheathed it and said, 'Indeed, by Allah, it is, and I have tested it and tested it again!' 'Let me see it,' said Abū Baṣīr. He gave it to him, and he struck him with it and killed him. The other man fled back to Medina and entered the mosque, terrified. When the Prophet ﷺ saw him, he said: 'This one has had a fright!' He went to the Prophet ﷺ and said, 'By Allah, my companion was killed and I barely escaped with my life!' Abū Baṣīr then arrived, and said: 'O Prophet of Allah! Allah has absolved you of any blame: you returned me to them, and then He saved me from them!' The Prophet ﷺ said: 'Woe betide his mother, what

324 Al-Bukārī, Ibn Hishām.

a firebrand! If only he had some help...' When Abū Baṣīr heard this, he realised that the Prophet ﷺ would send him back again to them, so he made for the coast. Meanwhile, Abū Jandal had escaped from them too, and he met up with Abū Baṣīr along with a group of others. They then began to waylay every caravan Quraysh sent out to the Levant, killing them and seizing their goods. Quraysh therefore sent a message to the Prophet ﷺ, asking him for the sake of Allah and kith and kin to send for Abū Baṣīr and the others, and promising that if they went to him they would be left alone. So the Prophet ﷺ sent for them.[325]

Thus the Prophet ﷺ kept his oath and loyally fulfilled its condition; and the Prophet's ﷺ virtue and far-sightedness was clearly manifested.

ʿAbdallāh ibn Abī al-Ḥamsāʾ said: 'I made a contract of sale with the Prophet ﷺ before he was sent on his mission, and I still owed him some of it, so I promised him I would meet him at a certain place to give it to him, but then I forgot. After three days, I remembered, I went to the place, and there he was ﷺ. He said: "My son, you have inconvenienced me! I have been here for three days awaiting you!"'[326]

An elderly woman came to the Prophet ﷺ. He asked her who she was, and she said, 'I am Jathāma al-Mazaniyya.' 'Nay,' he ﷺ said, 'you are Ḥassāna[327] al-Mazaniyya! How have you been since last we met?' She said, 'Very well, may my father and mother be ransomed for you, O Messenger of Allah.' When she had left, someone said: 'O Messenger of Allah, why did you give that old woman such a welcome?' He replied: 'She used to come and see us when Khadīja was still here; and keeping good relations is part of faith.'[328]

One day he ﷺ was sitting when his father by nursing[329] came to him ﷺ, so he laid down one of his cloaks for him to sit on. Then his mother by nursing came, so he ﷺ laid down part of his cloak from the other side for her to sit on. Then his brother by breastfeeding came, so the Messenger of Allah ﷺ stood for him, and bade him sit down in front of him.[330] He made clear his feelings towards the tribe of Hawāzin, in which he had paternal aunts, aunts by nursing, and nursemaids. One of them said to

325 Abū Dāwūd.

326 Abū Dāwūd, Ibn al-Jawzī.

327 Ḥassāna means 'very beautiful'. [t]

328 Al-Ḥākim, al-Bayhaqī and others.

329 I.e., the husband of the woman who suckled him ﷺ. [t]

330 Abū Dāwūd.

him, 'Had we nursed Nuʿmān bin al-Mundhir,[331] we would hope that he would have affection for us; and you are the best of all wards.' Upon this, he ﷺ gave them enough to fulfil all their hopes.[332] This is the greatest evidence of his loyalty and chivalry.

The Prophet ﷺ knew how parents must be shown reverence, kindness, and deference, following both the guidance of the Holy Qurʾān and the indications of his pure inclinations, noble character and sense of loyalty.

Asmāʾ bint Abī Bakr said: 'My mother came to me while she was yet an idolater, when the Messenger of Allah ﷺ made the covenant with Quraysh [meaning the Truce of Ḥudaybiyya]. Abū Bakr had divorced her in the days of the pagan ignorance. She brought me a gift, so I sent a message to the Messenger of Allah ﷺ, asking him: "My mother has come to me with a desire to see me. Should I let her in my house?" He sent me a reply: "Yes, let your mother in and keep your tie with her."'[333]

A man came to the Prophet ﷺ to ask permission to join the armed struggle. 'Are your parents alive?', the Messenger of Allah ﷺ asked him. He said that they were. 'Go and ask their permission, then,' he said; 'if they give you leave, then fight; if not, then have reverence for them.'[334] He also commanded sons to have love for those with whom their fathers were friends, because this is part of being loyal to one's father.

A man came to the Prophet ﷺ and said: 'O Messenger of Allah, I have wealth and a child, and my father needs my wealth.' He replied: 'You and your wealth belong to your father. Your children are one of your finest acquisitions, so you may partake of what they acquire.'[335]

Another manifestation of his ﷺ loyalty was the loyalty he showed to his wife Khadīja, of whom he would speak fondly; our lady ʿĀʾisha would sometimes hear this and become jealous, and once she said to him: 'Was she anything but an old woman, in whose stead Allah has given you something better?' He ﷺ became angry, and said: 'No, by Allah: Allah did not give me something better in her stead. She believed in me when the people disbelieved; and she trusted me when the people belied me; and she shared her wealth with me when the people refused me; and

331 An ancient king of the Arabs famed for his generosity. [t]

332 Ibn Hishām.

333 Al-Bukhārī.

334 Al-Bukhārī.

335 Ibn Mājah, al-Ṭabarānī.

Allah gave me a son by her, and by no other woman.'[336]

When a gift was brought to him ﷺ, he would say: 'Take it to so-and-so's house, for she was a friend to Khadīja, and she loved Khadīja'; and sometimes he would slaughter sheep and give them to Khadīja's friends. Once Khadīja's sister asked permission to see him, and he gave her a warm welcome. A woman once came to see him, and he welcomed her heartily and asked after her warmly. After she had gone, he said: 'She used to come to us when Khadīja was still here; and to keep good relations is part of religion.'

Another manifestation of his ﷺ loyalty occurred when Ḥalīma al-Saʿdiyya[337] came to see him after he married Khadīja, asking him to help her bear the burdens fate had brought her. He spoke to our lady Khadīja, and she gave Ḥalīma a camel and forty rams. She came to see him ﷺ again after the Battle of Ḥunayn, and when he saw her he said, 'Welcome, mother!', and spread out his cloak for her to sit on.

He had another wet-nurse named Thuwayba, who nursed him for a few days before he was given to the care of Ḥalīma. When he grew up and came to learn of this, he sought to repay this favour she had done him, and showed her kindness and generosity for as long as he was in Mecca; and even after he ﷺ emigrated to Medina, he still continued to keep ties with her and buy clothes for her.

When his sister by suckling Shaymāʾ was brought forth among the captives of Hawāzin, and he recognised her, he spread out his cloak for her to sit on and said, 'If you wish, you may stay with me, honoured and loved.'

He ﷺ would even command loyalty to animals in return for their services and labour. Laylā, the wife of Abū Dharr, came riding a she-camel belonging to the Messenger of Allah ﷺ after the Battle of Dhū Qard, and said: 'O Messenger of Allah, I vowed to Allah that I would slaughter her if Allah saved me on her back, and that I would eat of her liver and her fat.' The Messenger of Allah ﷺ smiled and said: 'How poorly you reward her: after Allah carried you on her back, and saved you by her means, you will then slaughter her? A vow is not valid if its object is a sin or something that does not belong to one. She is my camel, so return her to her kin with the blessing of Allah.'

336 Al-Bukhārī and Muslim, as well as others with various versions.

337 The Prophet's ﷺ wet-nurse.

His ﷺ Perfect Patience[338]

ALLAH SAID: [Be then, patient, as the strong-willed among the Messengers were patient; and hasten not for their sake] [46:35].

The patience of the Messenger of Allah ﷺ for the sake of Allah's cause was beyond that of the most patient of people; and the forbearance he showed ﷺ in the face of the persecution of his detractors was above the forbearance of all sentient beings. How severe was the harsh, shameless treatment he received from the impudent villains of Quraysh!

There is no doubt that vile and obscene language deeply impacts those of high moral rectitude, and affects them more than it does others; and acts of persecution work upon their souls much more than they do upon those who have no morals or manners. If this is so, then what about the disposition of our master the Messenger of Allah ﷺ, which is the embodiment of all perfections and virtues, and the source of them? Yet he would receive all this with a tranquil heart. Yet what effect do you imagine their offensive language and acts of persecution would have on him ﷺ?

Imam Aḥmad and al-Tirmidhī narrate, on the authority of Anas ﷺ, that the Messenger of Allah ﷺ said: 'I have been threatened in Allah's cause as no other has been threatened; and I have been hurt in Allah's cause as no other has been hurt; and I have been visited by thirty people in a single night and day, and neither I nor Bilāl had any food for a needy person to eat, save something concealed under Bilāl's armpit.'

The idolaters would confront him ﷺ with enmity, and all forms of persecution, whether in hordes, groups, or individually; even their women and children would be involved. Al-Ṭabarānī narrated that al-Ḥārith ibn al-Ḥārith said: 'I said to my father: "What is this horde?" He replied: "They are people who have gathered against one of their own who has left their way." We went down, and there we found the Messenger of Allah ﷺ, calling the people to the Oneness of Allah ﷻ, and to faith; and they were repelling him, and persecuting him, until midday arrived and they dispersed from around him.' A woman approached, her upper chest

338 See also *Our Master Muḥammad* ﷺ, Volume 1, pp 226-231.

inadvertently uncovered, carrying a vessel of water and a cloth. He 🌸 took them from her, and drank and made ablutions, and then raised his head and said: "Daughter, cover yourself, and worry not about your father." I said: "Who is this?" They replied: "It is Zaynab, his daughter 🌸.'"

It is reported that 'Urwa ibn al-Zubayr said to 'Abdallāh ibn 'Umar: 'What is the worst thing you saw Quraysh afflict the Messenger of Allah 🌸 with, of all the enmity they showed him?' He replied: 'I was amongst them when their nobles had gathered in the precinct, and said: "We have never seen the like of what we have borne from this man: he has ridiculed our aspirations, and insulted our forefathers, and criticised our religion, and divided our faction, and slighted our gods! We have borne from him a grave matter indeed!"

'Whilst they were in the midst of this, the Messenger of Allah 🌸 appeared to them, and they fell upon him in unison, and surrounded him, saying: "Are you the one who says such-and-such?", mentioning the criticism they had heard him speak against their gods and their religion. The Messenger of Allah 🌸 said: "Yes, I am the one who says this." I saw one of them take hold of his cloak 🌸. Abū Bakr stood between them, saying: "Will you kill a man for saying *My Lord is Allah*?" Then they left him be. That was the worst thing I saw Quraysh afflict the Messenger of Allah 🌸 with.'

Al-Bukhārī and Muslim narrate that Ibn Mas'ūd 🌸 said: 'Once the Messenger of Allah 🌸 was praying in the Sacred House [al-Bayt al-Ḥarām], and Abū Jahl and his companions were sitting there. Abū Jahl had slaughtered a camel the day before, and he said to his companions: "Which of you will take the intestines of the camel of the tribe of so-and-so, and throw them onto Muhammad's back as he prostrates?" The worst man of the lot, 'Uqba ibn Abī Mu'ayṭ, went and took it, and when the Prophet 🌸 prostrated, he threw them onto his shoulders. They began to laugh, leaning upon one another.

'I was standing there watching; if only I had the strength [or 'others with me'], I would have taken it off his back 🌸. The Prophet 🌸 remained in prostration, not rising, until someone went and told Fāṭima 🌸, who came (and she was still a young girl at this time) and removed it from him 🌸, and then confronted them and scolded them.

When the Prophet's 🌸 uncle Abū Ṭālib died, the idolaters intensified their persecution, and set upon him with all their severity. The Prophet

✲ decided to go to Ṭāʾif, in the hope that the tribe of Thaqīf would be a source of support and succour for him against his own people in Mecca. When he got there, however, they extended to him the worse possible welcome, and responded with the worst possible response. He only sought their aid, as al-Maqrīzī has said, because they were his relatives, and there was no enmity between them.

Al-Bukhārī and Muslim narrate that ʿĀʾisha ✲ said: 'I said: "O Messenger of Allah, was any day worse for you than the day of Uḥud?" 'He ✲ replied: "I encountered from your people what I encountered; and the worst that I ever encountered from them was on the day of al-ʿAqaba, when I presented myself to Ibn ʿAbd Yālīl ibn ʿAbd Kulāl, and he did not respond to me as I had hoped. I left, my head hanging in sorrow, and I did not recover until I had reached the Qarn al-Thaʿālib,[339] whereupon I raised my head, and saw above me a cloud that was giving me shade. I looked, and saw that within it was Jibrīl ✲, who called me, saying: 'Allah Almighty has heard the words of your people to you, and how they have rejected you; and He has sent to you the angel of the mountain, whom you may command to do with them as you like.' The angel of the mountain called out to me and greeted me, and said: 'O Muḥammad, Allah Almighty has heard the words of your people to you, and I am the angel of the mountain, whom He has sent to you, that you command me [al-Ṭabarānī's narration adds 'as you will']. If you desire it, I will cause the Akhshabayn[340] to tumble down upon them!" He ✲ said: "Nay, for I have hope that from their progeny will come forth those who worship Allah, and associate nothing with Him."'

Abū Nuʿaym narrated in al-Dalāʾil that ʿUrwa ibn al-Zubayr said: 'Abū Ṭālib died, and the severity of the persecution of the Messenger of Allah increased, so he set out to Thaqīf, hoping they would give him shelter, and support him. He found three men from the leaders of Thaqīf, the brothers ʿAbd Yālīl ibn ʿAmr, Khubayb ibn ʿAmr, and Masʿūd ibn ʿAmr. The Prophet ✲ opened himself to them, and told them of his troubles, and of what his people had done to him. One of them said: "If Allah sent you with anything, I will steal the hangings from the Kaʿba!" Another said: "By Allah, I will never speak another word to you again after this meeting! For, if you are a messenger from Allah, you are far too noble that

---

339   A small mountain one day-and-night's journey from Mecca.
340   The two mountains of Mecca, Abū Qabīs and Qaʿīqaʿān.

the likes of me should speak to you!" The third one said: "Could Allah find none to send but you?" They made what he had said to them known to all the people Thaqīf, who then gathered to ridicule the Messenger of Allah ﷺ, and sat before him in two rows either side of the path he walked, picking up stones. Every time he lifted his foot, or put it down, they pelted it with stones, ridiculing and disparaging him. When he had left the two rows behind, his feet streaming with blood, the Prophet ﷺ made for a vineyard of theirs, and sought the shade of one of the vines. He sat at its root, sorrowful and in pain, his feet bleeding.'

The narrations of Ibn Isḥāq and al-Ṭabarānī mention that 'Abdallāh ibn Ja'far ؓ said: 'When Abū Ṭālib died, the Prophet ﷺ went on foot to Ṭā'if, and called them to Islam; but they did not answer his call, so he sought the shade of a vine, and prayed two cycles of prayer, then said: "O Allah, unto You I complain of my weakness, and my helplessness, and my lowliness before the people. O Most Merciful of the merciful! You are the Most Merciful of the merciful, and You are the Lord of the Oppressed. To whom do you entrust me? To a distant enemy, who despises me? Or to a near one, to whom You have given power over me? If You are not angry with me, I care not; but Your protection would be for me the broader way! I seek refuge in the light of Your noble countenance, by which the heavens and the earth are lit, and the darkness is illuminated, and the affairs of this world and the next are rightly ordered, lest Your anger descend upon me, or Your wrath beset me! Yet it is Yours to reproach until You are well pleased; and there is no power and no might except through You."'

His ﷺ Perfect Asceticism

The Prophet ﷺ was the most ascetic of people; all you need to do to see this is reflect that his poverty was a matter of choice, not necessity; for despite his many conquests and the wealth that was brought to him, he completely turned away from the life of this world. He slept on straw mats which left visible marks on his blessed side, and when they offered to give him a soft mat to sleep on, he said: 'What have I to do with this world? My place in this world is but as that of a wayfarer who travels on a hot day, naps under a tree, and then leaves it behind him.'[341]

Allah offered him gold enough to fill the hollow of Mecca, but he ﷺ said: 'No, Lord; rather I will go hungry one day and eat my fill another; when I eat my fill, I will praise You and give thanks to You; and when I go hungry, I will seek Your aid and call upon you.'[342]

He ﷺ would always be happy with the least amount of worldly sustenance, and would say: 'O Allah, make the provision of Muḥammad's family [no more than] what meets their bare needs.'[343]

Our lady ʿĀ'isha said: 'The Messenger of Allah ﷺ never had a dinner large enough to last until supper, nor a supper large enough to last until the next dinner; and he never took two of anything: not two shirts, nor two cloaks, nor two loincloths, nor two pairs of shoes.'[344]

He ﷺ would never hoard things for himself; all the reports which state that he stored things mean that he stored them for his family. He ﷺ and his family never ate their fill of wheat bread three days in a row until he left this world.[345] He ﷺ never ate bread made from sifted flour from the day Allah sent him until he passed away.[346]

A month or two months would pass without a fire being lit in his ﷺ house, during which times only dates and water would be consumed.

341 Abū Yaʿlā.

342 Al-Tirmidhī, Aḥmad.

343 Muslim.

344 Al-Maqrīzī.

345 Muslim, Aḥmad.

346 Aḥmad.

Once Fāṭima took him a piece of bread. 'What's this, Fāṭima?', he said. 'It is a loaf I baked', she replied, 'and I could not feel at ease until I brought it to you.' The Prophet ﷺ said: 'Indeed, it is the first food to enter your father's mouth for three days.'[347]

At the time of his ﷺ passing, his shield was being held in mortgage by a Jew for thirty *ṣāʿ*[348] of barley, which he had taken to feed his family.[349]

Jābir said: 'When digging the trench, the Messenger of Allah and his Companions went three days without tasting any food. "O Messenger of Allah," they said, "there is a large boulder here, from the mountain." The Messenger of Allah ﷺ told them to sprinkle it with water ... and I noticed that the Messenger of Allah ﷺ had tied a stone to his belly.'[350]

Our lady ʿĀʾisha said: 'The Messenger of Allah ﷺ never once ate his fill of two kinds of food in the same day. If he ate his fill of dates, he would not eat his fill of barley; and if he ate his fill of barley, he would not eat his fill of dates.'[351]

ʿUtba ibn Ghazwān said: 'I once found myself in a group of seven, along with the Messenger of Allah ﷺ, and we had no food but acacia leaves, which we ate until our mouths were covered in sores.'[352]

Our lady ʿĀʾisha said: 'The Messenger of Allah ﷺ died having never eaten his fill of bread and oil twice in one day.'[353]

Anas said: 'I do not think that the Messenger of Allah ﷺ ever saw a piece of fine flat bread until he met with Allah ﷻ, nor ever saw a *samīṭ* lamb with his own eyes, until he met Allah ﷻ.' (A *samīṭ* is a young sheep whose wool is removed with boiling water and then roasted in its skin.)

347 Al-Bayhaqī, al-Ṭabarānī.

348 A measurement roughly equivalent to 2 litres.

349 Al-Bukhārī.

350 Al-Bukhārī, Muslim.

351 Ibn Saʿd.

352 Muslim.

353 Muslim.

His ﷺ Perfect Forgiveness

To forgive when one has the power to punish is like a mirror in which the finest image of the soul, and the loftiest of purposes, are reflected. The Holy Qurʾān imparted this noble quality to the Prophet ﷺ when it said: '*Hold to forgiveness, and enjoin what is right, and turn away from the ignorant*' [7:199]. He ﷺ manifested this quality in his words and his deeds, and encouraged others to adopt it as well. It is no secret how he dealt with the people of Mecca and Ṭāʾif, the champions of mischief and evil, when he entered Mecca as a victorious conqueror: his forgiveness embraced the entire city, including the chieftains and leaders who had transgressed in the land and gone to extremes in hurting him and persecuting him.

The Messenger of Allah ﷺ entered Mecca, but ʿIkrima ibn Abī Jahl, Ṣafwān ibn Umayya and Suhayl ibn ʿAmr were determined to fight, along with those they had managed to gather with them. They were routed and put to flight. Yet they then sought security from the Prophet ﷺ, and it was granted to them; and indeed, they were not only pardoned, but also given some of the spoils of Hawāzin, that their hearts might be reconciled.

Consider Ṣafwān ibn Umayya – the enemy, son of the enemy – who fled to Jeddah with the intention of making his way to Yemen by sea. ʿUmayr ibn Wahb went to the Messenger of Allah ﷺ and said: 'O Prophet of Allah, Ṣafwān ibn Umayya, the leader of his people, has fled from you and intends to leave by sea.' The Prophet ﷺ ensured his safety, saying: 'He shall be left alone.' ʿUmayr said: 'O Messenger of Allah, give me a token that he will recognise is from you.' The Messenger ﷺ gave him the turban he had worn when entering Mecca. ʿUmayr took it and found Ṣafwān just as he was about to embark, and said: 'Ṣafwān, my parents be your ransom! Beware of casting yourself into ruin! This is a token of safety from the Messenger of Allah, which I have brought to you.' Ṣafwān said, 'I fear that he means me harm.' ʿUmayr replied: 'Nay, he is more forbearing and noble than that!' They went back together to the Messenger of Allah ﷺ. Ṣafwān said to him: 'This man claims that you have assured my safety.' He ﷺ said: 'He speaks the truth.' Ṣafwān asked for two month's respite to make a decision. 'You shall have four month's respite', said the Prophet ﷺ.

Another man came to him ﷺ shortly before the Conquest, a man whose lampooning and persecution of the Messenger ﷺ had known no bounds: Abū Sufyān ibn al-Ḥārith ibn ʿAbd al-Muṭṭalib.[354] He asked permission to see the Prophet ﷺ, but the Prophet said: 'I have no need to see him, when he has brought dishonour upon me.' Now Abū Sufyān had a young son of his with him, and he said: 'By Allah, either he shall see me or I will take my son by the hand and go out into the desert until we die of thirst and hunger.' When the Messenger of Allah ﷺ heard this, his heart softened, and he agreed to see him, and forgave him. Upon this, Abū Sufyān said:

By your life, on the day I held a banner
For the victory of al-Lāt's knights over Muḥammad's,
I was like a traveller, lost on a dark night;
But now I have been guided, and I follow this guidance![355]

And in Mecca, as the Prophet ﷺ circled the Kaʿba, Fuḍāla ibn ʿUmayr intended to assassinate him. As he approached, the Prophet ﷺ said: 'Is that Fuḍāla?' 'Yes, O Messenger of Allah', he replied. The Prophet ﷺ said: 'What is it that you are thinking of?' 'Nothing,' said Fuḍāla, 'I am but invoking Allah ﷻ.' The Prophet ﷺ smiled, and said: 'Ask forgiveness of Allah!' He then placed his hand on Fuḍāla's chest, and peace entered his heart. Fuḍāla would later say: 'By Allah, by the time he raised it there was nothing of Allah's creation more beloved to me than him.'[356]

Once the people had settled down after the Conquest, the Messenger of Allah ﷺ stood by the door of the Kaʿba and said: 'There is no god but Allah, alone without partner. He has fulfilled His promise, helped His slave, and routed the clans, He alone. Every claim of glory, blood or wealth is, as of now, beneath my two feet, save for the custodianship of the House and the watering of the pilgrims. O men of Quraysh! Allah has relieved you of the conceit of pagan ignorance, and its pride in ancestry. All people are from Adam, and Adam is from dust!' He ﷺ

354 He was a poet who had composed satirical verses against the Prophet ﷺ.
355 Ibn Hishām.
356 Ibn Hishām.

then recited: '*O mankind! We have created you male and female, and made you into nations and tribes, that you may know one another. Surely the noblest among you in the sight of Allah is the most god-fearing of you*' [49:13]. He then said: 'O men of Quraysh! What do you think I shall do with you?' They said: 'We think well: a noble brother and the son of a noble brother.' He said: 'Go, for you are free.'

Consider also that he ﷺ had the whole of Thaqīf at his disposal, when their delegation had come to Medina after having been besieged and weakened by the Muslims. What did he do to them, when among them was a man such as ʿAbd Yālīl ibn ʿAmr ibn ʿUmayr, who had expelled the Prophet ﷺ from Ṭāʾif? (As for the other, Mālik ibn ʿAwf, the Prophet ﷺ had already forgiven him and returned to him his possessions and children.) The Messenger ﷺ returned their prisoner, buying him for a debt which he and his Companions incurred, and turning him over to his ﷺ own enemies, who had almost put an end to Islam at the Battle of Ḥunayn.

Another example of his ﷺ forbearance was that a rabbi of the Jews named Zayd ibn Saʿna studied the attributes of prophethood, and recognised their signs in the Messenger of Allah ﷺ, yet found that there were still two signs that needed testing. The first was *his forbearance will outstrip his wrath*, and the second was *severe mistreatment will only increase his forbearance*. Zayd would keep the company of the Messenger of Allah ﷺ often, and attempt to test him. One day, a Bedouin went to the Messenger of Allah ﷺ to complain about the difficult living conditions in a certain village. Zayd listened to this, and then said to the Messenger of Allah ﷺ: 'I will buy some dates from you', and took out eighty dinars and gave them to the Prophet ﷺ, who gave them to the man. They agreed that on a certain day, the delivery would be met; but Zayd came early. Zayd himself tells the tale:

'I approached the Prophet ﷺ and yanked his cloak firmly so that it came off his shoulders. Then I scowled at him and said, "Will you not give me what is mine, Muḥammad; for by Allah, you sons of ʿAbd al-Muṭṭalib are procrastinators, and I have spent enough time around you to know it!" ʿUmar became enraged and said, "Enemy of Allah! Do you say this to the Messenger of Allah? By Him who sent him with the truth, were I not wary of what would be lost, I would have your head!" The Messenger of Allah ﷺ looked at ʿUmar and smiled at his words, and then said: "Both I and he need something other than this: that you encourage me to repay properly, and that you encourage him to ask properly. Go, ʿUmar, and give him his due; and add another twenty *ṣāʿ* of dates to make up for the scare you gave him!'"

Upon this, Zayd's soul found peace and was content that he had found the signs he had been looking for. ʿUmar took him to repay his debt, and added the extra dates, and Zayd said to him: 'Do you know me, ʿUmar?' He asked who he was. 'I am Zayd ibn Saʿna', he said. 'The rabbi?', asked ʿUmar. 'The rabbi', said Zayd. 'Why, then,' said ʿUmar, 'did you behave this way towards the Messenger of Allah ﷺ, and say what you said to him?' He answered: 'I wanted to test his ﷺ forgiveness.'[357]

Another example of his ﷺ perfect forgiveness is found in the story told by Anas ؓ: 'I was with the Prophet ﷺ, who was wearing a rough-hemmed cloak, when a Bedouin came along and pulled the cloak fiercely so that it left a mark on his ﷺ blessed neck. The Bedouin then said: "O Muḥammad, load these two camels of mine with some of the wealth of Allah's that you have with you; for you will certainly not load them with your own wealth, or your father's wealth!" The Prophet was silent for a moment, and then said: "The wealth is Allah's, and I am His slave. Yet retribution in kind shall be exacted for what you did to me." "No it shall not", said the Bedouin. "And why is that?", asked the Prophet ﷺ. "Because", said the Bedouin, "you do not return one ill deed with another." The Prophet ﷺ laughed, then commanded that one of the man's camels be loaded with barley, and the other with dates.'[358]

At the Battle of Badr, Ṣafwān ibn Umayya lost his father and his brother, and Wahb, the son of ʿUmayr ibn Wahb, was captured. Ṣafwān and his cousin ʿUmayr therefore agreed, at the Ḥijr in the Sacred House, to assassinate the Messenger of Allah ﷺ, on condition that Ṣafwān assume all his debts and support his children if he were killed. ʿUmayr asked Ṣafwān to keep their conversation secret, in case the plan were revealed and news of it spread to Medina. Ṣafwān had a sword polished and then smeared it with poison and gave it to ʿUmayr, who set off for Medina to fulfil his mission. He dismounted by the door to the mosque and tied up his horse, then took up his sword and made for the Messenger of Allah ﷺ, who was inside. Upon his entry, the Messenger of Allah ﷺ said: 'What has brought you, ʿUmayr?' He replied, 'I have come to claim back

357 Al-Ḥākim, al-Bayhaqī, Ibn Ḥibbān.

358 *Al-Shifā*.

[my son] from you.' The Prophet ﷺ said: 'Then what condition did you ask of Ṣafwān in the Ḥijr?' ʿUmayr was startled by this, and said: 'What condition did I ask of him?' The Prophet ﷺ answered: 'In return for slaying me, you made him agree to take upon himself the responsibilities of your household. Yet Allah has come between you and that.' ʿUmayr said: 'I bear witness that you are the Messenger of Allah! Those words were spoken secretly between me and Ṣafwān in the Ḥijr, and no one but he and I heard them – yet Allah informed you of it! I believe in Allah and His Messenger.'[359] This shows how forgiving he was, even to those who wanted to kill him.

When the Prophet ﷺ went to Ḥunayn, one of those present was Shayba ibn ʿUthmān ibn Abī Ṭalḥa, whose father had been slain at the Battle of Uḥud. Shayba said: 'I thought that I would go along with Quraysh to Hawāzin at Ḥunayn, so that if they perchance fought I could take the opportunity to kill Muḥammad, and thus exact revenge for all of Quraysh.' Shayba used to say that even if all the Arabs and non-Arabs followed Muḥammad ﷺ, he would not.

Shayba continued: 'I was waiting for a chance to spring upon him, and kept feeling bolder and bolder as the time drew nearer.' He found his chance when the Muslims became divided from the Messenger of Allah ﷺ: 'I drew my sword and crept right up to him, and raised my sword, and as I was about to bring it down upon him a tongue of flame flashed up like lighting, and I covered my eyes in fear that I would be blinded.'

(Ibn Isḥāq's narration has it: 'I approached the Messenger of Allah ﷺ to slay him, yet something appeared and covered my heart, so that I could not.)

He said: 'The Messenger of Allah ﷺ then called me, saying: "Shayba, come to me." I went, and he placed his hand on my chest and said, "O Allah, protect him from Satan." By Allah, at that moment he became more beloved to me than my very hearing, my sight and my life, and Allah took the hatred out of me. He ﷺ then said: "Come and fight." I stood before him and fought with my sword; and Allah knows that I would have loved to protect him with my own life; even had I met my father then, were he alive, he would have fallen under my sword.'[360]

[359] Ibn Hishām.

[360] Abū Nuʿaym.

His ﷺ Perfect Justice

Justice means to give people their rights without prejudice, and to take people to task for their wrongs without favouritism or bias.

The Prophet ﷺ was endowed with justice that was rooted in divine instruction and Qurʾānic ethics; and from his youngest days, it was his natural disposition to be just. He took part in a covenant made by Quraysh to combat injustice and stand up for the oppressed, known as the 'Alliance of the Virtuous' (*Ḥilf al-Fuḍūl*). He ﷺ later said of this pact: 'I witnessed, in the house of ʿAbdallāh ibn Judʿān, a pact so excellent that I would not exchange my part in it for a herd of red camels; and if now, in Islam, I were called to it, I would gladly respond.'

He ﷺ would maintain justice and apply it to his own family, without giving consideration to social standing or ties of kin. When some men of the Helpers wanted to forgo their claim to the ransom of al-ʿAbbās, the Messenger of Allah's ﷺ uncle,[361] the Prophet ﷺ did not approve of this and said: 'You shall not remit even a single dirham of it.'[362] He did allow his daughter Zaynab's husband to be set free without ransom, however, only because he was clearly too poor to ransom himself – be well aware of this. Al-ʿAbbās, on the other hand, was known to be rich, so the Prophet ﷺ did not free him until he had paid his own ransom and the ransoms of those relatives of his who had been captured alongside him. Since the Prophet's ﷺ forgiveness enveloped all humanity, it is not surprising that his own son-in-law was also included in this forgiveness, just like anyone else.

His ﷺ justice was also manifested when he rebuked a man of the Helpers for his mistreatment of his camel, saying: 'Fear Allah in how you treat this beast; for he complained to me that you underfeed him and overwork him.'[363] He also commanded that two chicks be returned to their mother, who had become frantic at their loss. In these things is clearly manifested the spirit of the Prophet ﷺ in combating injustice, even for birds and beasts.

361 Who had been captured at the Battle of Badr, having not yet publicly embraced Islam.

362 Al-Bukhārī.

363 Abū Dāwūd.

Another instance where his ﷺ perfect justice was manifested was the occasion when Quraysh were concerned about the woman of the Makhzūm clan who had stolen. Seeing that no one else would dare do so, they asked Usāma ibn Zayd ﷺ, who was beloved to the Messenger of Allah ﷺ, to plead the woman's case to the Messenger of Allah ﷺ.

Usāma did so, but the Prophet ﷺ replied: 'Do you intercede against one of the bounds set by Allah Almighty?' He then stood and addressed the people, saying: 'The people who came before you only came to ruin because if one of their noblemen stole, they would leave him, whilst if one of their weak folk stole, then would punish him. By Allah, even if Fāṭima the daughter of Muḥammad stole, I would amputate her hand!'[364]

Another manifestation of his ﷺ justice was the occasion when, as he was dividing some wealth, a man came to him and rudely demanded a share of it. As the Prophet ﷺ was warding him off, he struck him with a stick that was in his hand, and cut his face. Immediately he said, 'Come and avenge yourself.' 'Nay,' said the man, 'I forgive you, O Messenger of Allah.'[365]

Another occasion when his ﷺ justice was manifested was related by a man of the confederate Arabs, who said: 'I was walking behind the Messenger of Allah ﷺ on the day of Ḥunayn. I was wearing heavy shoes, and I trod on his foot with them. He wafted the lash he was carrying in my direction, and said "In the Name of Allah, you hurt me!" I spent the following night rebuking myself, and saying "You hurt the Messenger of Allah!"; and only Allah knows the night I spent. In the morning, a man came looking for me, and I said to myself, "This, by Allah, is the repercussion of what occurred yesterday!" I went with him, sorely afraid. But when I came to the Prophet ﷺ, he said to me: "You trod on my foot yesterday and hurt me, and I wafted my lash at you; so here are eighty sheep for you to take."'[366]

Another manifestation of his ﷺ justice occurred in his final illness, when he ascended the pulpit and said: 'O people! If there is any of you whose back I scourged, then here is my back, that he may requite himself on it. And if there is any of you whose wealth I took, then here is my wealth, that he may requite himself from it. And if there is any of you

[364] Al-Bukhārī, Muslim.

[365] Al-Nasāʾī, Abū Dāwūd.

[366] Ibn Iṣḥāq.

whose honour I reviled, then here is my honour, that he may requite himself on it. Let no man say, "I fear that the Messenger of Allah ﷺ will bear me a grudge"; for it is not my nature, nor my way, to bear grudges. Indeed, the one of you I love the most is he who would claim from me what is rightfully his, or pardon me, that I may meet Allah with a clean conscience.' A man stood up and said, 'O Messenger of Allah, you owe me three dirhams.' He ﷺ replied: 'We do not belie anyone, nor ask him to swear; yet how is it that I owe you this?' He said: 'Remember, one day a needy person passed you by, and you told me to give him something.' The Prophet ﷺ said, 'Pay him, O Faḍl', addressing his nephew, the son of al-ʿAbbās.[367]

[367] Abū Yaʿlā, al-Ṭabarānī.

His ﷺ Perfect Humility

LEXICALLY, HUMILITY means to lower and humble oneself; conventionally, it means to forgo the concomitants of one's social status and pride, and to assume a lower position than one's equals; and for those of true insight, it means for a person to see himself as having no value, worth, or distinction, and to deem that he has been given more than he deserves.

Abū Zayd ﷺ said: 'As long as the servant [of Allah] thinks that there is anyone in the human race more evil than him, he is guilty of pride.' Someone asked him: 'So when is he truly humble?' He answered: 'When he does not pay any heed whatsoever to his own words or states.' Ibn ʿAṭāʾ Illāh says in the *Ḥikam*: 'The humble man is not the one who, when he humbles himself, sees himself as above his action; rather the humble man is the one who, when he humbles himself, sees himself as beneath his action.'

Now, humility is sometimes occasioned by a direct witnessing of the Lord's magnificence; and this is true humility, which cannot be displaced. Other times, humility is occasioned by the flaws a person sees in himself.

The first kind of humility is the one that quells the soul and melts it, displacing its egotism and uprooting from it the tree of pride and desire for power, so that it cannot thereafter be taken by arrogance or self-delusion. The second kind of humility causes the servant to ascend the ladder of virtue. Our Prophet ﷺ is the master of the humble, and the perfect and ample model of humility.

One example of his ﷺ humility: ʿUmar ibn al-Khaṭṭāb ﷺ relates that the Messenger of Allah ﷺ said: 'Do not laud me as the Christians lauded the Son of Mary; I am but a slave, so say: Allah's slave and messenger.'[368]

His ﷺ words 'do not laud me' meant: Do not exaggerate in praising me by saying something that is not true, as the Christians exaggerated in praising our master ʿĪsā by making him a god and a 'son of God'; they did so because they were blind to the indications and evidences of his contingent nature. His ﷺ words 'I am but a slave, so say: Allah's slave

368 Al-Bukhārī.

and messenger' (in another narration 'I am but Allah's slave') mean: I am but a slave and messenger (this is why he said 'so say: Allah's slave and messenger'); now this is an allusion to Allah's words '*Say: I am but a human like you; it is revealed to me…*' [18:110]. Yet the fact that he is Allah's slave and messenger does not mean that others are equal to him in slavehood to Allah, which means to bear witness to His lordship and never be heedless of it; for he ﷺ is the most perfect of all beings in this quality, which itself is the heart of human perfection.

Another example of his ﷺ humility: Anas ibn Mālik ؓ related that a woman came to the Prophet ﷺ and said to him: 'I have a need of you.' He ﷺ replied: 'Sit in any street of Medina you wish, and I will come and sit with you.'[369] Muslim's narration adds: 'So he spent some time in private with her on a certain street, until her need had been met.' Anas added that the Prophet ﷺ spent time in private with her, away from the eyes of the others who had been with him; this was so that no one else would hear her complaint, neither her companions nor his ﷺ. Al-Bukhārī narrates that a slave-girl would come and take ﷺ his hand, and lead him to wherever she needed him. This is a clear sign of his perfect humility. Al-Nasāʾī also narrates that he ﷺ would not disdain to walk with widows and the poor, and meet their needs.

Another manifestation of his ﷺ humility was that Allah gave him the choice whether to be a prophet-slave or a prophet-king, and he chose slavehood in his humility before Allah. This is affirmed in the ḥadīth of Abū Hurayra, as follows: Jibrīl sat with the Prophet ﷺ and looked to the sky, and an angel appeared and descended. Jibrīl said: 'That angel has not descended before, ever since he was created.' When he had come down, he said: 'O Muḥammad, your Lord has sent me to you: shall I make you a king, or a slave and a messenger?' Jibrīl said to him: 'Humble yourself before your Lord, O Muḥammad!' The Prophet ﷺ said: 'Nay, make me a slave and a messenger.'[370]

Another example of his ﷺ humility: Anas ibn Mālik ؓ is reported to have said: 'The Messenger of Allah ﷺ would visit the sick, attend funerals, ride donkeys, and answer the invitations of slaves. On the day of Banū Qurayẓa, he rode a donkey with a halter of palm fibres, and a

369 Al-Tirmidhī.
370 Ibn Ḥibbān.

saddle of palm fibres.'[371] His words 'he would ride donkeys' mean that he would do so though he had the ability to ride more imposing mounts. Concerning his words 'a halter of palm fibres', the halter is the rope placed in an animal's mouth to lead it, and palm fibres are the fronds at the base of the branches of a palm tree, used to make ropes and rough mats; and similarly, a 'saddle of palm fibres' is an extremely humble form of saddle.

He ﷺ would come near to ill people and sit by their heads and ask after them, saying 'How are you feeling?' He would also say to them: 'Worry not; it shall be a cause of your purification, by Allah's leave.' He would sometimes place his hand on the area of pain and say, 'In the Name of Allah: from every illness that harms you, may Allah cure you.'

Al-Ṭabarī relates in his *Mukhtaṣar al-Sīra* that the Prophet ﷺ rode a bareback donkey to Qubāʾ along with Abū Hurayra. The Prophet ﷺ said, 'I shall bear you.' 'As you wish, O Messenger of Allah', he said, and tried to mount, but could not. The Messenger of Allah ﷺ tried to pull him up, but they both fell off. The Prophet ﷺ mounted again and told him to join him, so he did, and they both fell off again. The Prophet ﷺ mounted and said it to him again, but Abū Hurayra said: 'By Him who sent you with the truth, I shall not throw you off a third time!'

Another example of his ﷺ humility: Anas ibn Mālik ؓ related that the Messenger of Allah ﷺ performed the pilgrimage on a camel with an old, worn-out saddle, upon which was a cloth worth less than four dirhams, saying: 'O Allah, make it a pilgrimage free of ostentation and vanity.'[372] Using such a saddle and such a cloth is an extremely humble way of performing the pilgrimage; for the pilgrimage should be a time of detachment and asceticism. His words 'O Allah, make it a pilgrimage free of ostentation and vanity' mean a pilgrimage that is sincerely devoted to Allah and meant to seek His pleasure alone, such that the people do not see it or hear about it, or speak words of admiration or praise about it, or laud it in their hearts. This was a supplication, and this supplication showed the extent of his humility, and his counting himself as just one of the people; for ostentation and vanity cannot afflict one who is divinely protected from sin. On the contrary, they afflict those who make the pilgrimage on expensive vehicles, wearing fancy clothes.

Another example of his ﷺ humility: Anas ibn Mālik ؓ said: 'No

371 Al-Tirmidhī.
372 Al-Tirmidhī.

one was more beloved to the people than the Messenger of Allah ﷺ. When they saw him, they would not stand up, because they knew how he disliked that.' This was due to his perfect humility and his amiable way of being with them, so that they preferred his will to their own. The reason he did not like them to stand for him was that he loved to be humble in acknowledgement of the Lord's favours, and to show that only the Lord of the worlds should be stood for. This does not mean it is wrong to stand for people of virtue, though, since it is also related that the Companions did indeed stand for the Messenger of Allah ﷺ. This ḥadīth has been explained as meaning that if they saw him ﷺ from afar and he was not coming towards them, they would not stand for him; or that if he repeatedly went out and came back to them in one gathering they would not stand every time. This does not deny that they would stand for him when he came to them the first time, and that when he left them [at the end of the gathering] they would stand for him again.

Another example of his ﷺ humility: Anas ibn Mālik relates that the Messenger of Allah ﷺ said: 'Were the gift of a trotter (*kurāʿ*) offered to me, I would accept; and were I invited to [eat] it, I would accept.'[373] The word *kurāʿ* here means the trotter of an animal, or the thin part of the shin.

Another example of his ﷺ humility: ʿĀʾisha ﷺ said: 'He ﷺ was a human being, of the human race: he darned his clothes, and milked his goats, and served himself.' Another narration has it: 'He stitched his clothes, and mended his shoes.' Another narration has it: 'He patched his clothes, and did all the work that men do in their homes.' Another narration adds: 'He would do housework, especially sewing.'[374] That is, he would do the same kind of housework that most people do, out of humility, and to guide others to humility. He would not disdain to do ordinary labour, as kings do. By saying this, she rebutted the false doctrine she had noticed the unbelievers held, namely that it is not fitting for a prophet to do the things that ordinary people do. ʿĀʾisha listed some of the tasks he would perform, saying:

'He would darn (*yaflī*) his clothes'; that is, he would inspect them to take out things like thorns, or patch holes in them, and the like; it does not mean, as some have imagined, that he would search them for lice, since

373 Aḥmad, al-Tirmidhī, Ibn Ḥibbān.

374 Al-Tirmidhī.

the bodies of the prophets cannot be infested with bugs. He would also 'milk his goats'; 'serve himself', that is, fetch his own water for ablutions, and the like; 'stitch his clothes', that is, patch them; and 'mend his shoes', that is, stitch them and mend any tears in them.

Al-Ṭabarī relates in *Mukhtaṣar al-Sīra* that once on a journey the Prophet ﷺ instructed his Companions to prepare a sheep that had been slaughtered. One man offered to skin it, another to cook it, and the Prophet ﷺ said: 'I shall fetch the firewood.' They said: 'O Messenger of Allah, we will take care of everything.' He replied: 'I know that you will, but I hate to be distinguished from the rest of you; and Allah hates for His slave to see himself as distinguished from his companions.'

All these ḥadīths clearly show the extent of his ﷺ humility, and his constant desire to go to lengths in humbling and lowering himself, and to show how little he thought of the precious things of this world and their allure, and how disdainful they are, and how what Allah has in store is better and more enduring. He ﷺ did not want his Companions to glorify him, or laud him as the Christians lauded Jesus the son of Mary, making him a god or a 'son of God' and thus going astray. He would also pay attention to people in need, listen to them and act to meet their needs, even if the person in need was a slave or a woman. He also kept the secrets of those in need, and did not publicise them or spread them; and he would take them to places where others could not hear their secrets.

He would also keep his situation secret from his Companions and not complain to them; he even mortgaged his shield to a Jewish man for thirty *ṣāʿ* of barley to feed his family, as we saw earlier.

The Perfect Form of His ﷺ General Manners

The Prophet ﷺ would use his right hand for eating, washing, giving and taking, and his left hand for cleaning after answering a call of nature and all other unpleasant tasks. When he sneezed, he would cover his face and stifle the sneeze with his clothing. When he sat, he would sometimes draw his knees up and wrap his arms around them, and would sometimes recline on his left side. He would sometimes lie down in the mosque, putting one foot on the other. When he walked, he would tread powerfully and firmly as though descending a hill. Abū Hurayra said: 'I was with the Messenger of Allah ﷺ at a funeral once. When I walked, he would outpace me, and if I jogged I would outpace him.'[375] He also said: 'I never saw anyone walk faster than the Messenger of Allah ﷺ; it was as though the ground were being folded up for him. We would exert ourselves [to keep up with him], though he did not seem to be making any effort at all.'[376]

He ﷺ liked optimistic speech, and when he went out to fulfil some need he would delight in hearing 'O guided one, O successful one!' Someone once said something that pleased him, and he said to them: 'We have received a good omen from your mouth!'[377] When something pleased him, his face would light up like the moon; and when he angered, his face would redden; and when he disliked something, it would be clear from his face. When he was concerned about something, he would stroke his beard much.

He disliked unpleasant names, and would change them for better ones. A woman named ʿĀṣiya ('Disobedient') once came to him, and he changed her name to Jamīla ('Beautiful'). Many Companions had the name ʿĀṣī ('Disobedient'), so the Prophet ﷺ changed their names to ʿAbdallāh ('Servant of Allah').

375 Aḥmad.

376 Al-Tirmidhī, Aḥmad.

377 Abū Dāwūd.

The Messenger of Allah ﷺ would swear an oath by saying: 'Nay, by Him who changes hearts', or 'By Him in whose hand is my soul', or 'Nay, and I ask Allah's forgiveness!'

Upon the conclusion of a gathering with his Companions, he would say: 'Glory be to You, Allah, and praise be to You. I bear witness that there is no god but You. I ask Your forgiveness, and turn in repentance to You.' Of this, he said: 'This is an expiation for all that took place in the gathering.'[378]

He ﷺ would wear wool, palm-fibre shoes, and rough clothing, and would eat *bashiʿ*. Anas said: 'We asked al-Ḥasan what *bashiʿ* is, and he said: "It is coarse barley, which he could only swallow with a draught of water."'[379]

When he ﷺ wanted to wear a new item of clothing, he would wear it on Friday and say as he put it on: 'Allah, praise be to You for clothing me with it. I ask you for the goodness in it, and the goodness in what it was made for; and I seek refuge with you from the evil in it, and the evil in what it was made for.'[380]

He ﷺ had a silver ring engraved with 'Muḥammad, the Messenger of Allah' (*Muḥammad Rasūl Allāh*): *Muḥammad* on one line, *Rasūl* on the next, and the Divine Name on the next. He wore it on his hand, and then Abū Bakr wore it after him, and then ʿUmar, and then ʿUthmān had it, until he lost it in the well of Arīs.[381] Narrations differ as to whether he wore it on the left or right hand.

He ﷺ would sometimes use henna,[382] and would frequently wet his beard and hair with water and comb them. Anas said: 'When he ﷺ lay down to sleep at night, he would set next to him his tooth-stick, water and comb; and when he awoke, he would clean his teeth and comb his hair.'[383] He would frequently apply oil to his head, and when he looked in the mirror would say: 'Praise be to Allah, who has beautified my appearance and my character, and made fine in me what is marred in others. Praise be to Allah, who has balanced my appearance and made it sound, and has

378 Al-Tirmidhī, Abū Dāwūd, Aḥmad.

379 Ibn Mājah, al-Ḥākim.

380 Al-Tirmidhī, Abū Dāwūd, Aḥmad, al-Ḥākim.

381 The well that used to be in front of the mosque at Qubāʾ; it has since dried up and filled in. This tale is told in the collection of al-Bukhārī and Muslim.

382 On his ﷺ hair and beard.

383 Al-Bayhaqī, al-Ṭabarānī.

ennobled the appearance of my face and beautified it, and has made me a Muslim.'[384]

He would trim his beard, both in length and in width, and cut his moustache short. He loved perfume, and would say: 'Beloved to me have been made women and perfume, and my eye's delight has been placed in prayer.'[385] He would perfume himself with musk and ambergris, but aloeswood (*ʿūd*) was the perfume he loved the most, as ʿĀʾisha said.[386]

384 Al-Bayhaqī, al-Ṭabarānī.

385 Aḥmad.

386 Al-Baghawī.

His ﷺ Etiquette of Eating

The foods he ﷺ loved the most were gourd, *tharīd* (a stew of meat and bread), sweets and honey. The meat he liked best was the foreleg and the meat from the back and shoulder. He also loved salad, dry bread and vinegar, cucumber with ripe dates, melon with ripe dates, and cucumber with salt. Other foods he ﷺ ate included stew, butter, curds, jerked meat, kebabs, chicken, bustard, palm cores, fresh and ripe dates, grapes, and *khabīṣ* (a mixture of butter, honey and flour cooked over fire). He would avoid foods with offensive smells like garlic, or things which he personally did not have a taste for, such as lizard. He would neither criticise food nor praise it: if he liked it he would eat it, and otherwise he would leave it. He would not eat charitable donations, and never reclined when he ate.

He would eat what was nearest to him, and sit on the floor and set his food on the floor to eat it. When he had finished eating and the tray had been taken away, he would say: 'Praise be to Allah: abundant, goodly, blessed praise; [praise which is] never enough, nor brought to an end, nor superfluous to [our] need, Lord!'[387] He would also say: 'Praise be to Allah, who feeds and is not fed; He blessed us by guiding us and giving us food and drink. Praise be to Allah, who feeds food, and gives drink, and clothes the naked, and guides the errant, and gives sight to the blind.'[388]

Fresh water would be brought to him from the outskirts of Medina. He would prefer water that had been left overnight to cool; it would be cooled for him in an old leather jug, because this cooled it best.

He would drink out of a rough-hewn wooden jug inlaid with iron, and another cup made of glass, from which he would also sometimes make ablutions. He would also drink milk, *sawīq* (a mash made from barley or dates), and honey from it.

The drink he loved the most was milk. He would say upon drinking it: 'Allah, bless us in it, and give us more of it.'[389] For everything else, he

387 Al-Bukhārī.

388 Al-Ḥākim.

389 Al-Tirmidhī, Ibn Mājah, al-Bayhaqī.

would say: 'Allah, bless us in it, and give us that which is better than it.' He would sometimes mix milk with water. He would drink in three sips, and praise Allah after finishing; sometimes he would praise Allah after every sip, and give thanks to Him after the last one. He would usually drink while sitting, and would occasionally drink while standing. He would personally give his Companions to drink, and then be the last of them to drink, saying: 'The one who gives drink to others, drinks last.'[390] When he drank, he would pass the cup to his right. Once he was sitting with a young boy at his right and the elders of the Companions on his left. He was given a drink, and after drinking said to the boy, 'Will you permit me to pass it to these others?' The boy said: 'No, I cannot give my share from you to anyone!'

He ﷺ would spend the evening conversing with the women of his household, speaking to them and listening to them before he slept. Before sleeping, he would make ablutions and apply kohl to each eye three times. He would lie down on his right side, and then say: 'Allah, to You I have surrendered myself, and to You I have turned my face, and with You I have sought protection for my back, desiring You and fearing You. There is no fortress nor refuge from You except with You. I believe in Your Book, which You have revealed, and in Your Prophet, whom You have sent.'[391] He said that anyone who says this and then dies in his sleep dies in a state of primordial perfection.[392] When he woke at midnight, or shortly before it or after it, he would rub his face three times and recite the last ten verses of sūrat Āl ʿImrān, and then make ablutions and pray.

When he ﷺ slept, only his eyes would sleep, and not his blessed heart.

He would perform cupping and advise others to do the same, saying: 'The best of your remedies is cupping.'[393] He would also use henna as a remedy: if he got a sore or a cut, he would put henna on it.

He would prefer to travel on Thursdays and Mondays, and when setting out he would say: 'Allah, You are the companion in travel, and the protecting watcher over our homes. Allah, I seek refuge with You from the trials of travel, the woes of what may be seen there, and the evil [that may await] upon homecoming. Allah, shorten our travel across the land,

390 Abū Dāwūd.

391 Al-Bukhārī, Muslim.

392 Al-Bukhārī.

393 Al-Bukhārī, Muslim.

and make our journey easy for us.'[394]

When he mounted, he would say '*Glory be to Him who has subjected this unto us, when we ourselves were not equal to it*' [43:13]. When bidding farewell to a traveller, he would say: 'I ask Allah to watch over your religion, your safety and the goals of your labour. May Allah equip you with piety, forgive your sins, and send goodness your way wherever you turn.'[395] If he made camp by night, he would say to the place where he was staying: 'My Lord and your Lord is Allah. I seek refuge with Allah from your evil and the evil of all within you, and the evil of all that passes over you. I seek refuge with Allah from the evil of every lion, snake, serpent, and scorpion, and from the evil of every dweller in the land, and from the evil of every sire and what he sires.'[396]

He ﷺ would pray on the back of his mount as he travelled, but only supererogatory prayers and not obligatory ones. When he returned from a journey, he would say: 'We return, repentant and full of praise for our Lord.'[397] When he went to his family, he would say: 'I return, I return, to our Lord repentant, may no fault of ours remain!'[398]

He would always return from journeys by day, at midmorning time. When he arrived, he would go to the mosque first and offer two cycles of prayer there, and sit and receive the greetings of his Companions.

He would not return to his family by night unless they had prior word of his coming; and he ﷺ would forbid others from doing so.

394 Muslim.

395 Al-Tirmidhī.

396 Abū Dāwūd, al-Tirmidhī.

397 Al-Bukhārī, Muslim.

398 Al-Bazzār, Abū Yaʿlā.

Part Four

The Perfection of His Glorious Feats and Unique Distinctions

"And your Lord shall give unto you, and you shall be satisfied"
[5:93]

His ﷺ Perfectly Clear Distinctions and Dazzling Miracles

Allah ﷻ singled out our master Muḥammad ﷺ with many graces and miracles, of which we shall now briefly mention the most well-known and authentic. We have also described some of them in more detail elsewhere in this book, but we wish to repeat them here so that they are all collected in one place.

One of them is that he was the first prophet to be created, and was a prophet when Adam was between spirit and body.[399]

Another is that Allah took a pledge from all the prophets – from Adam onwards – that they would believe in him and succour him. Allah says: *'And when Allah took the pledge of the prophets: 'Behold that which I have given you of Book and Wisdom; then there shall come to you a messenger, confirming what you possess: you shall believe in him and you shall help him'* [3:81]. Another is that glad tidings of his coming were given in the scriptures revealed before him. Another is that his line of descent from Adam was completely untainted by extramarital birth.[400]

Others are that when he was born, his mother saw emit from her a light that illuminated the palaces of Syria[401]; that a cloud would shade him on hot days[402]; that the shadow of a tree stretched out to him as he approached it[403]; that his ﷺ blessed breast was opened[404]; that Jibrīl whelmed him in his embrace three times at the onset of the Revelation; that the Qurʾān spoke about the different parts of his body, saying of his heart: '*The heart lied not of what it saw*' [53:11], and: '*The trusted Spirit brought it down, upon your heart*' [26:193-194], and of his tongue: '*Nor*

399 Al-Tirmidhī.
400 Al-Bayhaqī.
401 Aḥmad.
402 Abū Nuʿaym.
403 Al-Bayhaqī.
404 Muslim.

speaks he out of caprice' [53:3] and: *'Now We have made it easy by your tongue'* [44:58], and of his sight: *'The sight wavered not, nor did it stray'* [53:17], and of his face: *'Indeed We have seen the turning of your face unto the heavens'* [2:144], and of his hand and neck: *'Keep not your hand chained to your neck'* [17:29], and of his back and breast: *'Have We not expanded your breast for you, and lifted your burden from you, which so weighed down your back?'* [94:1-3]; and that his name is derived from Allah's name *al-Maḥmūd* (The Praised). Ḥassān said:

He honoured him with a name from His name,
He of the Throne is *Maḥmūd*, and this is *Muḥammad*.

Others are that he ﷺ was named *Aḥmad*, no one before him ever having this name[405]; that he would go to bed hungry and wake up fed, having been fed and watered by his Lord[406]; that he could see behind him as well as in front of him[407]; that he could see as well by the dark of night as by the light of day[408]; that his saliva would turn salt water fresh[409]; that his ﷺ voice carried further than other voices; that his hearing was more acute than that of others; that his eyes would sleep, but not his heart[410]; that he never yawned[411]; that he never had a nocturnal emission, and nor did any other prophet[412]; that his ﷺ sweat was more fragrant than musk[413]; and that if he walked next to a tall person, he would appear to be taller than them.[414]

Others are that the soothsayers lost their powers when he ﷺ was sent, and that the jinn could no longer listen for them; that the *Burāq* was saddled and bridled for him on the night of the Miʿrāj, whilst every other prophet had ridden it bareback; that he ﷺ was taken from the Sacred Mosque to the Aqsa Mosque, and then taken up into the heavens, where

405 Muslim.
406 Al-Bukhārī, Muslim.
407 Muslim.
408 Al-Bayhaqī.
409 Abū Nuʿaym.
410 Al-Bukhārī.
411 Ibn Abī Shayba, al-Khaṭṭābī.
412 Al-Ṭabarānī.
413 Abū Nuʿāym.
414 Al-Bayhaqī.

Allah showed him His greatest signs; that he was protected during the Miʿrāj so that his sight neither wavered nor went astray; that all the prophets (upon whom be blessings and peace) were brought forth, and he ﷺ led them all in prayer and the angels as well; and that Allah showed him Paradise and Hell; that he saw Allah Almighty; that He graced him with both vision and speech, speaking to him in the highest communion after having spoken to Mūsā on the mountain; and that angels went with him ﷺ wherever he went, walking behind him and fighting alongside him at the Battles of Badr and Ḥunayn.

Another is that it is incumbent upon us to invoke blessings and peace upon him ﷺ, as Allah says: '*Verily Allah and His angels invoke blessings upon the Prophet. O you who believe, invoke blessings upon him and greetings of peace*' [33:56].

Another is that he ﷺ was given the Glorious Book though he was unlettered, and did not read or write, and was never schooled. Another is that Allah protected the Book He sent to him, the Qurʾān, from any alteration or corruption, saying: '*Falsehood comes not to it from before it nor from behind it; a revelation from One All-Wise, All-Praiseworthy*' [41:42], and: '*It is We who have sent down the Remembrance, and We are its Guardians*' [14:9], guarding it from corruption, addition and subtraction. Were anyone to attempt to alter even a letter or a dot of it, the people of this world would recognise him as a liar. Even if an imposing elder were to change a letter of it, every child would say, 'You have read it wrong, Sheikh, it should be this.' This is not true of any other scripture, for they have all been subject to scribal errors, corruptions, changes, and other alterations, although the atheists, Jews and Christians have every motivation for attempting to corrupt it and discredit it.

Others are that his ﷺ Book encompasses all that the other scriptures contained; and that Allah made it easy for those who study it to memorise it, having said: '*Now We have made the Qurʾān easy for Remembrance*' [54:17]. Young children can commit it to memory in the shortest of time; yet when it comes to the other communities, not even one of them memorises their scripture, never mind great throngs of them.

Others are that the Qurʾān was revealed in seven different modes, to make it easier for us; that it is a lasting sign that will endure as long as the world does; and that he ﷺ alone was given the *āyat al-Kursī*, the *mufaṣṣal*, the *mathānī*, and the Seven Long Sūras. The *mufaṣṣal* sūras end with *sūrat al-Nās*; there is a difference of opinion as to where they begin, though al-Nawawī declared the soundest view to be that they begin with *sūrat al-Ḥujurāt*.[415] The *mathānī* is *sūrat al-Fātiḥa*[416], and the Seven Long Sūras are from *al-Baqara* to *al-Anfāl*.

Another is that he ﷺ was given the keys to the *khāzā'in* (stores); some say that the *khazā'in* are the stores of nourishment for the different species of life in the world, so that he apportions to each of them what they need. Thus, all the provision of sustenance in the world is divinely-bestowed by the hand of Muḥammad ﷺ, who holds the keys to it. Just as Allah alone possesses the keys to the unseen, so that no one knows it but He, He gave to this noble messenger ﷺ the distinction of possessing the keys to the *khazā'in*, and He gave him also the compendium of speech.

Another is that he ﷺ was sent to all mankind. Jābir and others relate that the Prophet ﷺ said: 'Each prophet was sent to his people alone, whilst I was sent to the red and the black'; another version has it 'to all people.' Others were that he ﷺ was succoured by dread for a distance of a month's journey, that battle-spoils were permitted to him and to none before him, and that the earth was made a pure place of prayer for him and his community.[417]

Another is that his ﷺ miracle will endure until the Day of Resurrection, whilst the miracles of the other prophets were confined only to the times of their occurrence, so that only reports of them remain. The Holy Qur'ān, on the other hand, remains the Prophet's ﷺ clear proof and invincible argument.

Others are that he ﷺ is the Seal of the prophets and messengers; that he was vouchsafed more miracles than any other prophet; that his Law will last until Judgement Day, and replaces the laws of all other prophets; that he will have the most followers of any prophet on the Day of Resurrection; that had the other prophets lived alongside him ﷺ they would have been bound to follow him; that he was sent to the jinn (according to all scholars); that he was sent to the angels (according to one opinion, declared the soundest by al-Subkī); and that he ﷺ was sent as a mercy to the worlds.

Another is that Allah addressed all the prophets by their names in the

415 *Mufaṣṣal* means 'separated', so called because they are the shortest of the sūras. [t]

416 Al-Bukhārī. *Mathānī* means 'oft-repeated'. [t]

417 Al-Bukhārī, Muslim.

Qurʾān, saying 'O Adam', 'O Nūḥ', 'O Ibrāhīm', 'O Dāwūd', 'O Zakariyyā', 'O Yaḥyā', and 'O ʿĪsāʾ; yet He addressed the Prophet ﷺ by saying 'O Messenger', 'O Prophet', 'O you who are wrapped in your raiment', and 'O you who are wrapped in your cloak'. Allah also forbade his ﷺ community from addressing him by his name, saying: '*Make not the calling of the Messenger among yourselves like your calling one of another*' [24:63], that is, do not call him by his name as you call one another by your names, raising your voices. Rather, say 'O Messenger of Allah' or 'O Prophet of Allah' with gravity and humility, and with a lowered voice. He also forbade that he ﷺ be addressed with a loud voice, saying: '*O believers, raise not your voices above the Prophet's voice, and be not loud in your speech to him, as you are loud one to another, lest your works fail while you are not aware*' [49:2], and that he ﷺ be called from behind the chambers, saying: '*Surely those who call unto you from behind the apartments, the most of them do not understand. And if they had patience, until you come out to them, that would be better for them*' [49:4-5].

Others are that he ﷺ is Allah's beloved, and that Allah graced him with both His love and His intimate friendship; that Allah swore to his prophethood by his own life, his city and his time; and that he ﷺ received Revelation in all its different modes of transmission.

Another is that Isrāfīl came down to him ﷺ, and never to any prophet before him. Al-Ṭabarānī narrates, on the authority of Ibn ʿUmar, that the Messenger of Allah ﷺ said: 'An angel descended upon me from the sky who had never descended upon any prophet before me, and nor will he ever descend on anyone after me. It was Isrāfīl. He said: "I am your Lord's messenger to you; He commanded me to give you to choose whether to be a prophet-slave or a prophet-king, as you desire." I looked at Jibrīl, who indicated to me that I should humble myself. Had I said "a prophet-king", mountains would have been turned into gold for me.'

Another is that he ﷺ is the master of the children of Adam: Muslim narrates, on the authority of Abū Hurayra, that he ﷺ said: 'I shall be the master of the sons of Adam on the Day of Resurection, and [I say this] without boasting. In my hand shall be the banner of praise, and [I say this] without boasting.'

Another is that his ﷺ past and future sins were forgiven for him, as Allah said: '*That Allah may forgive you your sins of the past and those to follow*' [48:2]. Al-Bayḍāwī said that this means 'all of those things in which you were remiss, such as you could be rebuked for them.'

Others are that he ﷺ is the noblest of all creation in Allah's sight, being superior to all the messengers and all the archangels; that his ﷺ demonic consort submitted to him[418]; and that the dead are asked about him ﷺ in their graves.

Another is that it was forbidden to marry his ﷺ wives after him, Allah having said: '*And his wives are their mothers*' [33:6]; that is, they are as forbidden to them as their own mothers. Allah forbade them from marrying his ﷺ wives after him as an honour and a unique distinction.

Another is that his ﷺ daughter's sons were considered to be his. He ﷺ said about al-Ḥasan: 'This son of mine is a nobleman (*sayyid*); all lines of birth and marriage will be severed before the Day of Resurection, save for his line of birth and marriage.' He ﷺ also said: 'All lines of birth and marriage will be severed before the Day of Resurection, save for my line of birth and marriage.'

Another is that it was forbidden for any man married to one of the Prophet's ﷺ daughters to take a second wife alongside her, since this would offend him, and to offend him ﷺ is forbidden by the agreement of all. Al-Miswar ibn Makhrama reported that ʿAlī ibn Abī Ṭālib proposed marriage to a daughter of Abū Jahl while he was already married to Fāṭima the daughter of the Prophet ﷺ. When Fāṭima heard of this, she went to the Prophet ﷺ and said: 'Your people are saying that you do not grow angry for the sake of your daughters! ʿAlī is to marry the daughter of Abū Jahl.' The Prophet went forth and addressed the people, testifying to Allah's Oneness and then saying: 'I gave one of my daughters in marriage to Abū al-ʿĀṣ ibn al-Rabīʿ, and he assured me of something and proved true to his word.[419] Fāṭima bint Muḥammad is a part of me, and I hate for anyone to cause her strife. By Allah, the daughter of the Messenger of Allah can never be joined with the daughter of the enemy of Allah in marriage to one man.' ʿAlī then forswore the engagement.[420] Another narration, also of al-Bukhārī and Muslim on the authority of al-Miswar, adds: 'My daughter is part of me; what alarms her alarms me, and what offends her offends me.'

Another is that there is no room for any independent reasoning

418 Muslim.

419 This may imply that Abū al-ʿĀṣ promised not to marry another woman while married to Zaynab (*Fatḥ al-Bārī*). [t]

420 Al-Bukhārī, Muslim.

[*ijtihād*] when it comes to the direction of his ﷺ *miḥrāb*, which needs no correction, whether to the left or to the right.

Another is that whosoever sees him ﷺ in their sleep has seen him in truth, for Satan cannot assume his form. Muslim's narration has it: 'Whosoever sees me in sleep shall see me in a waking state.' And no one can be given the agnomen *Abū al-Qāsim* (Father of Qāsim[421]), whether he be named *Muḥammad* or not, according to al-Shāfiʿī, although Mālik allowed this.

Another of his ﷺ unique distinctions is that anyone who was in his presence even for a moment is considered to be a Companion. The rank of Second Generation [*Tābiʿ*], on the other hand, is only given to those who spent a lengthy period in the company of a Companion, according to the soundest opinion of the scholars of *uṣūl*. The reason for this difference is the immensity of the prophetic rank and the light that it emits; the mere falling of his ﷺ gaze upon even a boorish Bedouin was enough to endow that person with wisdom. All his ﷺ Companions were just; for Allah said, speaking to those who were alive at that time: '*Thus We appointed you a midmost community*' [2:143], meaning a just community. The Prophet ﷺ said: 'Do not insult my Companions, for by Him in whose hand is my soul, were one of you to spend Uḥud's weight in gold he would not equal the measure of even one of them, nor even half of it.'[422] He ﷺ also said: 'The best of people are my generation, then those who follow them, then those who follow them.'[423]

Other unique distinctions of his ﷺ are that the one who prays addresses him ﷺ directly, saying 'Peace be upon you, O Prophet', and does not address anyone else; that if he ﷺ called anyone while they were praying, they were obliged to break the prayer and answer him; that to lie about him is not like lying about anyone else – since anyone who lies about him ﷺ may never be accepted as a narrator ever again, even if he repents, according to the soundest position of the scholars of *uṣūl*; that he ﷺ is divinely protected from all sins, major and minor, intended or unintended, as are the other prophets (peace and blessings be upon them all); that it is impossible for him ﷺ or any other prophet to fall victim to madness, lengthy unconsciousness or blindness, because they are all flaws; and that

421 This is one of the names of the Prophet ﷺ.

422 Al-Bukhārī, Muslim.

423 Al-Bukhārī, Muslim.

anyone who insults him or criticises him must be executed.[424]

Another of his ﷺ unique distinctions is that he was permitted to make special rulings for whomever he chose, such as when he made the testimony of Khuzayma equal to the testimony of two men. Al-Nuʿmān ibn Bashīr ﵁ reported that the Messenger of Allah ﷺ bought a horse from a Bedouin, but this Bedouin then denied that the sale had taken place. Khuzayma approached and said 'O Bedouin, I testify that you indeed did sell it.' The Bedouin said, 'Since Khuzayma has testified against me, then give me the price.' The Messenger of Allah ﷺ said: 'Khuzayma, you did not witness it, so how can you testify to it?' He replied: 'I believe you about the tidings you bring from Heaven; how, then, could I not believe you about the tidings of this Bedouin?' Upon this, the Messenger of Allah ﷺ made the testimony of Khuzayma equal to that of two men; and there was never anyone in the history of Islam whose testimony was equal to that of two men except Khuzayma.

Another example of this was his ﷺ dispensation for Umm ʿAṭiyya, permitting her to wail in mourning. Muslim narrates that she said: 'When the verse was revealed '*O Prophet, when believing women come to you, swearing fealty to you upon the terms that they will not associate with Allah anything, and will not steal, neither commit adultery, nor slay their children, nor bring a calumny they forge between their hands and their feet, nor disobey you in aught honourable…*' [60:12], this included funeral wailing [*niyāḥa*]. I said, "O Messenger of Allah, let this be for all save the family of [So-and-so], for they made me happy in the days of pagan ignorance, and so I must make them happy." He said: "For all save the family of [So-and-so]".'

Another example of this is his ﷺ excusing Asmāʾ bint ʿUmays from the mourning period. Ibn Saʿd narrated that Asmāʾ said: 'When Jaʿfar ibn Abī Ṭālib was slain, the Messenger of Allah ﷺ said to me: "Wear your mourning-dress[425] for three days, then do as you please."'

[424] Qāḍī ʿIyāḍ mentions this (in *al-Shifā*), as do others; their proof is taken from the Qurʾān, the Sunna and the consensus of the Muslims. Al-Khaṭṭābī said: 'I do not know of any disagreement among the Muslims that such a person must be executed if he is a Muslim.' The Mālikīs say that such a person is killed as a sinful Muslim (not an apostate), and that his repentance is not accepted, nor are any excuses of his that he said what he did accidentally or mistakenly. The Shāfiʿīs say that to do such a thing is an act of apostasy that takes one out of Islam into unbelief, so that such a person is unquestionably an apostate and an unbeliever.

[425] A black dress a woman in mourning would wear, which covered her head.

Another case of this was when he ﷺ allowed Abū Burda ibn Nayyār to offer the sacrifice of a female lamb[426]; though there is a difference of opinion as to whether this was a unique distinction.

Another instance of this was his ﷺ allowing the man to give a marriage-dowry of nothing more than the Qur'ān he had memorised; the Messenger of Allah ﷺ gave a woman in marriage to him in return for the sūra he had memorised[427], saying 'No one after you can offer such a dowry'; though there is a difference of opinion as to whether this was a unique distinction.

Another unique distinction of his ﷺ is that his fevers would be twice as bad as those other men suffered, so that the reward for them would be doubled.[428]

Another is that people offered his ﷺ funeral prayer in drove after drove with no imam, and without the usual funeral supplication[429]; and that he ﷺ was left for three days before being buried, and that his grave was lined with cloth, both of which would be reprehensible if done for any of us.

Another is that his ﷺ blessed body does not decay, nor do the bodies of any of the prophets (peace and blessing be upon them).[430]

Another is that he ﷺ left no inheritance, just as the other prophets (peace and blessings be upon them) did not. He ﷺ said: 'We prophets leave no inheritance.'[431]

Another is that an angel was set at his ﷺ grave to pass on to him the blessings that people invoke upon him.[432] Al-Ḥākim narrated this with an authentic chain of transmission, with the wording: 'Allah has angels who travel about the land, passing on to me the greetings of peace of my community.' Al-Asbahānī narrates it, on the authority of 'Ammār: 'Allah has an angel to whom he gave the power to hear all His servants: whenever someone invokes blessings upon me, he conveys them to me.'

Another is that the actions of his ﷺ community are shown to him ﷺ, and he seeks forgiveness for them. It is established that not a day passes but the Prophet ﷺ is shown the deeds of his community by morning and

426 Al-Bukhārī, Muslim.

427 Al-Bukhārī, Muslim.

428 Al-Bukhārī, Muslim.

429 Al-Bayhaqī.

430 Abū Dāwūd.

431 Al-Nasā'ī.

432 Aḥmad.

evening, and he recognises them by their marks and their deeds.[433]

Another is that his ﷺ pulpit stands above his pool (ḥawḍ)[434], as the ḥadīth reports (in one narration): 'My pulpit stands on a watered bank of Paradise.'[435] None of the scholars dispute that this is meant literally, and that it is a tangible reality; for the power of Allah knows no bounds, and every matter of the unseen which The Trusted One ﷺ conveys unto us must be believed. And what lies between his ﷺ pulpit and his grave is a meadow of Paradise.[436]

Another unique distinction of his ﷺ is that his grave will be the first to be opened at the Resurrection, as he ﷺ said: 'I shall be the first one for whom the earth is opened.'[437]

Another is that he ﷺ will be resurrected in the company of seventy thousand angels. With every dawn that rises seventy thousand angels circle about his grave, beating their wings, until in the afternoon they ascend and another seventy thousand angels descend; this will continue until the earth opens around him, whereupon he will come forth among seventy thousand angels to honour him ﷺ. He ﷺ will be the first to cross the Bridge,[438] and will be brought forth for the Resurrection riding upon the Burāq.[439]

Another is that at the Resurrection, he ﷺ will be clothed in the finest robe of Paradise. He ﷺ said: 'The people will be brought forth on the Day of Resurrection, and I and my community will stand on a hill; and my Lord will clothe me in a green robe.'[440]

Another is that he ﷺ will stand at the right side of the Throne, in a place where no other will stand, for which the first and the last will envy him.[441]

Another is that he ﷺ will be given the Glorious Station of Intercession (*al-Maqām al-Maḥmūd*).

433 Ibn al-Mubārak.

434 In Paradise.

435 The word used here is *turʿa*, which means a meadow in an elevated place; if it is in low land, it is called a *rawḍa*.

436 Al-Bukhārī (with the wording 'between my house and my pulpit').

437 Muslim.

438 Al-Bukhārī.

439 Al-Ḥāfiẓ al-Salafī.

440 Kaʿb ibn Mālik.

441 Ibn Masʿūd.

His Superiority to the Rest of the Prophets

1 – The first thing that indicates this is his ﷺ primordiality, meaning that his soul was created before their souls were. The proof of this primordiality is the ḥadīth reported by ʿAbdallāh ibn ʿAmr ibn al-ʿĀṣ, stating that the Prophet ﷺ said: 'Allah ﷻ wrote down the fates of creation fifty thousand years before He created the heavens and the earth, while His Throne was on the water.'

And one of the things which He wrote in the Remembrance – the Mother Book – was that 'Muḥammad is the Seal of Prophets'.[442] Another version has it: 'I was, in the sight of Allah, the Seal of Prophets while Adam was yet cast in his clay.'[443]

Another narration has it that someone asked him ﷺ: 'When was prophethood assigned to you?' He replied: 'When Adam was between spirit and body.'[444]

Another narration states that he ﷺ said: 'I was the first of the prophets to be created, and the last of them to be sent.'[445]

2 – Another proof is that Allah took a pledge from the prophets regarding him ﷺ, as He says: *'And when Allah took the pledge of the prophets: 'Behold that which I have given you of Book and Wisdom; then there shall come to you a messenger, confirming what you possess: you shall believe in him and you shall help him'* [3:81].

Thus He made all the prophets, as it were, his ﷺ disciples, and inspired them to follow him: had they lived to see him ﷺ, they would have been obliged to follow him.

Allah also mentioned him before the other prophets when He said: '*We have sent you inspiration, as We sent it to Nuḥ and the prophets after him*' [4:163].

3 – Allah addressed every prophet by his name, saying: '*O Adam! Dwell…*' [2:35], '*O Nūḥ! Go down…*' [11:48], '*O Ibrāhīm! Turn away…*' [11:76], '*O Mūsā! I have chosen you above all mankind…*' [7:144], '*O Dāwūd! We have*

[442] Muslim.

[443] Aḥmad, al-Bayhaqī, al-Ḥākim.

[444] Al-Tirmidhī.

[445] Abū Nuʿaym, Ibn Abī Ḥātim, Ibn Lāl; it is supported by similar narrations by al-Ḥākim, Ibn Ḥibbān and al-Tirmidhi.

made you...' [38:36], '*O ʿĪsā, Son of Maryam!*' [5:110], '*O Zakariyyā! We give you tidings...*' [19:7], and '*O Yaḥyā! Take the Book...*' [19:12]. Yet He did not address our Prophet ﷺ by his name, but rather honoured him by saying: '*O Prophet!*' [33:1] and '*O Messenger!*' [5:41]. And when He did mention his name to identify him, He linked it with his function as messenger, saying: '*Muḥammad is naught but a messenger; messengers have passed away before him*' [3:144], '*Muḥammad is the Messenger of Allah*' [48:29], and '*and believe in what is sent down to Muhammad – and it is the truth*' [47:2]. And when He mentioned him ﷺ alongside the Friend,[446] He mentioned the Friend by name and the Prophet ﷺ by his title, saying: '*Surely the people standing closest to Ibrāhīm are those who followed him, and this Prophet*' [3:68].

4 – Allah Almighty has told us that the earlier communities would address their prophets by their names, such as when they said: '*O Hūd! you hast not brought us a clear proof*' [11:53], '*O Ṣāliḥ! you hast hitherto been a source of hope among us*' [11:62], '*O Mūsā! Make for us a god, as they have gods*' [7:138], and '*O ʿĪsā Son of Maryam! Can your Lord...*' [5:112]; yet He forbade the Prophet's ﷺ community to address him by his name, saying: '*Make not the calling of the Messenger among yourselves like your calling one of another*' [24:63].

Ibn ʿAbbās said of Allah's words '*Make not the calling of the Messenger among yourselves like your calling one of another*' [24:63]: 'Do not say *O Muḥammad*, but say *O Messenger of Allah*.'

And the other prophets would debate with their communities about themselves: Nūḥ's people said '*We see you in manifest error*' [7:60], and he defended himself by saying: '*No error is there in me*' [7:61]; and Hūd's people said '*We see you in folly*' [7:66], so he said '*No folly is there in me*' [7:67]; and Pharaoh said to Mūsā '*Mūsā, I think you are bewitched!*' [17:101], whereupon Mūsā replied: '*Pharaoh, I think you are accursed*' [17:102].

But Allah took it upon Himself to argue for His Prophet ﷺ: when they called him a poet, Allah said '*We have not taught him poetry*' [36:69]; and when they called him a soothsayer, Allah said '*Nor is it the word of a soothsayer*' [69:42]; and when they called him errant, Allah said '*Your companion has not erred*' [53:2]; and when they called him mad, Allah said '*You are not, by your Lord's grace, a madman*' [68:2]; and when they

446 Ibrāhīm ﷺ. [t]

said '*You are but a forger*' [16:101], Allah said '*Nay, but most of them have no knowledge. Say: the Holy Spirit sent it down*' [16:101-102], and '*They only forge falsehood, who believe not in the signs of Allah; and those – they are the liars*' [16:105]; and when they said '*Only a mortal is teaching him*' [16:103], Allah replied to them: '*The speech of him at whom they hint is barbarous; yet this is clear Arabic speech*' [16:103].

5 – Allah ﷻ swore on the Prophet's ﷺ life, and oaths are only sworn on things of greatness. Ibn ʿAbbās is reported to have said: 'Allah neither created nor formed any soul nobler than Muḥammad ﷺ; and I never heard Allah swear by anyone else's life as He did when He said: '*Upon your life, they wandered blindly in their drunkenness*' [15:72].'

6 – Ibn ʿAqīl said: 'Greater yet than His words to Mūsā "*I have fashioned you for Myself*" [20:41] were His words: "*They who pledge allegiance unto you but pledge allegiance unto Allah*" [48:10].'

7 – (Ibn ʿAqīl continues) 'And His words: "*Nay, I swear by this land; and you are a dweller in this land*" [90:1-2] mean: I swear not by this land, and if I swear by this land, it is because you dwell in it.'

Another interpretation of this occurred to me, which is that Allah Almighty is saying '*I swear not by this land*' [90:1][447]; that is, 'Although this land is great, I shall not swear by it, because you dwell in it, Muḥammad, and you are greater still. Thus I shall swear by you; for how could I swear by something great when it contains that which is greater and nobler than it?'

8 – Allah spoke of the state of certain prophets and then declared than He had turned to them in forgiveness. He said: '*So the two of them ate of it, and their shameful parts were revealed to them, and they took to stitching upon themselves leaves of the Garden. And Adam disobeyed his Lord, and so he erred. Thereafter his Lord chose him, and turned again unto him, and guided him*' [20:121-122]; and He told us how Mūsā said: '*I killed one of them*' [28:33],

[447] This interpretation, as well as that of Ibn ʿAqīl, hinges on the understanding of the word *lā* at the start of the verse as meaning not 'Nay', as is the usual interpretation, but rather 'not.' Thus the verse can be translated either as 'Nay, I swear by this land', or 'I swear not by this land.' [t]

and then said '*Lord, forgive me!*' [7:151], and so He forgave him; and He said of Dāwūd: '*Said he, "Assuredly he has wronged you in asking for your ewe in addition to his sheep; and indeed many intermixers do injury one against the other…"*' [38:24], and then said '*We forgave him that*' [38:25]; and He said '*Certainly We tried Sulaymān…*' [38:34], and then said '*then he repented*' [38:34]. Yet He told us of how He forgave our Prophet's ﷺ sin without mentioning any specific sin, saying: '*That Allah may forgive you your sins of the past and those to follow*' [48:2].

The other prophets would also make requests for certain ranks and perfections for themselves, unlike our master Muḥammad ﷺ, whom Allah blessed with those ranks freely, without any request. This subject is extremely precious, and Allah has given my heart peace through that part of which He has deigned to show me; I shall now present the examples of this which have occurred to my heart.

Ibrāhīm broke the idols, while our Prophet ﷺ threw Hubal down from the roof of the Kaʿba, and then gestured towards three hundred and sixty idols, which fell down; this occurred on the day of the Conquest, as the *Ṣaḥīḥ* collections affirm.

Hūd was aided by the wind, while our Prophet, the Messenger of Allah ﷺ, was aided by a hurricane, which swept through his enemies on the day of the Battle of the Trench.

Ṣāliḥ was given a she-camel, while many camels prostrated themselves before our Prophet, the Messenger of Allah ﷺ, as the pure Sunna affirms.

Yūsuf was given half of all beauty, while the Messenger of Allah ﷺ was given all of beauty, as the ḥadīth states.

Water gushed forth from the rock for Mūsā, while water flowed from between the fingers of our Prophet, the Messenger of Allah ﷺ; and this was more incredible, for it is not so unusual for water to flow from rock as it is for it to flow from between flesh and blood.

Mūsā ﷺ had a staff, while the wailing and weeping of the tree trunk was all the more incredible. The story of the weeping tree trunk is related in the *Ṣaḥīḥ* collections; it states that the Prophet ﷺ used to give his sermons from a tree trunk which had been set up for him; but when the pulpit was made for him, he left the trunk, which began to weep and sob for him like a baby.

The mountains glorified Allah alongside Dāwūd, while it is affirmed that stones glorified Allah in the very hand of our Prophet ﷺ.

The winds were subjected to the will of Sulaymān, such that its morning course was a month's journey and its evening course was a month's journey, while our Prophet ﷺ was taken to Jerusalem, a month's journey, in a fraction of a night; and all within a month's journey were struck by dread of him, as the authentic ḥadīth says: 'I have been succoured by dread for a distance of a month's journey'; and he was taken up to the Throne, a journey of fifty thousand years.

Sulaymān understood the speech of birds, while our Prophet ﷺ understood the speech of the camel which complained about its master, and the speech of the stone which gave him greetings of peace, and other examples besides these.

The jinn were subjected to the will of Sulaymān, while the Qur'ān affirms that a group of the jinn went to our Prophet ﷺ and announced their faith. And if Sulaymān was able to fetter those of them who disobeyed him, then our Prophet ﷺ was able to catch hold of a demon that crept up on him, after which he let it go, saying: 'Were it not that my brother Sulaymān said '*Lord, forgive me, and give me a sovereignty that shall be given to none after me*' [38:35], I would have hung it from a pillar of the mosque for the children to play with', as is narrated in the *Ṣaḥīḥ* collections.

The jinn were helpers for Sulaymān, giving him their service; yet our Prophet's ﷺ helpers were the angels, who fought for him and repelled his enemies, as occurred at Badr and Ḥunayn.

ʿĪsā gave tidings of the unseen, while it is established that our Prophet ﷺ did this many times, for many people.

The Perfection of the Favours that will be Granted to Him ﷺ in the Hereafter, and to No Other

He will be the first person for whom the ground will be opened, the first intercessor, the first to be given leave to prostrate, the first to look upon the Lord of the worlds (at a time when the rest of mankind will be veiled from seeing Him), the first of the prophets to judge among his community, the first of them to pass across the Bridge with his community, the first of them to enter Paradise; and his will be the first community to enter Paradise. Allah gave him, besides these, other treasures and precious gifts beyond count.

Among these are that he ﷺ will be resurrected while riding a mount, and that he alone will be given the Glorious Station [*al-Maqām al-Maḥmūd*], and that he will bear the banner of praise and be followed by Adam and the other prophets. He will also be given unique leave to prostrate before the Throne, when Allah will teach him such words of praise and glorification that He never taught to any other, and will never teach to any other, thus ennobling him further and drawing him ever closer to Himself. And He will say to him, 'Muḥammad, lift your head: speak, and you shall be heard; ask, and you shall be given; intercede, and your intercession shall be granted.' No gift could be greater than this, save for the vision of the Almighty.

Another is that his ﷺ intercession and prostration will be repeated a second and a third time, when he will again praise Allah with the words He taught him; and Allah will say to him in each prostration: 'Muḥammad, lift your head: speak, and you shall be heard; ask, and you shall be given; intercede, and your intercession shall be granted.'

Others are that he ﷺ will stand on the right side of the Throne, where no other being will stand, so that he will be envied by the first and the last; that he will testify before the prophets and their communities that they delivered the message to them; that they will ask him to intercede for them to relieve them of their distress and weariness, and to shorten the time they will spend standing; that he will intercede for people who have already been condemned to Hell; that his Pool shall have more vessels in it than any other; that the believers will only enter Paradise by his intercession; that he will intercede for the raising of the ranks of people whose deeds would not have been enough to win them admission into Paradise; and that he has been given *al-Wasīla*, the highest level of Paradise. And there are more besides, by means of which Allah will increase the Prophet's ﷺ majesty, greatness, honour and nobility, for all of mankind and the angels to see. That is the grace of Allah, which He gives to whom He will; and Allah is of infinite grace.

As for his ﷺ being the first person for whom the earth will open, and the other things aforementioned, here are some of the ḥadīths pertaining to this:

Muslim narrates, on the authority of Abū Hurayra, that the Messenger of Allah ﷺ said: 'I shall be the master of the sons of Adam on the Day of Resurrection; and I shall be the first for whom the earth opens; and I shall be the first intercessor, and the first whose intercession is granted.'

Al-Tirmidhī narrates, on the authority of Abū Saʿīd, that the Messenger of Allah ﷺ said: 'I shall be the master of the sons of Adam on the Day of Resurrection, and [I say this] without boasting. In my hand shall be the banner of praise, and [I say this] without boasting; every prophet, from Adam onwards, shall be under my banner on that day. And I shall be the first for whom the earth opens, and [I say this] without boasting.'

Al-Tirmidhī and Abū Ḥātim narrate, on the authority of Ibn ʿUmar ؓ, that the Messenger of Allah ﷺ said: 'I shall be the first for whom the earth opens, and then Abū Bakr, and then ʿUmar; and then all those buried in al-Baqīʿ will be brought forth and gathered with me; and then I shall await the people of Mecca, until we meet between the Two Sacred Mosques.'

Al-Tirmidhī and al-Dārimī narrate, on the authority of Anas, that the Messenger of Allah ﷺ said: 'I shall be the first of mankind to emerge when they are raised, and I shall be their leader when they are called forth, and I shall be their orator when they listen, and I shall be their intercessor when they are confined, and I shall be the one who gives them glad tidings when they despair. Nobility and the keys will that day be in my hand, and the banner of praise will that day be in my hand. I am the dearest of the sons of Adam to my Lord, and a thousand servants will circle about me, as if they were precious eggs or scattered pearls.'

'Allāma Ibn al-Qayyim, author of *Ḥādī al-Arwāḥ*, narrates that the Messenger of Allah ✥ will be raised on the Day of Resurrection with Bilāl before him, calling the *adhān*.

Al-Ḥākim and al-Ṭabarānī narrate, on the authority of Abū Hurayra, that the Messenger of Allah ✥ said: 'The prophets will be raised upon mounts, and I will be raised upon the Burāq, and Bilāl will be raised upon a she-camel of Paradise, calling the *adhān* alone, and the Testimony of Faith in all truth; and when he reaches *I testify that Muḥammad is the Messenger of Allah*, the believers will testify to this, the first and the last of them.' Another narration has it: 'And when the prophets and their communities hear *I testify that Muḥammad is the Messenger of Allah*, they will say, "We testify to this!"'

Kaʿb al-Aḥbār related that he visited ʿāʾisha ✥, and the people present spoke of the Messenger of Allah ✥. Kaʿb said: 'With every dawn that rises, seventy thousand angels descend and fly about the grave, beating their wings and invoking blessings upon the Prophet ✥ until the afternoon, whereupon they ascend and another seventy thousand angels descend and fly about the grave, beating their wings and invoking blessings upon the Prophet ✥. Seventy thousand by night, and seventy thousand by day. This will go on until the earth opens for him and he emerges, amid seventy thousand angels to honour him.'

Al-Tirmidhī narrates, on the authority of Abū Hurayra ✥, that the Messenger of Allah ✥ said: 'I shall be the first for whom the earth opens, whereupon I shall be dressed in a cloak of Paradise[448], and then stand on the right side of the Throne, a place where no other creature will stand but I.'

Al-Bayhaqī narrated that the Messenger of Allah ✥ said: 'The first person to be dressed in clothes from Paradise will be Ibrāhīm, who will be dressed in a cloak of Paradise. Then a chair will be brought forth and set on the right side of the Throne. Then I will be brought forth, and dressed in a robe from Paradise that no man could fashion.' The ḥadīth goes on to state that he ✥ will sit on the chair to the right of the Throne.

---

448   Kaʿb's narration has 'a green cloak'.

Al-Bukhārī and Muslim narrate, on the authority of ʿAbdallāh ibn ʿAmr ibn al-ʿĀṣ, that the Messenger of Allah ﷺ said: 'My Pool has the span of a month's journey. Its water is whiter than milk, and its scent is sweeter than musk, and its cups are like the stars of the sky. Whosoever drinks from it once shall never thirst again.'

Muslim's version adds: 'Its sides are equal: it is as long as it is broad.' Umāma's narration adds: 'Its surface shall never darken.' A version narrated by al-Bazzār and al-Ṭabarānī on the authority of Anas adds: 'He who does not drink from it shall never be quenched of his thirst.' A version narrated by al-Tirmidhī and al-Ḥākim on the authority of Thawbān adds: 'The people who visit it most will be the poor folk of the Emigrants.' Al-Qurṭubī says in *al-Tadhkira*: 'The author of *al-Qawt* and others assert that the Pool will come after the Bridge; others say the opposite.'

Muslim narrates, on the authority of Abū Dharr: 'Into the Pool flow two streams from Paradise.'

Al-Tirmidhī narrates that Anas said: 'I asked the Messenger of Allah ﷺ who would intercede for me on the Day of Resurrection. He replied: "I will, if Allah wills it." I said: "Where, then, should I ask for it?" He said: "The first place you should seek me is on the Bridge." I said: "And if I meet you not on the Bridge?" "Then seek me at the Balance," he said. I said: "And if I meet you not at the Balance?" "Then seek me at the Pool," he said, "for I shall not miss these three places."'

Al-Qurṭubī said in *al-Mufhim*:

> Every morally responsible person should know and believe that the Almighty has singled out our Prophet Muḥammad ﷺ with the Pool, whose name, description and contents are clearly stated in several famous and authentic ḥadīths, which together impart definitive knowledge of this; for over thirty Companions related it from him ﷺ, including over twenty in the two *Ṣaḥīḥ* collections, and the rest in other collections. It is also something that became widely known and conveyed, the aforementioned Companions passing it on to the Second Generation, and they in turn to others, and so on. The early Muslims all affirmed it, as did those of the later Muslims who were of the *Ahl al-Sunna*.

Muslim narrated, on the authority of Abū Hurayra, that the Prophet ﷺ said: 'My community will come to me at the Pool, and I will give them to drink of it as a man gives his camels to drink.' They said, 'O Messenger of Allah, will you recognise us?' He replied: 'Yes, for you will have a mark that no others will have. You will come to me shining and bright, a result of your ablutions.'

Abū Saʿīd al-Nīsāpūrī narrated, on the authority of Anas, that the Prophet ﷺ said: 'My Pool has four pillars: the first in the hand of Abū Bakr al-Ṣiddīq, the second in the hand of ʿUmar al-Fārūq, the third in the hand of ʿUthmān Dhun-Nūrayn, and the fourth in the hand of ʿAlī ibn Abī Ṭālib. Thus, if anyone loves Abū Bakr and hates ʿUmar, Abū Bakr will not give him to drink; and if anyone loves ʿAlī but hates ʿUthmān, ʿAlī will not give him to drink.'

As for his ﷺ being honoured with intercession and the Glorious Station, Allah says: '*Perchance your Lord shall raise you in a glorious station*' [17:79].

The exegetes agree that the word 'perchance', when uttered by Allah, expresses a certainty. There is a difference of opinion as to the meaning of the 'glorious station'.

The first opinion, which Fakhr al-Dīn al-Rāzī considered the soundest and which al-Wāḥidī reported to be the consensus of the exegetes, is that it is the station of intercession. There are authentic ḥadīths that affirm this, such as that which al-Bukhārī narrates on the authority of Ibn ʿUmar, stating that the Messenger of Allah ﷺ was asked about the Glorious Station and replied: 'It is the intercession.' He also narrates that the Messenger of Allah ﷺ said: 'On the Day of Resurection, mankind will be arrayed in hosts, each community following its prophet and saying, "Intercede for us!" Eventually the intercession will be granted to me; and that is the Glorious Station.' This opinion is further supported by the famous prayer: 'Raise him to the Glorious Station for which he will be envied by the first and the last.'

The second opinion is drawn from Ḥudhayfa's words: 'Allah will gather mankind on a single plain, and not a soul will speak. The first to be called will be Muḥammad ﷺ, who will respond: "At Your service, and under Your command; all goodness is in Your hand, and evil touches you not! He is guided whom you guide. Your slave stands before You, and with You, and to You; there is no refuge from You save with You. Blessed and Exalted be you, glory be to You, Lord of the House!" This is the meaning of his words '*Perchance your Lord shall raise you in a glorious station*' [17:79].'[449]

[449] Al-Ṭabarānī, Ibn Mandah.

The third opinion is that it means simply 'a station whose final ends will be praised.'

If you say, 'Since the most commonly-held opinion is that the Glorious Station is the intercession, then what intercession is it?', the answer is that the intercession mentioned in the ḥadīths about the Glorious Station is of two kinds: the first is the universal intercession at the time of judgement, and the second is the intercession for the sinners to be taken out of Hell; but what occurs to me is that all these statements can be traced back to the universal intercession, since the Prophet's ﷺ being presented with the banner of praise, and the glorification he gives his Lord and the words he speaks before Him, are all features of the Glorious Station, when he will intercede at the judgement of mankind; the intercession for the sinners to be taken out of Hell, on the other hand, is but one of the things that will come after this moment.

Now the number of ḥadīths pertaining to the intercession for the sinful believers in the Hereafter is so high as to reach the level of mass-transmission (*tawātur*). Umm Ḥabība ؓ related that the Messenger of Allah ﷺ said: 'I was shown what my community will go through after me, and how they will spill one another's blood, and this saddened me. It was destined for them by Allah just as it had been for the communities [of old]. I asked Allah to grant me right to intercede for them on the Day of Resurrection, and He did so.'[450]

Abū Hurayra reported that the Prophet ﷺ said: 'Every prophet has a prayer which will definitely be answered when he makes it; I wish to save my prayer until I intercede for my community in the Hereafter.'[451] The narration of Anas has it: 'So I made my prayer an intercession for my community.' This was because of the intense compassion he ﷺ felt for us, and his good conduct in saving his answered prayer for the time we will need it most – may Allah reward him on our behalf with the best reward!

Al-Nawawī said that there are five kinds of intercession:

1 – For the relief of the terror of that moment.
2 – For some to enter Paradise without being reckoned.
3 – For some to enter Paradise even though they deserve to be punished.
4 – For some sinners to be taken out of Hell after entering it.

450 Al-Ṭabarānī, al-Ḥākim.

451 Al-Bukhārī, Muslim.

5 – For those in Paradise to be taken to higher ranks therein.

Those kinds which are given to him ﷺ alone are the first and second. As for his ﷺ honour of being the first to knock on the door to Paradise and the first to enter it, Muslim narrates on the authority of Anas that the Messenger of Allah ﷺ said: 'I shall have the most followers on the Day of Resurrection, and be the first to knock on the door of Paradise.'

Muslim also narrates that he ﷺ said: 'I will go to the door of Paradise on the Day of Resurrection and seek entrance. The doorkeeper will say, "Who are you?" I will say, "Muḥammad." He will say, "I was commanded to open for you, and for no one else before you."'

The whole Muḥammadan community will also attain unto this primacy, as an honour to their Prophet ﷺ: they will also be the first community to enter Paradise. Muslim narrates that the Prophet ﷺ said: 'We last will be the first on the Day of Resurrection: we will be the first to enter Paradise.'

Al-Ṭabarānī and al-Dāraquṭnī narrate, on the authority of ʿUmar ibn ʿAbd al-Khaṭṭāb ﷺ, that the Messenger of Allah ﷺ said: 'Paradise will be closed to all the prophets until I enter it, and closed to all communities until my community enters it.'

As for his ﷺ being honoured with the *Kawthar*, it is narrated in the *Ṣaḥīḥ* that the Prophet ﷺ said: 'Do you know what the *Kawthar* is?' They said, 'Allah and His Messenger know better.' He said: 'It is a river which my Lord has promised me, called *Kawthar* because of the abundance (*kathra*) of its waters and the immensity of its size and its goodness.' Al-Ḥāfiẓ Ibn Kathīr said: '[The ḥadīth of the *Kawthar*] is mass-transmitted by such a large number of ḥadīth narrators that it is completely certain.'

As for his ﷺ being favoured in Paradise with the *Wasīla*, the loftiest rank and the greatest favour, Muslim narrates, on the authority of ʿAbdallāh ibn ʿAmr ibn al-ʿĀṣ, that the Messenger of Allah ﷺ said: 'When you hear the muezzin, repeat what he says and then invoke blessings upon me; for whosoever invokes one blessing upon me shall have ten blessings from Allah. Then ask Allah to grant me the *Wasīla*; it is a station in Paradise fit only for one of Allah's slaves, and I hope that I will be that slave. Whosoever requests the *Wasīla* for me shall receive my intercession.'

The *Wasīla* is a level in Allah's sight and a name for the highest station of Paradise. It is the station of the Messenger of Allah ﷺ and his abode in Paradise, and the closest place in Paradise to the throne.

Since the Messenger of Allah ﷺ was the most ardent of all creatures in worshipping his Lord, and the one of them who knew Him best, feared Him most and loved Him strongest, his station is naturally the nearest station to Allah and the highest rank of Paradise; and he ﷺ instructed his community to request it for him so that, by this prayer, they would be drawn nearer to Allah and gain increased faith.

His ﷺ Perfect Eminence, as Affirmed by the Book of Allah[452]

MANY VERSES of the Qurʾān speak of the Prophet's ﷺ immense worth, lofty status, eminent rank and noble station; these include the following words of the Almighty: '*Verily Allah and His angels invoke blessings upon the Prophet. O you who believe, invoke blessings upon him and greetings of peace*' [33:56].

With these words, Allah affirms the station of the Prophet ﷺ in the Supreme Assembly,[453] where he is praised before the angels, who invoke blessings upon him; and He also commands the lower realm to invoke blessings and peace upon him. Thus he is praised by Allah and the inhabitants of the two realms, the higher and the lower.

Another example is Allah's words '*We have given you the Kawthar*' [108:1]. This verse implies a clear distinction for him ﷺ, since it expresses this in the past tense; He does not say 'We will give you'. This indicates that the gift has already been given; and there is no doubt that he who has already received glory and attention is nobler than one who will receive it in the future. It is as though Allah were saying, 'O Muḥammad, We readied the means of your everlasting happiness before you even came into this existence; so what does this say about your nature after you came into existence, and how you devoted yourself to Our worship? O noble slave, We did not give you this great favour because of your obedience; rather, We chose you through Our pure grace and favour, without any obligation.'

Another example is that Allah swore to the blessings He granted him ﷺ, and to his lofty status, saying: '*By the morning brightness, and by the night when it is still, your Lord has not forsaken you, nor does He hate you*' [93:1-3].

Another example is His words: '*Have We not expanded your breast for you*' [94:1].

452 The author ﷺ notes here: 'Much of the material in this chapter can also be found elsewhere in this book, but we wanted to collect it all in one place specifically devoted to it.' [t]

453 The assembly constituted by the superior angels and the spirits of past Divine Prophets in the higher heavens.

Another example is how He told him ﷺ of how He had pardoned him before issuing a rebuke, saying: '*Allah pardon you! Why did you give them leave?*' [9:43].

Another example is how Allah told him ﷺ of how the denizens of Hell will wish they had obeyed him, saying: '*Upon the day when their faces are turned about in the Fire they shall say, "Ah, would we had obeyed Allah and the Messenger!"*' [33:66].

Another example is how Allah ﷻ gave a testimony to his ﷺ prophethood in His words, quoting what Ibrāhīm and Ismāʿīl said when they built the Sacred House: '*Our Lord, accept this from us; you are the All-Hearing, the All-Knowing; and, our Lord, make us submissive to you, and of our seed a nation submissive to You; and show us our holy rites, and relent to us; surely you are the Relenting, the Merciful. And, our Lord, send among them a messenger, one of them, who shall recite to them your signs, and teach them the Book and the Wisdom, and purify them; you are the Almighty, the All-Wise*' [2:127-129]. Allah answered their prayer, and sent among the people of Mecca a messenger from them, with this description. The exegetes agree that the Prophet ﷺ is the one meant by this verse; and this is further strengthened by his ﷺ words: 'I am the prayer of my father Ibrāhīm, and the tidings of ʿĪsā.'[454] The scholars say that the 'prayer' means this verse, while the 'tidings of ʿĪsā' means what is mentioned in *sūrat al-Ṣaff*: '*And [I] bring tidings of a messenger who shall come after me, whose name is Aḥmad*' [61:6].

Another example is how Allah reminded the believers of how He blessed them by sending them this Prophet ﷺ, one of them, saying: '*Truly Allah was gracious to the believers when He raised up among them a messenger from themselves, to recite to them His signs and to purify them, and to teach them the Book and the Wisdom, though before they were in manifest error*' [3:164]. Allah gave the believers no greater blessing than the sending of Muḥammad ﷺ to guide them to the truth and the straight path. The reason this was the greatest of all blessings is that the blessing of the Prophet ﷺ completed all the good things of this life and the next, and perfected Allah's religion, which He chose for His servants.

Other examples are His words '*O Prophet, We have sent you as a witness, a bearer of tidings and a warner, calling unto Allah by His leave, and as a light-giving lamp*' [33:45-46], '*Allah knows that you are indeed His messenger*'

[454] Aḥmad, al-Ḥākim.

[63:1], and '*But Allah bears witness to that He has sent down to you; He has sent it down with His knowledge; and the angels also bear witness; and Allah suffices for a witness*' [4:166].

Another is that Allah tells us that the Prophet ﷺ was sent to all mankind, saying: '*Say: O mankind, I am the Messenger of Allah to you all*' [7:156] and '*We have sent you not, except to mankind entire*' [34:28].

Another is that Allah tells us that He made the Prophet ﷺ an intrinsic mercy, saying: 'We sent you not but as a mercy to the worlds' [21:107], and that He named him with two of His own Names, saying: 'Grievous to him is your suffering; anxious is he over you, full of tenderness and mercy [raʾūfun raḥīm] [455] for the believers' [9:128]. Ibn ʿAbbās said: 'He is a mercy for the righteous and the sinful alike, because if ever a prophet was belied, Allah would destroy those who belied him; but as for our Prophet ﷺ, he is a mercy to the believers in the guidance he brings them, and a mercy to the hypocrite in the protection from being killed he affords him, and a mercy to the disbeliever by the postponement of the chastisement he gains through him; for Allah says: 'Allah would not chastise them while you were among them' [8:33].'

Another example is how Allah tells us that revelation and prophethood have now come to an end, for there shall be no messenger or prophet after him ﷺ, as He says: '*Muḥammad is not the father of any man among you, yet he is the Messenger of Allah and the Seal of the Prophets*' [33:40].

Another is that Allah tells us that the previous scriptures such as the Torah and Gospel prophesised the Messenger of Allah's ﷺ coming, saying: '*They who follow the Messenger, the Unlettered Prophet whom they find written down with them in the Torah and the Gospel*' [7:157].

Another is that Allah describes him ﷺ in the Qurʾān as having reached the most perfect level of moral character, saying: '*Verily, you are of a tremendous nature*' [68:4].

ʿĀʾisha ﷺ also alluded to this when she said: 'His nature was the Qurʾān.' His speech was in conformity with the Qurʾān and an explanation of it; his knowledge was the knowledge of the Qurʾān; his will and his deeds were defined by what the Qurʾān commands and recommends; if he turned away from anything, it was because the Qurʾān forbade it; he desired all that it desired; he rejected all that it rejected; he disliked all that it disliked; he loved all that it loved; he strove to implement its

455 *Al-Raʾūf* and *al-Raḥīm* are Names of Allah ('the Tender, the Merciful)'. [t]

instructions. Thus she ﷺ expressed her perfect knowledge of both the Qur'ān and the Messenger ﷺ in the finest way by saying, 'His nature was the Qur'ān.'

Another example of this is how Allah ﷻ swore on the morning brightness to the blessings He granted him ﷺ, and to his lofty status, saying: '*By the morning brightness, and by the night when it is still, your Lord has not forsaken you, nor does He hate you; and the last shall be better for you than the first*' [93:1-4].

This was in response to the occasion when his enemies said 'Muḥammad's Lord has forsaken him!' after the Revelation had not come to him for a time. These verses were then revealed, conveying these divine blessings and favours. Allah denied that He would ever forsake His Prophet ﷺ or hate him; that is, 'He has not forsaken you since He first took you into his care, and He has not hated you since He first loved you.' '*And the last shall be better for you than the first*' [93:4]. This verse speaks of his ﷺ totality, and indicates that every successive state he reached would be better than that which preceded it, and also that the Hereafter would be better for him than what came before it. He then made him ﷺ a promise which comforted his eyes and expanded his breast, vowing to give unto him so that he would be satisfied: '*And your Lord shall give and give unto you, and you shall be satisfied*' [93:5]. This included all that He would give unto him: the Qur'ān, guidance, the spread of his call, his ascendancy of his message over his enemies both during his lifetime and that of his caliphs and those who followed them; and also what He would give him in the Hereafter: the intercession and the Glorious Station, and the gifts He would give him in Paradise: the *Wasīla*, the Lofty Station, and the *Kawthar*. All in all, this verse indicates that Allah would give him ﷺ everything that satisfied him. It is narrated in the *Ṣaḥīḥ* that Allah Almighty said to him: 'We shall not disappoint you regarding your community.' Someone said about this:

In *al-Ḍuḥā* we read 'thy Lord shall give',
And our hearts were gladdened by that gift;
For far be it, O Messenger of Allah,
That you be satisfied if one of us be punished!

Allah then told him of the favours He granted him, and commanded him to receive them with the appropriate gratitude, saying: '*Has He not found you an orphan and sheltered you?*' [93:6], and so on until the end of the sūra.

Another example of this is how Allah swore to his ﷺ truthfulness and absolved him of any caprice in his speech, saying: '*By the star as it sets, your companion has not erred, nor speaks he out of caprice*' [53:1-3]. He swore by the star to the innocence of His Messenger ﷺ from the misguidance and error his enemies attributed to him. Reflect on His words '*your companion has not erred*'; He did not say 'Muḥammad', in order to rebut them by emphasising to them the fact that he ﷺ was their companion, and they knew him better than anyone, and knew well his states, words and deeds. They did not know him to ever have lied, erred or gone astray, and they found no fault with him at all. Allah alluded to this elsewhere with his words '*Or do they not know their own Messenger?*' [23:69].

He then declares His Messenger's ﷺ speech pure of any capricious source, saying: '*nor speaks he out of caprice; it is but Revelation, revealed*' [53:3-4]. Al-Awzāʿī narrated that Ḥaṣṣān ibn ʿAṭiyya said: 'Jibrīl would bring down the Sunna to the Messenger of Allah ﷺ just as he brought down the Qurʾān to him, teaching it to him.'

He then gives us a description of the one who taught him ﷺ the Revelation and the Qurʾān, saying: '*There has taught him one of terrible power*' [53:5], namely Jibrīl; and there is no doubt that to praise the teacher is to praise the student. This is akin to what He says elsewhere: '*One of power, with the Lord of the Throne secure*' [81:20].

He then says: '*And He revealed unto His servant that which He revealed. The heart belied not what it saw*' [53:10-11]. He tells us that the Prophet's ﷺ heart believed what his eyes saw, and that the heart believed the eyes, not like one who sees something differently to how it actually is so that his heart belies his sight. Nay, his heart believed what his eyes saw.

Another example of this is how Allah described the reality of how the Prophet ﷺ met with Jibrīl and took from him, explaining the mode of transmission by saying: '*No! I swear by the slinkers, the runners, the sinkers; by the night swarming, by the dawn sighing – truly this is the word of a noble Messenger*' [81:15-19], as He said in *sūrat al-Najm*: '*There has taught him one of terrible power*' [53:5]. This power prevented any demons from coming near him, or subtracting anything from the Revelation or adding anything to it. '*One of power, with the Lord of the Throne secure*' [81:20], that is, having a secure position; and this 'with-ness' is a 'with-ness' of ennoblement, honour and distinction. '*Obeyed*' by Allah's archangels, who carry out his commands and follow his opinion, and '*moreover trusted*' [81:21] with Allah's Revelation and Message; for Allah made him immune to any treachery or error.

So these are five attributes of the Qur'ān's mode of transmission. Muḥammad ﷺ heard it from Jibrīl, and Jibrīl heard it from the Lord of the worlds; and besides the majesty and glory of this transmission, Allah also took it upon himself to attest to it personally.

He then declares His Messenger Muḥammad ﷺ to be pure and free of what his enemies said of him, saying: '*And your companion is no madman*' [81:22]. This is something that they already knew, and did not doubt; even if they said otherwise, they knew that they were lying.

He then speaks of how the Prophet ﷺ saw Jibrīl ﷺ, saying: '*He truly saw him on the clear horizon*' [81:23]; that makes it clear that what is meant here is a physically present angel which can be seen with the eyes and perceived with the sight. '*He is not niggardly with the unseen*' [81:24]. Ibn ʿAbbās said: 'He is not a miser with what Allah reveals unto him.' The exegetes are unanimous that 'the unseen' here means the Qur'ān and the Revelation. The word *ḍanīn*, 'niggardly', can also be read *ẓanīn*, 'untrustworthy'; that is, this messenger, Muḥammad ﷺ, is not untrustworthy with the Qur'ān, but rather is trusted with: he will not add anything to it, or take anything away from it.

Another example of this is how Allah swore by him ﷺ when He said: '*Upon your life, they wandered blindly in their drunkenness*' [15:72], and swore by his land when He said: '*Nay, I swear by this land; and you are a dweller in this land*' [90:1-2], the 'land' here being Mecca; and He swore by his lifetime when He said: '*By time, verily man is in loss*' [103:1-2].[456]

Another example of this is how Allah described him ﷺ as being a light and a shining lamp, saying: '*There has come unto you from Allah a Light, and a Book Manifest*' [5:15], and how He commanded us to obey him and follow his Sunna, saying: '*O you who believe! Obey Allah and His Messenger*' [8:20], thus making His obedience and His Messenger's obedience one, linking them together, just as He made the pledge of allegiance to the Prophet ﷺ a pledge of allegiance to Allah, saying: '*They who pledge allegiance unto you but pledge allegiance unto Allah*' [48:10].

Another example of this is how Allah commanded, in His Sacred Book,

[456] This is according to the opinion that *al-ʿaṣr* here means 'the time of the Prophet ﷺ'. [t]

that good manners be shown towards the Prophet ﷺ, saying: '*O believers, advance not before Allah and His Messenger*' [49:1]; that is, do not pre-empt the Messenger of Allah ﷺ in anything until Allah has delivered judgement on the Messenger's tongue. Consider the good etiquette of Abū Bakr al-Ṣiddīq ؓ with him ﷺ when he was leading the people in prayer in the Messenger of Allah's ﷺ absence. When the Prophet arrived, he gestured to Abū Bakr that he should continue to lead the prayer, but Abū Bakr ؓ moved back into the front row so that the Prophet ﷺ could assume the position of imam.[457] When the Prophet ﷺ asked him why he had done this, he replied: 'It is not for the son of Abū Qaḥāfa to lead the Messenger of Allah ﷺ in prayer.' Consider, then, how Allah decreed that Abū Bakr ؓ would inherit the position of imam later on.

Al-Ḍaḥḥāk said that this verse means: 'Do not make a judgement without consulting the Messenger of Allah ﷺ'; others say it means 'Do not command anything until he commands it, and do not forbid anything until he forbids it.'

Thus it is correct etiquette to refrain from pre-empting the Prophet ﷺ in any command, prohibition, permission or action until he has commanded, forbidden or allowed it, as Allah commands in this verse – and this will remain the case until the Day of Resurrection, and has not been abrogated. Thus to advance before his Sunna, even after his passing, is the same as advancing before him during his lifetime; and there is no difference between the two for anyone with a sound mind.

Another element of the good manners that must be shown to him ﷺ is that voices must not be raised above his voice, as Allah says: '*O believers, raise not your voices above the Prophet's voice, and be not loud in your speech to him, as you are loud one to another, lest your works fail while you are not aware*' [49:2]. This implies that the believer should not speak in the Prophet's ﷺ presence as a slave would speak in his master's presence; rather, his voice should be even lower than that of a slave with his master. And if raising one's voice above the Prophet's ﷺ voice causes one's works to fail, then what about raising opinions and ideas above his Sunna and what he ﷺ brought? It is related that when this verse was revealed, Abū Bakr said: 'By Allah, O Messenger of Allah, I will henceforth speak only to you as a bearer of secrets does.' And after this verse was revealed, ʿUmar

[457] Sayyid Muḥammad ibn ʿAlawī ؓ only alludes to this story in passing here; I have added some detail (from al-Bukhārī's narration), since readers may not be familiar with it. [t]

ﷺ would only speak to the Prophet ﷺ in a whisper, so that he would have to ask him to repeat himself.

It is related that Abū Jaʿfar, the Commander of the Faithful, debated with Imam Mālik in the Mosque of the Messenger of Allah ﷺ. Mālik said to him: 'O Commander of the Faithful, raise not your voice in this mosque, for Allah chided certain people, saying '*raise not your voices above the Prophet's voice*', and praised certain people, saying '*Surely those who lower their voices in the presence of Allah's Messenger, those are they whose hearts Allah has tested for piety; they shall have forgiveness and a mighty wage*' [49:3]; and He criticised certain people, saying: '*Surely those who call unto you from behind the apartments, the most of them do not understand*' [49:4]. His sanctity in death in as his sanctity in life.' Upon hearing this, Abū Jaʿfar calmed down.

Another aspect of good manners with him ﷺ is not to call him as we call one another. Allah says: '*Make not the calling of the Messenger among yourselves like your calling one of another*' [24:63]. There are two interpretations of this:

The first: Do not call him by his name, as you do with one another; call him 'O Messenger of Allah', 'O Prophet of Allah', with reverence and humility.

The second: Do not respond to his calls to you as you do to the calls you make to one another, where the one called may answer if he likes, or ignore the call if he likes. Rather, if he calls you, you must answer him, and you do not have the right to fail to do so. A quick response to him is obligatory, and to leave him without his leave is forbidden.

Another aspect of good manners with him ﷺ is that if they were all gathered together for a speech, a military engagement or an encampment, none of them would ever go off to do anything without first seeking his ﷺ permission, as Allah says: '*Those only are believers, who believe in Allah and His Messenger and who, when they are with him upon a common matter, go not away until they ask his leave*' [24:62].

Another aspect of good manners with him ﷺ is that his words can never be questioned, but only the interpretations of his words can be questioned; and no statement of his can be challenged by an analogy, but rather analogies must be abandoned if they contradict his statements; and his words can never be interpreted in such a way as denies their apparent meaning in deference to a whim that is claimed to be 'rational', when in fact it is ignorant and devoid of truth; and nothing he taught needs the approval of anyone else before it is accepted. To do any of these things is bad manners with him ﷺ, and indeed is insolence towards him. The essence of all good manners with him ﷺ is to have perfect deference to him, to obey his commands, and to meet his words with acceptance and belief without allowing vainglorious fancy to goad oneself into preferring the opinions of other men over his. Deference, unquestioning acceptance and obedience must be devoted exclusively to the Messenger ﷺ, just as worship is devoted exclusively to the One who sent him; these, then, are two exclusive devotions[458] without which there can be no salvation.

The Qurʾān is filled with verses guiding to the proper manners one should have with him ﷺ.[459] When the idolaters said '*Thou, upon whom the Remembrance is sent down – you are assuredly mad!*' [15:6], Allah answered the Prophet's ﷺ enemies Himself, without any intermediary, saying: '*Nūn. By the Pen, and what they inscribe, you are not, by the blessing of your Lord, a man possessed*' [68:1-2].

When they said '*What, has he forged against Allah a lie?*' [34:8], Allah answered them for him: '*Not so; but those who believe not in the Hereafter are in chastisement and far error*' [34:8].

When they said '*You are not an envoy*' [14:43], Allah answered them: '*Yā Sīn, by the Wise Qurʾān, you are truly among the envoys*' [36:1-3].

When they said '*What, shall we forsake our gods for a poet gone mad?*' [37:36], Allah answered: '*No indeed; but he brought the truth, and confirmed the Envoys*' [37:37], affirming his veracity, and then gave a warning to his enemies: '*Now certainly you shall come to taste the painful chastisement*' [37:38].

When they said '*He is a poet for whom we await Fate's uncertainty*' [52:30], Allah responded: '*We have not taught him poetry; it is not seemly for him. It is only a Remembrance and a Clear Qurʾān*' [36:59].

When they said, as Allah tells us, '*This is naught but a calumny he has forged, and other folk have helped him to it*' [25:4], Allah responded: '*Thus they have committed a wrong and a falsehood*' [25:4]; and He replied to their

458 Translating *tawḥīdān*, literally 'two forms of declaring unity'. This idiomatic expression is used by Ibn al-Qayyim in *Madārij al-Sālikīn*, and by Ibn Abī al-ʿIzz al-Ḥanafī in *Sharḥ al-Ṭaḥāwiyya*, among others. [t]

459 The author ﷺ adds a footnote here saying: 'We have already seen some of this in the chapter on the Prophet's ﷺ eminence in the Qurʾān; we repeat it here with some additions, for another purpose.' [t]

words '*Fairy-tales of the ancients*' [25:5] by saying: '*Say: He sent it down, who knows the secret in the heavens and earth*' [25:6].

When they said than the Revelation was inspired by Satan, Allah said: '*Not by the devils has it been brought down*' [26:210].

When he ﷺ recited to them the news of what happened to the ancients, al-Naḍr ibn al-Ḥārith said: '*We could say the like of this; this is naught but the fairy-tales of the ancients*' [8:31], and Allah responded: '*Say: If men and jinn banded together to produce the like of this Koran, they would never produce its like, not though they backed one another*' [17:88].

When al-Walīd ibn al-Mughīra said '*This is naught but a trumped-up sorcery; this is nothing but mortal speech*' [74:24-25], Allah responded: '*Even so not a Messenger came to those before them but they said, "A sorcerer, or a madman!"*' [51:52], by way of consoling the Prophet ﷺ.

When they said 'Muḥammad's Lord has forsaken him', Allah responded: '*Thy Lord has not forsaken you, nor does He hate you*' [93:3].

When they said '*What ails this Messenger that he eats food, and walks in the markets?*' [25:7], Allah responded: '*And We sent not before you any Envoys, but that they ate food, and walked in the markets*' [25:20].

When the enemies of Allah among the Jews envied him for having married several times, saying 'He is concerned with nothing but marriage', Allah responded: '*Or are they jealous of the people for the bounty that Allah has given them? Yet We gave the people of Abraham the Book and the Wisdom, and We gave them a mighty kingdom*' [4:54].

When they found it far-fetched that Allah would sent a human being as a messenger, saying, as Allah tells us, '*And naught prevented men from believing when the guidance came to them, but that they said, "Has Allah sent forth a mortal as Messenger?"*' [17:94] (for they were ignorant of the fact that people are more at ease with their own, and feel more separated from those who are not like them), Allah answered them: '*Say: Had there been in the earth angels walking at peace, We would have sent down upon them out of heaven an angel as Messenger*' [17:95]. That is, had the people of earth been angels, their messenger would have been an angel; but since the people of earth are human beings, their messenger had to be a human being.

The Perfection of His ﷺ Worship

The Prophet's ﷺ worship was constant and uninterrupted, night and day. Our lady ʿĀʾisha ﵂ was asked: 'How was the Messenger of Allah's ﷺ spiritual action? Did he devote it to certain days [and not to others]?' She replied: 'No, his action was constant; and who among you could do what the Messenger of Allah ﷺ could?'[460]

The Messenger of Allah ﷺ never left his regular supererogatory prayers and acts of worship in his whole life. Umm Salama is reported to have said: 'In the time before the Messenger of Allah ﷺ died, he stepped up his [supererogatory] prayers, offering them while seated. The action he loved the best was the one which the servant did consistently, even if it were only a little.'[461]

His ﷺ sweetest pleasure and fondest repose was in worship. He ﷺ would say: 'Arise, O Bilāl, and give us peace with prayer!'[462] He also said: 'The comfort of my eye has been placed in prayer.'[463]

His ﷺ way of worship was that if he ever performed an act of worship, he would continue to do so consistently and regularly. ʿĀʾisha ﵂ related that the Messenger of Allah ﷺ said: 'Take on that action which you can manage; for Allah does not lose interest until you lose interest. The action most beloved to Allah is the most consistent, even if it is only a little.' ʿĀʾisha added: 'And when he ﷺ performed an act of worship, he would be consistent in it.'[464]

He ﷺ would regularly offer night vigils, usually in the early part of the second half of the night. Our lady ʿĀʾisha said: 'He would sleep in the first part of the night, and keep vigil in the latter part.'[465]

The Prophet ﷺ said that this vigil after sleeping was the most beloved form of night vigil: 'The most beloved form of vigil to Allah is the vigil of Dāwūd: he would sleep for half the night, pray for a third of it, and

460 Abū Dāwūd.

461 Ibn Ḥibbān.

462 Aḥmad.

463 Al-Nasāʾī, Aḥmad.

464 Abū Dāwūd.

465 Al-Bukhārī, Muslim.

then sleep for a sixth of it.'[466] This is so that one can have a break from the rigours of the vigil, and so that after the vigil the body can rest and be relieved of the weariness and physical fatigue of staying awake, which is not the case if one simply stays up all night. Another wisdom of this is that it allows one to offer the dawn prayer and begin one's daily activities with freshness and vigour. In terms of the prayer, this method is also better for avoiding ostentation, since if one sleeps the final sixth of the night he will appear to be relaxed and fresh when he awakes, which better conceals his nightly actions; this is mentioned by al-Ḥāfiẓ Ibn Ḥajar in *Fatḥ al-Bārī*. Furthermore, this method allows the one who keeps the night vigil to partake in the blessings of the Lord's ﷻ manifestations of grace in the final two thirds of the night.

He ﷺ would also recite certain formulas and Qur'ānic passages before he slept; it is related that he would not sleep until first having recited the sūras of *Banī Isrā'īl* (*al-Isrā'*) and *al-Zumar*.[467] It is also related that he ﷺ would not sleep until having first recited the sūras of *al-Sajda* and *al-Mulk*.[468] It is also related that he would recite the *Musabbiḥāt*[469] before lying down to sleep; and he said: 'In them is a verse worth a thousand verses.'[470]

He ﷺ would also offer the midmorning (*ḍuḥā*) prayer regularly; sometimes he would offer two cycles (which is the least number that can be offered), sometimes four (which he did most often), sometimes six, sometimes eight, and sometimes twelve (which is the best and greatest number that can be offered).

After offering the dawn prayer, he ﷺ would sit cross-legged in his place and invoke Allah until the sun had fully risen.[471] He would offer supererogatory prayers after the sunset prayer which differed in number: sometimes he would keep praying from sunset until the evening prayer[472], and sometimes he would offer six cycles after the sunset prayer, saying: 'Whosoever offers them consistently will have all his sins forgiven, even

466 Al-Bukhārī, Muslim.

467 Al-Tirmidhī, Aḥmad.

468 Al-Tirmidhī, al-Nasā'ī.

469 The six *Musabbiḥāt* (so called because they all begin with various conjugations of the verb *sabbaḥa*, meaning 'to extol and glorify') are the chapters *al-Ḥadīd*, *al-Ḥashr*, *al-Ṣaff*, *al-Jumu'a*, *al-Taghābun*, and *al-A'lā*. [t]

470 Aḥmad and the *Sunan*.

471 Muslim.

472 Al-Nasā'ī.

if they be as many as the foam of the sea.'[473] He also said: 'Whosoever offers six cycles of prayer after the sunset prayer, not speaking any ill word between them, will have them counted for him as equal to twelve years of worship.'[474]

He would supplicate often and encourage others to do the same. When he supplicated, he would raise his hands to level with his shoulders, palms facing the sky if he was praying for some good to be gained and palms facing down if he was praying for some tribulation to be avoided.[475] He would raise his hands higher than usual when praying for rain, seeking Allah's urgent aid, or seeking succour against an enemy. When raising his hands to supplicate, he would not put them down again before wiping his face with them.[476] He would face the *qibla* when supplicating[477], and would like to repeat his supplication three times[478], and would ask Allah's forgiveness three times. He would prefer to make comprehensive supplications, and would usually not do otherwise.[479] 'Comprehensive' here means supplications that combined, in succinct words, the good of this life and the next. One of his comprehensive supplications was: 'O Allah, our Lord, give us goodness in this world, and goodness in the Hereafter, and spare us from the torment of hellfire.'[480]

Another of his comprehensive supplications was: 'O Allah, make good for me my religion, which is the safeguard of my affairs; and make good for me my worldly life, wherein is my living; and make good for me my afterlife, whereto shall be my return; and make life a means of increase for me in all that is good, and make death a means of repose for me from all that is evil.'

Another was: 'O Allah, I seek refuge with You from discord, and hypocrisy, and evil conduct.'[481] The books of the Sunna record many of his comprehensive supplications, which he would say upon different occasions, times and circumstances.

473 Al-Ṭabarānī.
474 Ibn Mājah, al-Tirmidhī.
475 Abū Dāwūd.
476 Al-Tirmidhī, al-Ḥākim.
477 Al-Tirmidhī.
478 Ibn Mājah.
479 Abū Dāwūd, al-Ḥākim.
480 Al-Bukhārī, Muslim.
481 Abū Dāwūd.

He ﷺ would also glorify Allah often throughout the night and day. Rabīʿa ibn Kaʿb said: 'I used to serve him by day, and when night came I would go to the Messenger of Allah's ﷺ door, where I would hear him say over and over: "Glory be to Allah, glory be to my Lord", until I was overcome with sleep.'[482]

He ﷺ would also ask forgiveness of Allah often throughout the day and night, both in prayer and outside of it, and in all his gatherings and situations. He would say: 'By Allah, I ask forgiveness of Allah and turn to Him in repentance more than seventy times a day.'[483] Ibn ʿUmar said: 'We once counted the Messenger of Allah ﷺ say, in a single gathering, "Lord, forgive me and relent unto me; You are the Relenting, the Merciful", one hundred times.'[484] Another version has it 'You are the Relenting, the Forgiving.' He would also sometimes say: 'I ask forgiveness of Allah, besides whom there is no god, the Living, the All-Sustaining, and I turn to Him in repentance' more than one hundred times in a single gathering.[485]

He ﷺ would also fast often. Sometimes he would fast for so many days that people would say, 'He will never stop fasting!'; other times he would go so long without fasting that the people would say, 'He will never fast!' He would fast three days out of every month, and also fast on Mondays and Thursdays and encourage others to do the same, saying: 'They are the days when deeds are presented; so I love to make it so that, when my deeds are presented, I am fasting.'[486] He ﷺ would honour the blessed day of his birth, Monday, by fasting on it, saying: 'This was the day I was born.'[487]

He would also endeavour to fast for most of the month of Shaʿbān, and would sometimes fast constantly. When the month of Ramaḍān came, he would make more effort in his vigils than at any other time, and would make more effort in the final ten nights of it, making a spiritual retreat therein and spending the whole night in worship.

482 Al-Ṭabarānī.

483 Al-Bukhārī.

484 Abū Dāwūd, Ibn Ḥibbān, al-Tirmidhī.

485 Al-Nasāʾī.

486 Al-Tirmidhī, al-Nasāʾī, Aḥmad.

487 Muslim.

His ﷺ Perfect Fear of Allah

The Messenger of Allah ﷺ feared Allah more than any other person. This was because, as Allah says, *'Those truly fear Allah, among His servants, who have knowledge'* [35:28]; and he ﷺ knew Allah better than anyone, as the ḥadīth states:

The two *Ṣaḥīḥ* collections tell us that ʿĀʾisha said: 'The Messenger of Allah ﷺ did something and thus made it lawful, yet some people were still averse to it. When news of this reached the Prophet ﷺ, he said: "What is wrong with certain people, that they are averse to something I do? By Allah, I know Allah better than any of you, and fear Him more than any of you."'

This ḥadīth makes clear his ﷺ superiority over all mankind in knowledge of Allah and fear of Him, and shows that Allah gave him the highest and most perfect station of knowledge and fear.

Anas said: 'The Messenger of Allah ﷺ gave a sermon to us, the like of which I had never heard. He said: "Knew you all what I know, you would laugh little and weep much!" He then said: "Paradise and Hell were shown to me, and never have I seen good and evil the like of which I saw today. Knew you all what I know, you would laugh little and weep much!" Never was a day more grievous for the Companions of the Messenger of Allah ﷺ than that day. They covered their heads, and sobbed.'[488]

This ḥadīth indicates the depth of his fear of Allah, and how much he wept in fear of Allah.

Another aspect of his ﷺ perfect fear of Allah was that he ﷺ was always in a state of humility and lowliness before his Lord in all that he did, whether in prayer and worship, or worldly affairs. His reverence in prayer was such that a sound could be heard from his chest like the sizzling of a cooking pot. ʿAlī said: 'We had no mounted knight on the day of Badr except al-Miqdād; and [on the night before the battle] I saw that all of us were sleeping except for the Messenger of Allah ﷺ, who was under a tree, weeping as he prayed, until the dawn.'[489] And when he ﷺ entered Mecca

488 Al-Bukhārī, Muslim.

489 Aḥmad.

on the day of the Conquest, he entered in a state of humility to his Lord – may Allah send his best and noblest blessings upon him, and upon his Family and his Companions!

Part Five

The Perfection of His Political and Military Leadership

"O Prophet, struggle with the unbelievers and hypocrites, and be you firm with them!" [9:73]

His ﷺ Perfect Wisdom in Dealing with Matters of Politics

The recorded life of our Prophet and Master Muḥammad ﷺ gives us a clear picture of his perfect wisdom and the brilliant political strategy he employed in dealing with issues, solving problems, facing difficulties, making deals, and establishing covenants, and how skilful and far-sighted he was. By this, he was able to attain advantages both obvious and subtle, bring benefit, ward off harm, cut off the means to harm, arrange things in the best way, and succeed in a way that no one before him had. Yet this unparalleled success did not change him in any way; he remained a merciful, righteous, humble, ascetic and devoted worshipper. It is true beyond any possible dispute that his life, leadership of the Muslim community, way of ruling, and delivery of the Message constitute together the greatest guide – which he showed us with action, not merely words – of what a model ruler should be, in all his circumstances and affairs.

When he ﷺ came to Medina, the events of Buʿāth[490] were still fresh in the minds of the tribes of Aws and Khazraj, and the ancient enmity between them was still provoking new instances of conflict; the Jews were also fanning the flames of conflict between them, fearing what would happen if things changed. As for the companions of the Prophet ﷺ who emigrated to Medina, they had no power or strength at all, no more than any other refugees who seek the aid of people who have no love for their families or tribes.

Because of all this, their position was extremely delicate. But the Prophet ﷺ handled the situation with his wisdom, sound strategy and perfect intellect, proving that he was fit to handle any grave situation. He immediately began the construction of the mosque, which was the foundation he placed for both religious and worldly good, becoming thereafter a place of worship, a centre of leadership, and the base for the dissemination of the call to Allah. The believers were given their education

490 A particularly savage battle between the two tribes. [t]

there in the best of environments and the finest of circumstances; and all administrative, political and military plans were formed there; and delegations were received there; and knowledge was imparted there.

One example of his ﷺ sound policy in his early days in Medina was how, when he saw that the community was divided because of their different religious beliefs, he set about making a system that safeguarded the rights of all and preserved religious freedom and the sanctity of life, property and honour, and made all of them equally responsible for defending the city from any outside aggression, so that they were united in their common interest in times of both war and peace. All this was enshrined in a charter which read:

In the Name of Allah, the Infinitely Good, the Merciful. This is a written statement of Muḥammad, the Prophet ﷺ, making a pact between the believers and Muslims of Quraysh and Yathrib[491], and all who follow them, join them and fight alongside them, that they are one community, distinct from all others.

The charter then affirmed that if the Jews were to join them in this pact, they would be given succour and security, and the Muslims would not allow them to be wronged or aid anyone against them, and that the Jews of Banū ʿAwf would be united with the believers in one community, the Jews having their religion and the Muslims having theirs, together with their freedmen and all their citizenry. It then affirmed that the rest of the Jews who joined the pact would also be granted all that had been granted to the Banū ʿAwf.

The charter then affirmed that the Jews and Muslims alike would have to bear their own expenses, and that they were bound to succour one another against anyone who waged war against those who were party to the charter. They were also bound to seek mutual advice and consultation, and to uphold loyalty as a guard against treachery.

The charter also stated that Yathrib would be a sanctuary for those who were party to the charter, and that a stranger given protection would be treated as well as his host as long as he caused no harm and committed no crime. It also stated that a woman could not be given sanctuary without her kin's consent. It further stated that if any dispute or quarrel arose

[491] The old name of Medina. [t]

between the parties to the charter that might put it at risk, the matter would be referred to Allah ﷻ and to Muḥammad, the Messenger of Allah ﷺ.

This charter inadvertently put the Messenger of Allah ﷺ in a position of political power over Yathrib, for a pact such as this would always be invoked whenever a dispute arose, and there was no other pact to be invoked besides this one. From that moment, the cornerstone of the Islamic State was set down.

Thus the Messenger of Allah ﷺ put an end to the chaos and power struggles, and made it so that the final decision was always referred to Allah, meaning to His Law and His Messenger, the discharger of this Law. Before that, power was determined by brute force: mob rule, which did not distinguish between the guilty and the innocent.

Another example of his ﷺ sublime and rightly-guided polity was the occasion when a dispute arose between a man of the Helpers and a hired hand of ʿUmar ibn al-Khaṭṭāb, during the campaign of Banū al-Muṣṭaliq. The Helper called for help from the Helpers, and the hired hand called for the help of the Emigrants, and the two groups almost came to blows. This was further exacerbated by Ibn Ubayy ibn Salūl, the chief of the hypocrites, who took advantage of the situation, having alongside him a young man named Zayd ibn Arqam. 'Have they gone so far as this?', said Ibn Ubayy. 'They seek to take precedence over us, and crowd us out of our own land. Naught will fit us and them but the old saying, "Fatten your dog and it will feed upon you." By Allah, when we return to Medina, the mighty of us will cast out the lowly!' Zayd ibn Arqam told the Messenger of Allah ﷺ of what Ibn Ubayy had said, whereupon ʿUmar said: 'O Messenger of Allah, send someone to kill him!' Yet this wise leader replied: 'How shall it be then, ʿUmar, when the people say that Muḥammad slays his companions?' He saw that it was enough to break camp and move off, leaving with the army at an hour at which he had never been known to move off before. He took them off that very day, and they travelled all afternoon and all through the night and into the next day, until the heat of the sun forced them to stop, weary and exhausted. When they finally pitched camp, the men had no sooner touched the ground than they fell asleep.

The wise prophetic reason for making them travel through the day and the night without halting was to prevent them from dwelling on the incident which had stirred up their feelings of patriotic rivalry. In this way, Allah guarded them from the evil of that moment, a consequence of this wise and brilliant strategy.

Now when Ibn Ubayy's son 'Abdallāh – who was one of the finest Muslims – heard about what his father had said, he went to the Messenger of Allah ✤ and said, 'I have heard that you wish to see 'Abdallāh ibn Ubayy slain because of what you have heard he said. If you really intend to do so, then command me to do the deed, and I shall bring you his head. By Allah, you know that there is no one among the Khazraj more dutiful to his father than I; and I fear that if you command anyone but me to slay him, I will look upon my father's killer walking among the people, and kill a believer in revenge for a disbeliever – and surely I would go to Hell for doing so.' And what was the reply of this wise, kind, merciful messenger, who knew the nature of the human soul so well? Calmly and kindly, he replied: 'No, 'Abdallāh. Rather be gentle with your father, and we shall treat him well as long as he is with us.'

This way of dealing with the situation had a lasting effect in preventing further evils; for from then on, whenever Ibn Ubayy the hypocrite tried anything similar, his people upbraided him and took him to task for his actions, and reminded him of what the Messenger of Allah ✤ had said.

And by doing this, the noble Messenger ✤ wanted to show 'Umar ✤ the depth of his balanced and judicious political acumen. In later times he said to him: 'See you not, 'Umar, that had I slain him as you told me to, I would have aroused the wrath of folk who, if I were to order them to slay him now, would willingly do so, their hearts overflowing with love and esteem for the Messenger of Allah?' 'Umar replied: 'By Allah, I know that the command of the Messenger of Allah is more blessed than mine!'

Another of the praiseworthy decisions he ✤ made that show his rightly-guided political acumen was his decision on the day of Ḥudaybiyya to assent to the conditions of the Treaty which seemed, on the surface, to spell humiliation and ignominy for the Muslims. Some of them objected to this, even our master 'Umar ✤, because the Muslims had not yet discerned the great wisdom and sound polity that the Prophet ✤ was employing. After some time had passed, however, the Muslims began to realise the importance of this truce, and the great good that it spelled.

One of the Treaty's benefits was the protection of the weak Muslims in Mecca, and the preservation of their blood, which would otherwise have been spilled had fighting broken out, because they were living among the unbelievers. Another of its benefits was that it was a cause for many of the unbelievers of Quraysh to embrace Islam because of the time they spent with these Muslims who lived among them. This inspired them to go to Medina, the centre of faith and Islam, and hear from the Muslims the sayings of the Prophet ﷺ, and the clear miracles he had performed, and the beautiful story of his life, and the open call to his prophethood, and all the other things that caused them to enter Allah's religion in droves. The Muslims realised after all this that their being barred from the Sacred House and forced to turn home may have appeared a defeat, but was in fact a great triumph and source of power for them. Thus Allah debased the idolaters where they had sought glory, and overwhelmed them where they had sought triumph: '*Yet glory belongs to Allah, and to His Messenger, and to the believers!*' [63:8].

His ﷺ Perfect Courage

Courage is one of the loftiest of virtues; indeed you might say that it is the guardian of the virtues, defending them from all that would touch them. Our Lord ﷻ allotted His prophets (upon whom be blessings and peace) a greater share of this courage, just as He gave them a greater share of all the virtues.

The reason it was always His wise way to give them this unrivalled level of courage is that whenever He wants to assign a task to someone, He prepares him for this task, and gives him the power he needs to do it. Now the task of the prophets, which Allah has given to them, is to call mankind to the truth; and this call cannot be made without the prophet's confronting his people with what he has been sent to convey, and asking them to yield to it and to cast aside their current ways, never to return to them.

Whosoever would like to see how courageous the prophets were need only read what the Holy Qur'ān says on the matter. Take our master Hūd ﷺ, who said to his people, as Allah Almighty tells us: '*I call Allah to witness; and witness you, that I am quit of that which you ascribe as partners besides Him; so try your guile on me, all of you, and give me no respite*' [11:54-55].

And take our master Mūsā: when his people said to him '*We shall be caught*' [26:61], he replied bravely: '*Nay! My Lord is with me; He shall guide me*' [26:62].

The prophets were the bravest of all people, and he ﷺ was one of the prophets, and thus was, alongside them, the bravest of people. Indeed, he was the bravest of all the prophets, because he was sent to all mankind while the prophets who came before him were only sent to their own people; and the divine wisdom would not apportion equal amounts of courage to one who stands before some people and one who stands before *all* people.

So in his courage, steadfastness and firmness in the face of the most awful terrors, he ﷺ had the highest position which no other can attain, and whose summit no one can know but He who gave it to him. It was because of this that he ﷺ participated in all the many battles he attended in his military life; and it is not known that he ever held back from his position even a single foot, or a single finger's breadth. This made him, for his Companions, a leader who inspired the utmost confidence and obedience, so that the young and old of them alike would be quick to heed his signals – not only because he was the Messenger of Allah, but because of the courage they witnessed from him, which made their own valour seem like nothing to them in comparison, despite the fact that many of them were heroes in their own right, whose courage has become the stuff of legend. Our master ʿAlī ibn Abī Ṭālib ؓ attested to this with complete frankness when he said: 'When times became hard, and eyes became red, we would seek the protection of the Messenger of Allah ﷺ, so that no one would be closer to the enemy than he.'[492]

An example of this is the tale narrated by Jābir ؓ, who said: 'We were with the Prophet ﷺ during the campaign of Dhāt al-Riqāʿ, when we came to a shady tree, which we left for the Prophet ﷺ. An idolater came along, while the Prophet's ﷺ sword was hanging from the tree. He took it, and said to him: 'Do you fear me?' The Prophet ﷺ said: 'No.' The man said, 'But who will protect you from me?' He replied: 'Allah.'[493]

Another example of this is what he ﷺ did with Ubayy ibn Khalaf at the Battle of Uḥud, when that accursed man spurred his horse towards the Messenger of Allah ﷺ, and some men from among the Muslims made to stop him. Yet the Prophet ﷺ said, 'Let him come!' He then took a spear from the companion al-Ḥārith ibn al-Ṣimma, and leapt forward with it, whereupon they scattered like flies from a bolting camel's back. The Prophet ﷺ then turned to Ubayy and thrust him in the neck with a thrust that made him sway atop his horse several times. Ubayy returned to his people and said, 'Muḥammad ﷺ has slain me!' They told him he was fine, but Ubayy replied: 'If what afflicts me now were to afflict all people, it would surely kill them! Did he not say: "It is I who will slay you"? By Allah, had Muḥammad but spat upon me, he would have slain me!'[494]

Another example of this is found in the words of our master Anas ؓ, as narrated by al-Bukhārī and Muslim: 'The Messenger of Allah ﷺ was

492 Aḥmad, al-Ṭabarānī, al-Nasāʾī.

493 Al-Bukhārī, Muslim.

494 ʿAbd al-Razzāq, Ibn Saʿd, al-Bayhaqī.

the best of people, the most generous, and the bravest. The people of Medina were alarmed [by a strange sound] one night. Some people went out towards the source of the sound, and met the Messenger of Allah ﷺ on his way back, for he had gone before them to see what was going on. He was riding bareback on one of Abū Ṭalḥā's horses, his sword round his neck, saying "Worry not!"'

Another of his ﷺ great and famous stands – and they were all great – was the stand he took on the day of the Battle of Ḥunayn. Al-Bukhārī and Muslim – and the Qur'ān – relate that all save a few of his Companions ﷺ took flight and left him on that day. Al-Bukhārī and Muslim agree that he ﷺ was riding a mule, and Muslim's narration has it that al-ʿAbbās ﷺ said: 'When the Muslims and unbelievers met in battle, the Muslims took flight, whereupon the Messenger of Allah ﷺ began to spur his mule before the disbelievers; and I had hold of the Messenger of Allah's ﷺ mule's bridle, trying to slow it down.'

Al-Bukhārī and Muslim also agree that he ﷺ cast a handful of dust into the faces of the unbelievers. Muslim narrates, on the authority of our master Salama ibn al-Akwaʿ ﷺ, that he ﷺ got off his mule and took up a handful of dust, and said: 'Abased be the faces!', flinging it into their faces. Every single one of them found his eyes filled with dust from that handful, and they turned their heels and fled, routed by Allah ﷻ.

Another of Muslim's narrations has it that al-ʿAbbās ﷺ said: 'By Allah, as soon as he flung his pebbles at them I saw them began to break and scatter!' Another narration of Muslim has it that he ﷺ said as he flung the pebbles: 'Be routed, by the Lord of the Kaʿba! Be routed, by the Lord of the Kaʿba!'

They also agree that he said, at that crucial moment:

I am the Prophet, no lie!
I am the scion of ʿAbd al-Muṭṭalib!

Al-Bukhārī and Muslim also agree that their enemies were archers; and the Qur'ān tells us that in the end the tide turned in favour of the believers. They also agree that this took place after his Companions had returned to him ﷺ, responding to the rallying-cry he ﷺ had commanded his uncle al-ʿAbbās to make.

His ﷺ Perfect Military Leadership

When one looks at the Prophet's ﷺ biography and how he waged military campaigns and dealt with his enemies, one sees many events that show the greatness of his leadership and his perfect knowledge and expertise in the ways of warfare, and his excellent management of armies, even though he did not study the arts of war or military science in any school or academy. This can clearly be seen in the battles he fought, the defensive plans he drew up, and the military tactics he established. On many occasions he gained victory though his army was the smaller; and he entered Mecca, the nerve-centre of the enemy's campaigns and plots, as a conqueror; and he defeated the Jews and put an end to their influence after they had reneged on so many of their treaties and refused to stop their plotting and scheming. His policy was not one of aggression, subjection and wrongdoing, but rather one of defence, resistance and justice.

In all this, Allah combined in the Prophet ﷺ perfect character, sound polity, and impeccable management, so that all things were put in their proper places.

One occasion that showed his ﷺ military brilliance, leadership and concern was when he arrayed the ranks and inspected the troops at the Battle of Badr, straightening the ranks of his Companions himself, with an arrow in his hand to direct them; he would tell one to come forward, and another to go back. As he was straightening the ranks, he commanded Sawād ibn Ghaziyya to stand in line, and pricked him in his belly with the arrow as he did so. Sawād said, 'O Messenger of Allah, you have hurt me, and Allah has sent you with truth and justice, so give me my requital.' The Messenger of Allah ﷺ laid his belly bare and said, 'Take it.' Sawād stooped and embraced the Prophet ﷺ, and kissed his belly instead. 'What made you do that, Sawād?', said the Prophet. Sawād answered: 'O Messenger of Allah, we are now faced with what you see; and I desired that at my final moment with you, my skin should touch your skin', and the Prophet ﷺ beseeched Allah to bless him.

And on the day of Uḥud, he inspected the troops, accepting some and sending others back: Usāma ibn Zayd, ʿAbdallāh ibn ʿUmar, Zayd ibn Thābit, Abū Saʿīd al-Khudrī and others presented themselves to him, and he sent them all back.

He ﷺ also arrayed the ranks and flanks of his Companions on the day of Uḥud, setting up the necessary protection at the rear of the Muslims, and commanding the archers to remain at their posts at all costs, no matter what condition they saw their brothers in arms to be in, until they received a command from him ﷺ to do otherwise. He was among the foremost strategist of the arts and ways of war, utilising the best means to defeat and rout the enemy by causing discord among them, breaking their ranks, wearing them down and hemming them in.

An example of this is how he ﷺ accepted al-Ḥubāb ibn al-Mundhir's plan at Badr. When the Prophet ﷺ arrived at Badr, he stopped and dismounted at the first well they came to. Al-Ḥubāb said: 'O Messenger of Allah, has this place been revealed to you from Allah as the only place we may stop, so that we cannot go beyond it or pull back from it, or is it merely a matter of opinion, war and strategy? The Prophet ﷺ answered that it was merely a matter of opinion, war and strategy. Al-Ḥubāb then said: 'In that case, O Messenger of Allah, this is not the best place to halt. Let us continue on until we reach the well nearest to the enemy, halt there, and stop the well up and build a cistern upon it, and fill it with water, so that we can drink whilst they cannot.' The Messenger of Allah ﷺ said, 'Your opinion is indeed sound', and he went with some men to the nearest well to the enemy and halted there, stopped up the well, and build a cistern upon it. It filled with water, and each man filled his drinking vessel from it.

Another famous example of his leadership in this field was how he sent people to spread discord in the ranks of the enemy to sabotage them. One such occasion was at the Battle of the Confederates, when Nuʿaym ibn Masʿūd al-Ashjaʿī ؓ came to the Prophet ﷺ and said: 'I have embraced Islam, and my people do not know it; command me to do as you please.' He ﷺ replied: 'You are but one man among us, so draw them off us if you can, for war is deception. Go and sow discord among the ranks of the enemy, and use your wiles to disrupt them.'

Nuʿaym went to Banū Qurayẓa, a Jewish clan with whom he had been friendly, and said to them: 'You know of my love for you, and the special relationship we have.' 'You speak the truth,' they said, 'you are beyond suspicion in our eyes.' He told them that Quraysh and Ghaṭafān had come from Mecca and gathered near Medina, preparing to attack the Prophet ﷺ and his Companions, and that the Banū Qurayẓa, Jews who resided in Medina had already agreed to join them in that. 'They are not like you,' he said; 'the city is your city, and in it are your possessions and your women and children. You cannot flee elsewhere. If they have the chance to prevail, they will take it; otherwise, they will return home, leaving you to him [Muḥammad ﷺ and his Companions] in your own city; and you do not have the power to stand against him alone. Do not fight with them unless they give you some of their noblemen as hostages, as a guarantee that you will continue to fight Muḥammad with them until you defeat him.' They approved of Nuʿaym's plan.

Nuʿaym then went to Quraysh and said to Abū Sufyān: 'You know of my love for you and my dispute with Muḥammad. Something has come to my attention which I feel duty bound to pass on to you, as sincere counsel; keep, then, my secret.' They agreed. Nuʿaym said: 'The Jews regret what they have done, and have sent a message to Muḥammad telling him so, and offering to appease him by seizing some noblemen of Quraysh and Ghaṭafān and slaying them, and then joining him to fight the rest until they are utterly destroyed. And Muḥammad has accepted their offer! Therefore, if the Jews request hostages from you, do not give them a single man.'

Nuʿaym then went to Ghaṭafān and said: 'You are my people and my clan, and the people I love most, and I do not imagine that you could ever mistrust me.' 'You speak the truth,' they said, 'you are beyond suspicion in our eyes.' 'Keep then my secret,' Nuʿaym said. They agreed, and he told them the same thing he had told Quraysh.

Allah decreed for His Messenger ﷺ that Abū Sufyān and the heads of Ghaṭafān sent ʿIkrima with a delegation representing the two tribes to the Banū Qurayẓa, with the message: 'We are not residents of this land, and our camels and horses are exhausted. Prepare for battle, that we might set upon Muḥammad and settle our conflict with him.' So the Jews of Qurayẓa sent a message back to Quraysh and Ghaṭafān: 'It is the Sabbath, and we shall not break it, for some of us broke it once and there befell them that which you yourselves need not fear [i.e. they were destroyed].

In any case, we shall not fight alongside you until you give us some of your men that we may keep until we have defeated Muḥammad; for we fear that if the battle becomes too hard for you, you will return to your homes [Mecca and the surrounding areas] and leave us alone with this man [Muḥammad] without the power to fight him.' Quraysh and Ghaṭafān said: 'By Allah, what Nuʿaym said was true!' So they sent a message to the Banū Qurayẓa: 'By Allah, we shall not fight alongside you until you too give us hostages!' They refused, and thus Allah divided them; and He then sent a fierce wind upon them on a sorely cold night, which knocked over their pots, tore down their tents, and set them fleeing.

The Tactics He ﷺ Employed to Conceal Things from His Enemies

The Prophet ﷺ would conceal his war strategies from his enemies so that they would not be aware of them and prepare defences against them, or recruit extra troops. In doing so, he ensured that many lives were spared.

Kaʿb ibn Mālik said: 'The Messenger of Allah ﷺ never set out for a battle without making it seem that he would do otherwise, until that Battle [of Tabūk] came along...'[495]

At the Battle of Badr, he went himself to seek out information about Quraysh: he and Abū Bakr ﷺ rode until they found an Arab elder, whom they questioned about Quraysh, Muḥammad and his Companions, and all he had heard about them. The old man said: 'I shall tell you nothing until you identify yourselves.' The Prophet ﷺ replied: 'If you tell us, we will tell you.' 'Quid pro quo?', asked the man. 'Yes', said the Prophet ﷺ. The old man said: 'I have heard that Muḥammad and his Companions went out on [such-and-such] day; and if the one who told me was telling the truth, they are today in [the place where the Messenger of Allah ﷺ indeed was]. I also heard that Quraysh went out on [such-and-such] day; and if the one who told me was telling the truth, they are today in [the place where Quraysh indeed were].'

When he had finished telling what he knew, he asked, 'Where are you from?'. The Messenger of Allah ﷺ replied: 'We are from water', and then they departed. 'From water?', said the man to himself. 'Does he mean from Iraq?'

Another example of his ﷺ wise strategy was that when Quraysh violated the Treaty of Ḥudaybiyya, they sent Abū Sufyān to Medina to ask the Prophet ﷺ to renew the pact and extend its duration. Upon arriving, he said: 'O Muḥammad, I was absent from the Treaty of Ḥudaybiyya, so I have come to renew it.' The Prophet ﷺ said: 'That is why you have come?' Abū Sufyān said yes. 'Has something happened?', asked the Prophet ﷺ.

[495] Al-Bukhārī, Muslim.

'Allah forbid!', said Abū Sufyān, 'we remain steadfast upon our pact and our treaty, and have not erred from it at all.' The Prophet ﷺ replied: 'Then it still stands.'

Behold this rightly-guided prophetic course of action. He ﷺ did not rebuke Abū Sufyān for breaking the pact, nor declare war on him, so that they would not begin thinking of war or making preparations for it. Because of this, they were not aware of it until the Prophet ﷺ had almost reached Mecca with his armies.

His ﷺ Concern for Knowing the Condition, Numbers, Preparedness and News of His Enemies Before Meeting Them in Combat

At the Battle of Badr, the Prophet ﷺ sent ʿAlī, Zubayr, and Saʿd ibn Abī Waqqāṣ in a delegation of his Companions to the wells of Badr to undertake a reconnaissance mission for him. They found the water-bearers of Quraysh there, and seized two of them. the Prophet ﷺ began to question them himself, asking them about Quraysh. 'By Allah,' they answered, 'they are behind the far bank of yonder dune.' He asked how many there were, and they answered that there were many. 'How many do they number?', he asked. They said they did not know. 'How many [animals] do they slaughter a day?', he asked. 'Sometimes nine and sometimes ten', they answered. The Prophet ﷺ said: 'Then there are between nine hundred and one thousand of them.' He then asked them, 'What noblemen of Quraysh are among them?' They replied: "ʿUtba ibn Rabīʿa, Shayba ibn Rabīʿa, Abū al-Bakhtarī ibn Hāshim, Ḥakīm ibn Ḥazzām, Nawfal ibn Khuwaylid, Abū Jahl, Umayya ibn Khalaf, al-Naḍr ibn al-Ḥārith'; and they listed other chieftains of Quraysh besides these. The Messenger of Allah ﷺ went to the people and said: 'Behold, Mecca has thrown unto you the dearest morsels of her liver!'[496]

And at the Battle of Ḥunayn, before the fighting had begun, He ﷺ approached ʿAbdallāh ibn Abī Ḥadrad al-Aslamī and commanded him to go to the enemy and stay with them, and bring back tidings of them. He set off and entered their camp, and circled about them, gathering information to take back. One thing he had heard was Mālik saying to his companions: 'Muḥammad has never really fought anyone before now; he has only encountered whelps with no knowledge of warfare, and thus defeated them. On the morrow, bring out your livestock, women

[496] That is, 'has sent you her dearest sons.'

and children and array them behind you, and then get in ranks. Let the attack come from you, and break the sheaths of your swords, so that you meet them with twenty thousand sheath-broken swords! Wage war as one man, and know that victory comes to those who strike first.' ʿAbdallāh went back to the Messenger of Allah ﷺ and told him what he had heard.

And at the Battle of the Confederates, the Messenger of Allah ﷺ sent Ḥudhayfa to discover news of the enemy. Ḥudhayfa himself later told the story of that dangerous mission: 'We were with the Messenger of Allah ﷺ at the Trench, and he ﷺ said: "Will any man go and see for us what they are doing, and then return? The Messenger of Allah ﷺ guarantees that he shall return; and I ask Allah that he be my companion in Paradise." No man put himself forward, because of their intense fear, hunger and cold; and when no one came forward, the Messenger of Allah ﷺ called me, and I had no choice but to come forward when he called me. "Ḥudhayfa," he said, "go and enter amid the people and see what they are doing; and do nothing before coming to us." So I went and entered their midst, and found that the wind and Allah's other hosts had been unleashed upon them, not leaving a single pot, fire or structure of theirs alone. Abū Sufyān stood up and said, "People of Quraysh! Let each of you look to see who your sitting companion is!" I took the hand of the man next to me and said, "Who are you?" He told me his name. Abū Sufyān then said: "People of Quraysh! By Allah, you are not in your place of residence, and the camels and horses are exhausted, and Banū Qurayẓa have betrayed us, and we have heard something about them which displeases us. The wind has assailed us as you have all seen, leaving no pot unturned, no fire burning, and no structure standing. Be gone, then, for I am surely going!" He went to his camel, whose leg was tied, and sat upon it. He then spurred it, and it stood up on three legs; by Allah, he did not even untie the cord binding its leg until it was standing! Had the Messenger of Allah ﷺ not commanded me to do nothing until I came to him, I would have slain him with an arrow. I then returned to the Messenger of Allah ﷺ and found him standing in prayer. I told him what I had seen; and Ghaṭafān heard what Quraysh had done, and they too hurried off home.'

Now this story of our master Ḥudhayfa ibn al-Yamān should not be mistaken for the story of our master al-Zubayr; the latter says that al-Zubayr went to find out if the Banū Qurayẓa had reneged on their pact with the Muslims by agreeing to fight alongside Quraysh against the Muslims. Al-Bukhārī and others narrate, on the authority of Jābir, that the Prophet ﷺ said on the day of the Confederates: 'Who shall bring me news of them?', meaning the Banū Qurayẓa, as al-Wāqidī makes clear. Al-Zubayr said: 'I shall.' He then said again, 'Who shall bring me news of them?' 'I shall', said al-Zubayr. He then said a third time, 'Who shall bring me news of them?' 'I shall', said al-Zubayr. The Prophet ﷺ then said: 'Every prophet has a disciple (*ḥawārī*)[497]: my disciple is al-Zubayr.'

[497] This is the word used in the Qur'ān for the Disciples of Christ ﷺ. It is said to mean 'worthy vicegerent' or 'helper' (*Fatḥ al-Bārī*). [t]

His ﷺ Use of Threats and Fear-Inspiring Warnings to His Enemies Before Meeting Them in Battle

Another example of his ﷺ strategy in this regard was that when he came to Wādī Fāṭima he ordered every Muslim to light a fire so that Quraysh would see them and alarmed by how many there were. They lit ten thousand fires, and when Abū Sufyān saw them, dread gripped his heart and he said, 'What are all these fires, like the fires of ʿArafa?' (It was their custom to light fires on the night of ʿArafa.)

Abū Sufyān and Budayl ibn Warqāʾ had set out that night to conduct reconnaissance; and the sight of the fires had a profound effect on them. They began speaking about it with concern, fear and anxiety; and this was a major reason for Abū Sufyān's eventual response and his request for security from the Messenger of Allah ﷺ for the Meccans.

Another example of his great strategy in battle was his announcement that whoever entered Abū Sufyān's house would be guaranteed safety. This was the height of good strategy and wisdom.

His ﷺ wise strategy was also manifested when he ordered al-ʿAbbās to keep Abū Sufyān at the narrow end of the valley so that he would see Allah's hosts passing before him. As each tribe passed with its banner, Abū Sufyān asked al-ʿAbbās who they were. Al-ʿAbbās later recounted: 'I said, "That is Sulaym", and he said, "What have I to do with Sulaym?" Then another tribe passed and he asked me who they were. I told him it was Muzayna, and he said, "What have I to do with Muzayna?" This went on until all the tribes had gone by; with every tribe that passed, he asked me who they were, and when I told him he said, "What have I to do with them?" And when the Messenger of Allah ﷺ passed by in his green[498] company of the Emigrants and Helpers, of whom only the eyes were visible because of their steel armour, he said: "Glory be to Allah! ʿAbbās, who are they?" I said: "That is the Messenger of Allah ﷺ with

498 They looked green because of their steel armour. [t]

the Emigrants and Helpers." He said: "No one could have any power or might over them!'"

Another example is what he did with the Banū Naḍīr when they locked themselves in their fortresses. He ﷺ laid siege to them and ordered that their date-palms be cut and burned; now he ﷺ only did this to a few of them, and left the rest unharmed. The Qurʾān then condoned his ﷺ action, both the cutting of some and the sparing of the rest, saying: '*Whatever palm-trees you cut down, or left standing upon their roots, that was by Allah's leave*' [59:5].

Part Six

The Perfection of His ﷺ Ethics in Guiding and Teaching the Muslim Community, and His Kindness Towards All of Them Generally, and Towards His Family and Companions Especially

"And had you been harsh and hard-hearted, they would have scattered from about you" [3:159]

The Most Complete Ḥadīth on the Prophetic Character

One of the most complete descriptions we have of the Prophet ﷺ is the ḥadīth that al-Ḥusayn ؓ related from his father ʿAlī ibn Abī Ṭālib ؓ, in which he spoke about many aspects of his ﷺ character. With respect to his ﷺ interactions with others and the way he would behave towards them, ʿAlī ؓ says in this famous ḥadīth:

'His custom regarding the part of his time he devoted to his community was to give preference to the people of distinction, and to divide his time according to their religious merit. Some of them had one need to ask of him, others two, others more; so he would busy himself with them, and would engage them with that which would benefit them, and the whole community,[499] answering their questions, and informing them of what was required of them, saying: "Let he who is witness to this inform those who are absent; and let me know the need of those who are unable to let me know themselves, for he who informs a ruler of the need of those who cannot speak for themselves will have his feet made firm for him by Allah on the Day of Resurrection." Nothing else would be mentioned in his presence, and he would not accept anything else from anyone. People would go to him searching, and would not leave except having been granted a taste[500]; they would go out as guides to the good.'

Al-Ḥusayn ؓ then asked his father about what the Prophet's ﷺ customs were when he was out of the house. ʿAlī ؓ replied: 'The Messenger of Allah ﷺ would hold his tongue, except in regard to matters that

[499] 'He would busy himself with them' means that he would be busy with answering their requests and questions, and meeting their needs; and 'he would engage them' means that he would direct them to those things wherein lay their benefit. What this means is that he ﷺ would not let a single moment pass without giving any benefit to the community; and he would not leave his companions idle, but would engage them with what was good for them, and for the whole community.

[500] This means that people would visit him in search of what would benefit their religious and worldly lives, and ameliorate their souls, and teach them their way to felicity; and by the time they left, they would have been honoured, and their requests granted.

concerned him.[501] He would make people feel comfortable, and would not frighten them off.[502] He would honour the noblemen of every tribe, entrusting their people to them.[503] He would be cautious of people, and be careful around them, without denying any of them his cheery disposition and fine character.[504] He would miss his Companions [in their absence], and ask people about others.[505] He would praise what was good, and support it; and he would condemn what was vile, and deplore it. He was consistent, never contradictory.[506] He was never inattentive, fearing that the people would be become heedless, or distracted. He was prepared for any situation.[507] He never fell short of the truth, nor went beyond it.[508]

'The people who were close to him were the best of people; and the finest of them in his sight were the ones who sincerely advised the most people; and the greatest of them in his sight were the ones who were the most beneficent, and helpful.'

Al-Ḥusayn ☙ then asked his father about the Prophet's ☙ gatherings. 'Alī ☙ replied: 'The Messenger of Allah ☙ would not sit or stand without making mention of Allah ﷻ. He would not reserve places for himself; and he forbade others from doing so. When he came to a gathering of people, he would sit wherever he found a place, and would command

---

[501] So he ☙ would only speak about things that concerned him.

[502] He ☙ would make them comfortable by his kind companionship and pleasant conversation, and would not frighten them off by being coarse, or harsh, or using hurtful words.

[503] That is, he would honour the nobleman of a tribe with the generosity and kind welcome that he was due; and he ☙ would place him in a position of authority over his people, and entrust their affairs to him. This was born of his good judgment and acumen, and his appreciation for status.

[504] That is, he would be cautious around those people who were new to Islam, without testing them with weighty matters; and he would be careful around them, without denying them his kind companionship and pleasant conversation, and his ☙ cheery disposition.

[505] That is, he ☙ would especially miss his companions, and would also ask after the whole community in general. He would ask those people who knew about others, and about what state they were in, whether good or bad, or in comfort or poverty, or ease or hardship, or happiness or grief; and he ☙ would rejoice at what made them rejoice, and grieve over what made them grieve, and would strive to assist them with their problems and misfortunes.

[506] This means that all of his words and deeds ☙ were completely balanced.

[507] For every situation that might arise, he was well prepared; and for every eventuality, he was ready with whatever he needed for it.

[508] So he ☙ was perfectly upright upon the side of truth, neither negligent nor excessive, neither falling short of the truth nor going beyond it; and this was the case for all of his affairs (*Our Master Muḥammad*, Volume 2, p. 41).

others to do the same. He would give everyone he sat with their share of his company, so that no one he sat with would imagine that anyone was dearer to him than them. If anyone sat down with him, or sought his advice in something, he would bear with them patiently, until they were the ones to leave.[509]

'If someone asked him for anything, they would not leave except with either what they asked, or a reassuring word. He accommodated the people with his kindness and good character, and became like a father to them; and before him, they were all equal. His gatherings were gatherings of knowledge, modesty, patience, and security. Voices were not raised therein, nor were honours affronted,[510] nor were any sins reported.[511] The people were equal; they would compete for precedence according to their piety. They were humble, revering the elderly, having mercy on the young. They would put the needy first, and take good care of the stranger.'

Al-Ḥusayn ؇ then asked his father about the Prophet's ﷺ manners with those whom he sat with. 'Alī ؇ replied: "The Messenger of Allah ﷺ was always cheery of disposition, easy-going, and compassionate. He was not boorish, or coarse, or raucous, of vulgar, or critical,[512] or niggardly; he did not over-praise[513] or jest.

'He would ignore that which he disliked.[514] He would not dash the hopes of anyone who hoped for something from him, and they would not be disappointed. He withheld from himself three things: debate, excess, and that which did not concern him; and he withheld from the people three things: he would never criticise or disparage anyone, and he would not

---

[509]   That is, his patience would outlast the one who was sitting with him or seeking his counsel, however long they spoke for; and he ﷺ would never be the first to stand up and leave, or stop the conversation; and he would not reveal to them any sign of boredom or weariness.

[510]   This means that people's honours were not disparaged in his ﷺ gatherings, nor were they exposed to defamation or slander or the like. Rather, his ﷺ gatherings were free of all ugly speech and evil conduct.

[511]   The word here is *falatāt*, which means the errors or sins a person makes. What is meant here is that no sins were committed in his gatherings ﷺ in the first place, since none of those who attended his ﷺ gatherings committed any sins there that could have been disclosed; rather, the gatherings were places of decorum and virtue.

[512]   That is, he ﷺ would not criticise people, animals, or food.

[513]   He did not over-praise the lawful enjoyments of this world.

[514]   He would ignore and pay no mind to any speech or behaviour that he disliked on the part of his companions at the gathering, out of kindness and tenderness for them.

seek to shame anyone, and he would not speak about anything unless he hoped to be rewarded (by Allah) for it. When he spoke, his companions would bow their heads as though upon them were birds; and when he fell silent, they would speak. They would not talk over one another in his presence; they would give their attention to whoever was speaking until he finished, and their discourse in his presence was the discourse of the first of them.[515] He would laugh at what made them laugh, and marvel at what they marvelled at. He would bear the coarse speech and questioning of strangers, so that even his Companions would be keen to bring them to him.[516] He would say: "If you see a person in need, help them." He would never accept praise except that which was appropriate.[517] He would never stop anyone from speaking until they had gone on far too long, in which case he would stop them either with a word, or by standing.'

Another aspect of his ﷺ perfect etiquette in dealing with people is that he would ignore the inane remarks of those who sought to sow discord, and accept their statements at face value, even if they were expressions of their foul intentions and evil desires.

One example of this was the occasion when a group of Jews came to visit the Messenger of Allah ﷺ and greeted him with the words al-sām ʿalaykum ('death be upon you'), to which ʿĀʾisha responded: 'Nay, upon you be death and curse!' The Prophet ﷺ said to her: 'Allah loves gentleness in all things.' 'Did you not hear what they said?', she asked him. He replied: 'I said and upon you.'[518]

He ﷺ knew full well that they said *sām* ('death') instead of *salām* ('peace') deliberately (and on another occasion they said *silām*, which means 'stone'); but he took their words at face value, while preserving the dignity of the Muslims by answering 'and upon you.'

515 That is, the first person to speak at the gathering would be the first to have arrived.

516 That is, the Companions would seek to bring strangers to the Prophet's gatherings ﷺ so that they could benefit from the questions they would ask.

517 That is, praise that was balanced, neither exaggerated nor understated.

518 Muslim.

His ﷺ Kindness to His Family and Relatives

The Prophet ﷺ was a kind companion to his wives and the rest of his family, treating them with benevolence, amiability, love and generosity. He encouraged us to do the same, saying: 'The best of you are the best to their families; and I am the best of you to my family'[519], and 'The believers with the most complete faith are they who have the best characters, and are the kindest to their families.'[520]

Our lady ʿĀʾisha was asked how he ﷺ was when alone with his household, and said: 'He was the mildest of people, smiling and laughing.'[521]

One example of the kind companionship he ﷺ gave his family is found in the words of our lady ʿĀʾisha ﷺ, narrated in the *Ṣaḥīḥ*: 'I was playing with dolls in the Prophet's ﷺ house, along with some playmates of mine. When the Prophet ﷺ came in, they would hide from him in another room, or behind a curtain, and he would send them to me one by one to play with me.'

Al-Ḥāfiẓ Ibn Ḥajar says in *Fatḥ al-Bārī*:

> This ḥadīth is proof that it is permissible to make dolls for girls to play with; this is an exception to the prohibition of making images. This was ʿIyāḍ's opinion, which he attributed to the majority of scholars, saying that they allow for such toys to be sold for girls to teach them, while they are still young, the affairs of the household and children. Some scholars say that this was abrogated.

Aḥmad narrated, on the authority of ʿĀʾisha, that the Prophet ﷺ came to her while she was playing with dolls and a toy horse. He asked her what it was, and she said 'It is the horse of Sulaymān', and he smiled at what she said.[522]

519 Al-Tirmidhī.

520 Al-Tirmidhī.

521 Ibn Saʿd.

522 Imam Aḥmad declared it to be singular (*gharīb*).

The *Ṣaḥīḥ* also relates that the dolls were in ʿĀʾisha's possession when he ﷺ was betrothed to her. Al-Safārīnī quotes Ibn Ḥazm as saying that children alone are permitted to play with images, and no one else, and that aside from this all images are forbidden, even if they are embroidered on cloth.[523]

Another example of the kind companionship he ﷺ gave to his family was the story, related by al-Sāʾib ibn Yazīd, of how a woman came to the Messenger of Allah ﷺ, who said: 'O ʿĀʾisha, do you know her?' 'No, Prophet of Allah', she replied. 'She is a songstress of [such-and-such tribe]. Would you like her to sing for you?' ʿĀʾisha said yes, and the woman sang for her.[524]

Look at this model of prophetic kindness; he ﷺ sent for someone to sing for ʿĀʾisha, doing it for her without her having to ask.

Another example of the kind companionship he ﷺ gave to his family was when he raced with his wife ʿĀʾisha. He raced her once and she beat him; and then after some time had passed he called her to race him again. As our lady ʿĀʾisha tells it, 'I had grown fat and plump by then, and he won the race, and began to laugh, saying, "This [pays you back] for that!"'

He was also at his family's service,[525] helping them with their household tasks. He would also listen to his wives and joke and laugh with them with amiability and kindness. He once listened to a story about ten women who each vowed to tell all about their husbands, each of them describing her husband, both the good and the bad. The one telling this story was his wife, our lady ʿĀʾisha ﷺ, and he listened to her raptly and attentively.[526]

We should not neglect to mention also his ﷺ kindness to his foster-mother Ḥalīma al-Saʿdiyya and her daughter (his sister by nursing) Shaymāʾ. And because of these two, he was generous and kind to the whole Banū Saʿd tribe; thus she was the most blessed woman for her people.

523 Al-Safarānī, *Sharḥ Manẓūmat al-Adab.*

524 Aḥmad, al-Ṭabarānī.

525 Al-Bukhārī.

526 Al-Bukhārī and Muslim. See *Our Master Muḥammad* ﷺ, Volume 1, pp 73-78 for the story.

His ﷺ Kind Way of Conversing With People

The Prophet ﷺ would always listen attentively to those who spoke to him or asked him questions, and would welcome them and treat them kindly.

Anas said: 'I never saw the Prophet ﷺ speak to a man in confidence, then turn his head away from him; the other man would always be the one to turn away first.'[527]

And ʿAmr ibn al-ʿĀṣ said: 'The Messenger of Allah ﷺ would turn his face towards and converse with even the most wicked of people, in order to gain their affection.'[528]

When Greeting People

When he ﷺ greeted someone and shook his hand, he would not let go until the other man let go.[529] He was the cheeriest of people in countenance, and the quickest to smile. When someone approached him, he would welcome them. He once said to ʿAmmār when he approached him: 'Welcome to the good, sweetly-perfumed one!'[530] When his Companions came to sit with him, he would ask after them, saying 'How are you? When the person responded : 'I am well, praise be to Allah!', the Prophet ﷺ would reply: 'May Allah make you well!' When a nobleman or well-respected person came to see him, he would honour them and spread his cloak and robe out for them to sit on. One day Jarīr al-Bajalī came to visit him, but could not find a space because of all the Companions in attendance, and so sat at the door. The Messenger of Allah ﷺ took off his cloak and offered it to him. Jarīr took it, and drew it to his face and began to kiss it, weeping. He tossed it back to the Prophet ﷺ, and said: 'I would never sit on your clothes; may Allah honour you, as you have honoured

527 Abū Dāwūd.

528 Al-Tirmidhī, al-Ṭabarānī.

529 Al-Bazzār, al-Ṭabarānī.

530 Al-Tirmidhī.

me!' The Prophet ﷺ looked right and left, and said: 'If a nobleman comes to you, honour him!'[531]

He ﷺ would also invite elders to speak or ask questions first before the rest of their people, saying: 'Make way for the eldest, make way for the eldest!'

He ﷺ would always extend, to those who sat with him, relaxed and wholesome companionship with both his words and his manner, without stifling them or repressing them. If they spoke about something, he would join them in conversation, as long as it was not of a sinful nature. Khārija ibn Zayd said (quoting his father): 'When we would speak about the life of this world, he would speak about it with us; and when we spoke about the Hereafter, he would speak about it with us; and when we spoke about food, he would speak about it with us.'[532]

Jābir ibn Samura said: '[The Companions] would speak about the time of ignorance, and they would laugh; and he would smile with them.'[533]

He ﷺ would also joke with his Companions to amuse them. One example of this was the occasion when a man came to him to request an animal to ride. He ﷺ said to him: 'I will give you the child of a she-camel.' 'O Messenger of Allah,' the man replied, 'what will I do with the son of a she-camel?' The Prophet ﷺ replied: 'Are camels born of anything but she-camels?'[534]

He ﷺ would also joke with a man from the countryside named Zāhir, saying: 'Zāhir is our countryside, and we are his townsfolk!'[535]

Ibn Bikār narrated, on the authority of Zayd ibn Aslam, that a woman named Umm Ayman al-Ḥabashiyya came to the Messenger of Allah ﷺ, saying: 'My husband invites you.' 'Who is your husband?', he asked. 'Is he the one with the white in his eyes?'

'There is no whiteness in his eyes', she said. 'Indeed, there certainly is whiteness in his eyes', he replied. 'No, by Allah', she said. The Prophet ﷺ said: 'Everyone has whiteness in their eyes!'[536]

Another example was the occasion when an old woman came to the Prophet ﷺ and said: 'O Messenger of Allah, pray for me that I will enter

531 Al-ʿAskarī.

532 Al-Tirmidhī, al-Ṭabarānī.

533 Muslim.

534 Al-Tirmidhī, Abū Dāwūd, Aḥmad.

535 Al-Tirmidhī.

536 I.e. the white of the eye that surrounds the iris. [t]

Paradise.' He replied: 'O mother of so-and-so, no old woman will enter Paradise.' The woman turned to go, weeping, but then the Prophet ﷺ said: 'Tell her that she will not enter Paradise as an old woman, for Allah Almighty says [faithful lovers, equal in age] [56:37].'[537] This means that all in Paradise will be the same age.

He ﷺ would also frequently smile in his Companions' faces when he met them and conversed with them, out of kindness to them and a desire to make them feel comfortable.

Umm al-Dardā' said: 'Abū al-Dardā' would always smile when he spoke, and so I said to him: "Stop, for people say you are a madman!" Abū al-Dardā' said: "I never saw or heard the Messenger of Allah ﷺ speak except that he smiled."'[538] So Abū al-Dardā' would smile when he spoke, following the example of the Messenger of Allah ﷺ.'

A man named ʿAbdallāh but known to the Companions as Ḥimār ('Donkey') used to make the Messenger of Allah ﷺ laugh. He would bring a skin of clarified butter or honey and give it to the Messenger of Allah ﷺ, and then later bring its owner and say, 'Pay him for it!' Our Sheikh, al-Kattāni, mentions in *al-Tarātīb* that his biography is given in *al-Iṣāba*, as is the biography of Suwaybiṭ ibn Harmala al-ʿAbdarī, who also got up to many acts of tomfoolery, one of which made the Prophet ﷺ and his Companions laugh for a whole year.[539]

Another example of the kind companionship he ﷺ gave his Companions was the occasion when the Abyssinians came and played with their spears in the mosque, and the Chosen Prophet ﷺ brought ʿĀ'isha to watch them, leaning on his shoulder.[540] One narration has it that the Abyssinians were dancing and saying, 'Muḥammad is a righteous man!'[541]

It is also confirmed that one of the great Companions danced before the Prophet ﷺ as he looked on. Ibn Saʿd reports that the Prophet ﷺ said to Jaʿfar: 'You resemble me both in appearance and in character.' Upon this, Jaʿfar stood and danced in a circle around the Messenger of Allah ﷺ. Another narration has it that he ﷺ said to ʿAlī: 'You are of me and I am of you', and said to Zayd: 'You are our brother and our liege.' All three

537 Al-Tirmidhī.

538 Aḥmad.

539 See *Our Master Muḥammad* ﷺ, Volume 1, pp 193-194.

540 Al-Bukhārī.

541 Aḥmad.

of them then stood and danced around him and before him.[542] A version narrated by Abū Dāwūd states that Jaʿfar and Zayd stood and danced; al-ʿIrāqī said that this narration is sound, and al-Ḥāfiẓ al-Suyūṭī said: 'This was because of the ecstasy he felt upon hearing those words; and the Prophet ﷺ did not rebuke him.'

Furthermore, al-Bayhaqī narrated, on the authority of al-Muṭṭalib ibn ʿAbdallāh, that the Messenger of Allah ﷺ said: 'Sport and play, for I hate to see any harshness in your religion.'

Al-Ḥākim narrated on the authority of ʿĀʾisha that he ﷺ said: 'Have you any amusements [*lahw*]? For the Helpers love amusement.' This is evidence that the soul may be given recreation when it is bored, and polished when it is rusty, by lawful means of amusement and play. For the most part, the Prophet's ﷺ laugh was no more than a smile.

He would also be kind to children, greeting them and patting their heads.[543] He would sometimes line up ʿAbdallāh, ʿUbaydallāh, and several of the children of al-ʿAbbās, and then say: 'Whoever reaches me first will win [such-and-such].' They would then race to him, and jump on his ﷺ back and chest, and he would hug and kiss them.[544]

And when he returned from a journey, the children of his household would joyfully rush out to meet him because they knew of his kindness and compassion. He would sit one of them in front of him on his horse, and another behind him ﷺ.

He ﷺ was the most dignified, well-mannered and noble of people. Khārija ibn Zayd said: 'The Messenger of Allah ﷺ was the most dignified person in any gathering he attended; he showed almost nothing of himself.'[545] This means that he ﷺ would not expel anything from his nose or mouth, or cut his nails.

WHEN INTERACTING WITH PEOPLE

He ﷺ would always repay a kindness with a greater kindness. He served the delegation of the Negus himself when they came to him. His Companions said to him: 'We will suffice you', that is, we will accommodate them and serve them for you. He ﷺ said: 'They were generous to our

542 See al-ʿIrāqī's *Takhrīj al-Iḥyāʾ*.
543 Ibn Ḥibbān.
544 Aḥmad.
545 Abū Dāwūd.

companions, and I would like to repay them.'[546]

He ﷺ would never let a good turn go unrewarded, nor deny the favour and kindness that anyone did for him; rather, he would remind them of it and repay it with something even better. He honoured the whole tribe of Hawāzin and pardoned them because of how one of them had nursed him; and he honoured his sister-by-nursing Shaymāʾ bint Ḥalīma when she came to him, because of how her mother had done him the kindness of nursing him.

He would also honour the friends and relations of his wife Khadīja because of her goodness and favour, which he never forgot. Indeed, he would show gratitude for things far lesser than that. Abū Ayyūb once saw a feather in his ﷺ beard and quickly took it out, whereupon he ﷺ said to him: 'May Allah remove from you all that you dislike.'[547] ʿAmr ibn Akhṭab al-Anṣārī saw a hair in the vessel from which the Prophet ﷺ was drinking, and quickly took it out, whereupon the Prophet ﷺ said, 'Allah, make him beautiful!' The narrator said that in later years he saw ʿAmr at the age of ninety, and there was not a single white hair in his beard.[548]

And at the Battle of Badr, he ﷺ forbade that Abū al-Bakhtarī ibn Hishām be slain, in return for the generosity he had shown the Muslims in Mecca, and how he had defended the Messenger of Allah ﷺ and refused to persecute him; indeed, he even sent a great deal of food to the Banū Hāshim during the boycott; and when Abū Jahl rebuked him for this, Abū Sufyān said, 'Leave him alone; he is but a noble man who looks after his family ties.' And he had striven to annul the hostile document which Quraysh had written against the Prophet ﷺ.

He ﷺ would also miss his Companions; and we have seen in the ḥadīth of Hind ibn Abī Hāla[549] that ʿAlī said: 'He ﷺ would miss his companions, and ask people about others...'' meaning that he ﷺ would ask after them when they were absent from him.

Anas also said: 'If the Prophet ﷺ missed a man from amongst his brethren for three days, he would ask after him. If he was away, he would pray for him; and if he was in town, he would go to him; and if he was sick, he would visit him.'[550]

546 Al-Bayhaqī.

547 Al-Ṭabarānī.

548 Aḥmad, al-Ṭabarānī.

549 That is, the one above in which al-Ḥusayn ﷺ asks ʿAlī ﷺ to describe the Prophet ﷺ. [t]

550 Abū Yaʿlā.

He ﷺ would visit his companions in order to honour them and make them happy. He ﷺ would often visit the Helpers,[551] and would sometimes pray in the houses of those he visited,[552] in order to pass on his blessing (*baraka*) to them, and so they could seek blessings from the place where he prayed.

He would also visit weak and sick Muslims, and attend their funerals,[553] cheering them up so that they would be set at ease and forget their poverty and their worries. He would say to them, 'Rejoice, poor folk of the Emigrants, in the perfect light that shall be yours on Day of Resurrection: you shall enter Paradise half a day before the rich – and that means five hundred years!'

In his dealings with people he ﷺ would be extremely modest and humble, broad-hearted, forbearing and generous, forgiving and merciful, and more patient than even the most patient of people. He was the most just of Allah's creatures in upholding the rights of Allah and rights of mankind. He preserved bonds of love, maintained covenants, and kept promises, even if it was difficult for him to do so. He withstood the boorishness of Bedouins and treated them kindly, meeting their harshness with sweet-natured speech and conduct.

The way he ﷺ interacted and dealt with his Companions gave them complete self-esteem and confidence in themselves; he did this by seeking their counsel. He encouraged us to follow this lofty principle by saying: 'He whose counsel is sought is in a position of trust'[554], and saying: 'He who seeks [Allah's] aid in decisions will not be disappointed; and he who seeks [people's] advice will not feel regret.'[555]

Abū Hurayra said: 'I have never seen anyone seek counsel from his companions more than the Prophet ﷺ did.'

The Prophet ﷺ sought counsel from his Companions on many occasions, including at the Battle of Badr when they faced Quraysh. One example was how he ﷺ sought their counsel at Badr about where they should make camp. He also sought their counsel at Uḥud about whether they should set out or remain where they were; most of them said they should set out, so they did. He also sought their counsel about the truce

551 Aḥmad, al-Tirmidhī.

552 Al-Bukhārī (*al-Adab al-Mufrad*).

553 Abū Yaʿlā, al-Ḥākim.

554 Aḥmad, with variants in the *Sunan*.

555 Al-Ṭabarānī.

on the day of the Trench. And on the occasion of the Lie (*al-Ifk*), he said to them: 'Give me your counsel.' When they gave him good counsel, he took it and acted upon it, and announced that it was correct and good, to honour the one who gave it and encourage him, and to give esteem to the opinion he had reached, based on his experience.

The Way He ﷺ Set Minds at Ease

One aspect of his ﷺ perfect etiquette in interacting with people was how he set their minds at ease and made them feel comfortable.

There are many famous accounts of this, including his ﷺ words, as narrated by al-Bukhārī on the authority of Abū Hurayra: 'Were it not for the Emigration, I would be a man of the Helpers.'

This means 'I would ascribe myself to their hometown, Medina'; or 'I would call myself after their name and ascribe myself to them', according to the way the Arabs would swear oaths of ascription; but the special distinction of the Emigration had already come to pass and prevented this from every happening, because it was too noble and lofty to be replaced by anything else. It is clear, then, that his ﷺ reason for saying this was to please them and make them feel comfortable, to praise them for their piety, and to set their minds at ease. He did not mean to suggest that he was renouncing the lineage of his forefathers, for this is clearly forbidden – especially since he ﷺ already had the most noble of all lineages.

Another instance of this was how he ﷺ addressed the Helpers after having given battle-spoils to others but not them, speaking to them words that set their minds at ease and gave them great and immeasurable joy. He said: 'Are you not content that they go home with their spoils, whilst you go home with the Messenger of Allah? Verily, were the Helpers to go one way, I would follow them down the way they took.'[556]

Another instance of this was his words to a man of the Helpers who asked the Prophet ﷺ to place him in a position of authority, but was not granted that. The Prophet said to him: 'You shall encounter [a time of] nepotism[557] after me; so be patient, until you meet me at the Pool.'[558]

Another example of this was how when the Prophet ﷺ entered Mecca to make the lesser pilgrimage which had been delayed before, Ḥamza's

[556] Al-Bukhārī.

[557] The man thought that perhaps he was more suited to the role he sought than the one to whom it was assigned; the Prophet ﷺ therefore assured him that no such preferential treatment would be given in his time.

[558] Al-Bukhārī.

daughter followed them calling, 'Uncle! Uncle!' 'Alī ؓ took her hand and said to Fāṭima ؓ: 'Here is your uncle's daughter; carry her.' 'Alī, Zayd and Jaʿfar then began to argue over her. 'Alī said: 'I deserve her the most, for she is my uncle's daughter.' Jaʿfar said: 'She is the daughter of my uncle; and her maternal aunt is my wife.' Zayd said: 'She is my brother's daughter.' The Prophet ﷺ gave her over to her maternal aunt, saying: 'The maternal aunt is like the mother.' To 'Alī, he said: 'You are from me, and I am from you.' To Jaʿfar, he said: 'You resemble me in appearance and character.' And to Zayd, he said: 'You are our brother and our freedman.'[559] Thus he ruled in favour of Jaʿfar, and spoke words to please the other two men as well.

Other narrations of this incident indicate that it was something else which prompted these words. Usāma ibn Zayd reported (as his son relates) that 'Alī, Jaʿfar and Zayd ibn Ḥaritha gathered together, and Jaʿfar said: 'I am the most beloved of us to the Messenger of Allah ﷺ.' 'Alī said: 'I am the most beloved of us to the Messenger of Allah ﷺ', and Zayd too said: 'I am the most beloved of us to the Messenger of Allah ﷺ.' 'Let us go to the Messenger of Allah ﷺ and ask him', they said. Usāma said: 'They came and asked leave to see him, and he said, "Go out and see who is there." I told him that it was Jaʿfar, 'Alī and Zayd. (I didn't say 'my father.'[560]) He told me to let them in, so they came in and said, "O Messenger of Allah, whom do you love the most?" "Fāṭima", he said. "We mean of all men", they said. He replied: "As for you, Jaʿfar, my appearance resembles yours, and your character resembles mine; and you are from me and my family tree. And as for you, 'Alī, you are my son-in-law and the father of my son[561]; and I am from you and you are from me. And as for you, Zayd, you are my freedman, and are from me and to me, and the most beloved of people to me."'[562] See, then, how he ﷺ set each of their minds at ease, and made them all happy.

Another example of this was his ﷺ words: 'Salmān is from us, the People of the Household.'[563]

---

559   Al-Bukhārī.

560   Usāma makes a point here to say that he didn't say 'my father is here', but rather named his father as Zayd. [t]

561   I.e.my grandchild. [t]

562   Aḥmad, al-Ḥākim.

563   Al-Ṭabarānī, al-Ḥākim.

His ﷺ Excellent Way of Rebuking and Censuring

Rebuking is a form of discipline and refinement, and the Prophet ﷺ would make use of it when it was needed, as a means of educating or alerting. But he ﷺ would use different methods and forms of rebuke according to circumstance and necessity; sometimes he would rebuke with a gesture, other times with an elliptical expression, and other times with a direct expression; or he might do so by turning away, or ostracising; and sometimes he would do so by the traces of anger which showed on his blessed face.

An example of this was the occasion when he ﷺ saw ʿAbdallāh ibn ʿUmar wearing two robes died with safflower; and since that was forbidden, he ﷺ said to him: 'Did your mother tell you to wear that?'[564] He ﷺ went no further with his rebuke than this, because it was enough to set the matter straight and make clear what was right; and therefore the authentic narration tells us that as soon as Ibn ʿUmar got home, he burned the clothes.

Sometimes he ﷺ would use sterner rebukes; not because the person being rebuked needed it, or could not get the message without sternness, but rather in order to convey another important teaching. An example of this was the occasion when Muʿādh ibn Jabal ؓ led his people in prayer in the mosque and made the prayer very long, so that a person in the congregation who had a pressing need was forced to curtail his prayer and leave. When Muʿādh heard of this, he called the man a hypocrite – and at that time, of course, such a word was extremely serious, because it meant unbelief. The man therefore came forward in a state of some agitation and worry, and complained about Muʿādh's lengthening of the prayer and his subsequent charge of hypocrisy. Upon hearing this, the Prophet ﷺ rebuked Muʿādh firmly, saying: 'Are you a mischief-monger, Muʿādh? Are you a mischief-monger, Muʿādh? Are you a mischief-monger, Muʿādh?' He did this to set the man's mind at ease and to show due concern for

[564] Muslim.

his complaint; for otherwise, the issue of lengthening the prayer required nothing more than a simple announcement that the imam should make the prayer light, especially since Muʿādh was one of the most well-versed people in the Shariah.

Another example of this was how he ﷺ firmly rebuked Abū Dharr ﵁: Abū Dharr said to his slave, 'You son of a black woman!' The slave complained of this to the Prophet ﷺ, who said to Abū Dharr: 'You are a man in whom there is a remnant of pagan ignorance! Did you insult him by reviling his mother?' This was a stern rebuke for Abū Dharr, and something less might have been sufficient; but the Prophet ﷺ took into consideration the state of the servant who had made the complaint, who had found refuge in the bosom of Islam, which does not distinguish between colours and races. Therefore he ﷺ wanted to set his mind at ease and satisfy him, and let him know that he was concerned about his situation and his complaint.

Sometimes he ﷺ would use prison as a means of correction. The Prophet ﷺ did not have a custom-built jail for that function, nor did Abū Bakr ﵁ during his rule; at that time, prison meant simply to restrain an individual so he could not move about freely, whether in a house or a mosque. Abū Dāwūd narrates that the Prophet ﷺ once imprisoned a man after a charge was brought against him; and it is narrated in the *Ṣaḥīḥ* that he ﷺ imprisoned Thumāma ibn Uthāl by binding him to a pillar of the mosque. The *Sīra Ḥalabiyya* also narrates that he ﷺ imprisoned the Banū Qurayẓa in Medina in the house of Bint al-Ḥāritha, a woman of the Helpers, before having them executed.

Sometimes the one who brought the charge, or his agent, would be made responsible for imprisoning the guilty party himself. Abū Dāwūd and Ibn Mājah narrated, on the authority of al-Harmās ibn Ḥabīb, that his grandfather[565] said: 'I took a debtor of mine to the Prophet ﷺ. He told me to take hold of him, and then said to me, "O brother of the Banū Tamīm, what do you wish to do with your prisoner?"' This remained the mode of imprisonment during the time of the Messenger of Allah ﷺ and Abū Bakr; then ʿUmar ﵁ bought a house in Medina and made it a jail.[566]

Another means of correction he ﷺ would employ was scourging: he

565 The original has 'his father'; the correction is from Abū Dāwūd, Ibn Mājah, al-Bayhaqī, and al-Ṭabarānī. [t]

566 See Suyūṭī, *Tārīkh al-Khulafāʾ*, chapter on ʿUmar ﵁.

scourged someone for murdering their slave,[567] and scourged Misṭaḥ ibn Uthātha and those who spread rumours about the Lie [*al-Ifk*]; and the story of this is well-known.[568]

Another means of correction he ﷺ employed was banishment. It is established that he banished al-Ḥakam ibn Abī al-ʿĀṣ to Ṭāʾif[569]. And he commanded it, saying: 'An unmarried fornicator receives one hundred lashes and a year's banishment.'[570] He also sentenced a hired hand who fornicated to lashes and a year's banishment, and gave the same sentence to the hermaphrodite who would visit women illicitly.

Another means of correction he ﷺ employed was ostracising, as occurred in the story of Kaʿb ibn Mālik, one of the three who refused to go out to the Battle of Tabūk,[571] in return for which the Prophet ﷺ ostracised them and refused to speak to them, and commanded everyone else to do the same.

They suffered so sorely on account of being ostracised by the Chosen Prophet ﷺ and his Companions that, as the Qurʾān says of them: '*The earth for all its vastness was straitened for them, and their souls were straitened, and they thought that there was no refuge from Allah except in Him*' [9:118].

The Almighty's words 'for all its vastness' meant that despite the vastness of the earth, they could find no place where they felt at ease because of their worry and woe; this illustrates their utter desperation. Even their own souls and hearts were straitened with misery and loneliness because of their delayed repentance, so that they had no room for any joy or solace.

In Kaʿb's own words: 'This went on until the world I knew was unrecognisable to me, not the same thing I had known before.' (Another narration has it that he said: '...the very walls became unrecognisable to us, and not the same walls we had known before.') This is how the one who is miserable and depressed come to see all things, until finally he even sees himself that way. Another narration has it that he said: 'This went on until [we] were utterly cowed, and had become like monks.'

He ﷺ also punished certain people by ordering that their hands and feet be amputated and their eyes branded. This occurred in the famous

567 See Ibn al-Ṭallāʿ, *Aqḍiyat al-Rasūl* ﷺ.

568 See *al-Iṣāba* and *al-Istīʿāb*.

569 See *al-Iṣāba* and *al-Istīʿāb*.

570 Muslim.

571 The other two being Hilāl ibn Umayya and Mirāra ibn al-Rabīʿ.

and authentic story of the men of ʿUrayna, narrated by al-Bukhārī on the authority of Anas, who said: 'Some men came from ʿUkl and ʿUrayna but did not get on well with the climate of Medina. The Messenger ﷺ commanded them to go out and join the camel-herd and drink their urine and milk.[572] They went out, and when they became well they murdered the Prophet's ﷺ camel-herder and drove the camels away. News of this came at the start of the day, so we set out after them, and they were caught before midday. He commanded that their hands and feet be cut off and their eyes branded, and that they be sent out into the stony, barren land, to vainly seek water.' (One narration adds 'until they died.') According to Ibn Abī ʿAwwāna, on the authority of ʿAqīl, who heard it from Anas, two of them were crucified, two had their hands and feet amputated, and two had their eyes branded. If this is authentic, it means that their punishments were diverse.

Muslim narrated that Anas said: 'The Prophet ﷺ only branded their eyes because they had branded the eyes of the camel-herder.' Al-Bukhārī also alludes to this narration.[573]

It is also related that the Prophet killed one person in battle with his own blessed hand; it was Ubayy ibn Khalaf. What happened was that the Prophet ﷺ took a spear from the hand of al-Ḥārith ibn al-Simma and thrust Ubayy in the neck with a thrust that made him sway atop his horse several times, and broke one of his ribs, resulting in his death. Al-Ḥāfiẓ al-Bābilī relates in his *Sīra* that this was the only occasion when the Prophet ﷺ killed someone with his own hand.[574]

He ﷺ also punished by means of burning and demolition of property: Ibn Hishām narrates, on the authority of ʿAbdallāh ibn Ḥātim, who heard it from his father, that the Messenger of Allah ﷺ was told that some of the hypocrites were gathering in the house of Suwaylim the Jew and urging people not to go out to Tabūk. The Prophet ﷺ therefore sent Ṭalḥa ibn ʿAbdallāh with a group of men and commanded them to burn down Suwaylim's house, which they did.

And during the expedition of Tabūk, he ﷺ was inspired with news of the 'Mosque of Discord' [*Masjid al-Ḍirār*],[575] and so sent a group of his Companions to demolish it and burn it down. He sent for Mālik ibn al-

572 As medicine. [t]

573 *Kitāb al-Jihād, Bāb idhā aḥraq al-mushrik*[u] *al-muslim*[a] *hal yuḥraq.*

574 Al-Zurqānī, *al-Mawāhib.*

575 Built by the hypocrites to use as a base for spreading discord among the Muslims. [t]

Dakhsham and Maʿn ibn ʿUdayy al-ʿAjlānī and said: 'Go to this mosque, established by wicked men, and demolish it and burn it.' They set off and did as they were bid.

The Prophet ﷺ also cut down and burned some of the date palms of the Banū Naḍīr.

The Perfect Education He ﷺ Gave the Muslim Community, and His Devotion to Teaching the Qurʾān

The Prophet ﷺ was intensely devoted to the teaching of the Qurʾān, especially in the case of young children. There is no doubt that there is a great benefit in this, which is that children are guided to the belief that Allah is their Lord, and that this is His Speech; and so that the spirit of the Qurʾān pervades their hearts, and its light penetrates their thoughts, perceptions and senses; and so that the child is taught the doctrines of the Qurʾān from an early age, and grows up with love for the Qurʾān, attachment to it, and deference to its commandments and prohibitions, imbibing its ethics and following its guidance.

For this reason, the parents and guardians of the Muslim community have always been careful to teach the Qurʾān to their children; and this is one of the foundations of Islam, ensuring that they retain their primordial nature as they grow up, and that the lights of wisdom reach their hearts before caprice can get to them and overwhelm them with sin and error. A poet said of this:

Passion for it came to me ere I knew what passion was,
And thus it entered an empty heart, and settled there.

He ﷺ would also stipulate that delegations of Arabs who came to embrace Islam must have the Qurʾān read to them and the religion taught to them, and appoint people to make the call to prayer for them.

The Companions ﷺ and the righteous early Muslims who came after them taught the Qurʾān to their children just as the Chosen Prophet ﷺ had, in perfect obedience to his instructions; in doing so, they sincerely vied with one another to attain unto the goodness and blessings that he

ﷺ guaranteed, by Allah's leave, to those who do so, saying: 'Whosoever teaches his child the Qur'ān by sight[576] will be forgiven; and whosoever teaches it to him from memory will be resurrected by Allah in a form as radiant as the moon when it is full, and it will be said to his child: "Recite", and every time he recites a verse, Allah ﷻ will raise the father a degree, until he has finished reciting all the Qur'ān he has.'[577]

Al-Ṭabaranī narrated, on the authority of Abū Hurayra, that he ﷺ also said: 'Every father who teaches his child the Qur'ān in this world will be crowned on the Day of Resurrection with a crown in Paradise, by which the people of Paradise will know him as one who taught the Qur'ān to his child in this world.' Imam Aḥmad's narration adds: '[The child's] parents will be dressed in two robes more valuable than this whole world, and they will say: "How have we come to be wearing these?" It will be said: "By the Qur'ān your child learned."' (Al-Ṭabarānī's narration has it: 'By teaching your child.')

Ibn Khaldūn says in his *Muqaddima*, on the subject of the virtue of teaching children:

> Be aware that teaching children the Qur'ān is an essential part of the religion, which has been adopted and continued by its adherents in every corner of the Muslim world. This is because it ensures that the first claim to hearts is staked by the firm faith and doctrine the verses of the Qur'ān impart. Thus the Qur'ān has become the foundation of teaching upon which all the rest of education is built ... Islamic custom has always been to begin education with the study of the Qur'ān, in order to obtain blessing, and to protect the child from the lunacies and perils of youth by ensuring that the Qur'ān reaches him before they do.

The Holy Qur'ān is the broadest treasury of knowledge for humanity, and the Book that '*falsehood cannot approach, neither from the front nor the rear; it is a Revelation from one Wise and All-Praiseworthy*' [41:42]. It is the mighty tome from which the community of Islam have derived and drawn all manner of sciences, as Allah says: '*We have neglected nothing in the Book*' [6:38]; and He says: '*And We have sent down on you the Book,*

[576] I.e., from a written page. [t]

[577] Al-Ṭabarānī (the author points out here that al-Haythamī declared the chain of narration to contain narrators unknown to him). [t]

making clear all things' [16:89]. And the Prophet ﷺ said: 'There shall be manifold civil strife.' 'What is the way out of them, O Messenger of Allah?', they asked. 'The Book of Allah,' he said, 'in which there are tidings of what will come after you, and news of what came before you, and a verdict on what is now with you.'[578]

Indeed, it is the first encyclopaedia known to humanity, by its own attestation.

Now the first people to study at the school of the Qurʾān, to be educated by its guidance and guided by its education, and to base their way of life upon it, were the noble Companions, who were eager to study and teach the Qurʾān in obedience to the Prophet's ﷺ words: 'Learn the Qurʾān and read it; for the Qurʾān shall be, for the one who learns it, reads it and prays with it [by night], like a pouch filled with musk whose fragrance floats everywhere'[579], and his ﷺ words: 'The best of you is he who studies the Qurʾān and teaches it.'[580]

The Prophet ﷺ would teach them, alongside the Qurʾān itself, the proper etiquette of those who memorise the Holy Qurʾān, so that they would know its right over them and respect and honour it. He would say to them: 'He who reads the Qurʾān thereby draws prophethood in between his two sides, although no revelation comes to him. It does not befit the one who possesses the Qurʾān to speak words of anger with the angry, nor words of ignorance with the ignorant, whilst the Word of Allah is in his breast.'[581]

578 Al-Tirmidhī.

579 Al-Tirmidhī, Ibn Mājah.

580 Al-Bukhārī.

581 Al-Ḥākim.

Exegesis of Qur'ān

Another subject given special attention in the prophetic circles of knowledge was the exegesis of Allah's Mighty Book. The chosen Prophet ﷺ would give them his own exegesis of certain Qur'ānic verses; and he said to them: 'Never do people gather in one of Allah's houses, studying the Book of Allah and reciting it to one another, save that great inner peace (*sakīna*) descends upon them, mercy enfolds them, the angels surround them, and Allah mentions them to those who are with Him.'[582]

Al-Qārī says in *Sharḥ al-Miskāh*: '"Reciting it to one another" means reading it to one another to correct (their memorisation of) its words, or to discover its meanings.'

Al-Suyūṭī asserts in *al-Itqān* that the Prophet ﷺ explained all of the Qur'ān to his Companions, or most of it. This is supported by the ḥadīth narrated by Aḥmad and Ibn Mājah stating that one of the final verses to be revealed was the verse pertaining to indirect heirs [4:176], and that the Messenger of Allah ﷺ passed away before he had explained it. This implies that he ﷺ *did* explain to them everything else that was revealed, but did not explain this verse to them because he passed away so soon after it was revealed. Otherwise, there would have been no reason to say this about this one verse.

As for the ḥadīth narrated by al-Bazzār in which ʿĀ'isha said: 'The Messenger of Allah ﷺ never explained any of the Qur'ān except for a few verses Jibrīl taught him', it is *munkar*[583] according to al-Ḥāfiẓ Ibn Kathīr. Ibn Jarīr and others interpreted it to mean that she was referring to verses which he was uncertain of, and so asked Allah about, who sent their explanations to him on the tongue of Jibrīl.

582 Muslim. This is a reference to the *malā'ika muqarrabūn*, those angels nearest the Throne: '*Those who bear the Throne and those around it hymn the praises of their Lord, believe in Him, and pray forgiveness for those who believe: 'Our Lord! Your Reach is over all things in mercy and knowledge. Forgive, then, those who turn in repentance and follow Your path, and preserve them from the torment of the Fire!*" [40:07] [t]

583 A *munkar* ḥadīth is one with a weak chain whose content is contradicted by a ḥadīth with a stronger chain. [t]

History and Tales of Old

Another subject to which the Prophet ﷺ gave special attention, and taught to his Companions, was that of historical events and the stories of the communities of old; and he devoted time to the study of this field, in obedience to Allah's words: '*Remind them of the Days of Allah*' [14:5]. That is, remind them of the events Allah destined for the communities of old, that they may follow the path of those who are guided. History is the search for the roots of bygone communities and the discovery of their identities, stories, knowledge, vestiges, customs, rises and falls; and it is something that intellectuals compete in, and kings take pride in, and all people aspire to know.

Allah Almighty told us, in the Qur'ān, about what happened between the prophets and their communities, and guided us to recognise the successive cycles of time, change, expansion, contraction, prosperity and destruction.

Now he ﷺ would devote certain times to teaching: either every day (without being too strenuous), or every other day (one day to relax so that the next day can be approached with vigour), or once a week on Fridays. This differs according to circumstances and individuals; it is determined by need, along with a careful appraisal of people's enthusiasm.[584]

This Muḥammadan Sunna is the best way to encourage people to attend circles of knowledge and learning, and inspire them to come with a thirst for knowledge and an attachment to it.

584 *Fatḥ al-Bārī.*

Literacy

LITERACY WAS another field given special attention in the noble prophetic era. ʿAbdallāh ibn Saʿīd ibn al-ʿĀṣ taught people to write in Medina, on the instructions of the Messenger of Allah ﷺ.[585]

ʿUbāda ibn al-Ṣāmit said: 'I taught some of the People of the Ledge [*Ahl al-Ṣuffa*][586] how to write the Qurʾān.'[587]

Abū al-Wafāʾ Naṣr al-Hawarīnī al-Maṣrī said in *al-Maṭāliʿ al-Naṣriyya*:

> Arabic writing did not become prevalent until over a year after the prophetic Emigration. This was because when the Helpers captured over seventy of the leaders of Quraysh, as well as more of the commoners, at the Battle of Badr in the second year after the Emigration, they set a sum of money for the ransom of each captive; and each one of those who could not pay was told instead to teach one of the children of Medina to write, and would not be freed until he had done so. In that way, writing became prevalent, and began to spread to every area Islam conquered.
>
> It is further related in the *Sīra* literature that each one of these idolaters would teach ten boys to write, and then be allowed to go his way.

585 *Al-Istīʿāb.*

586 The *Ṣuffa* was a ledge in the back of the Prophet's ﷺ Mosque which, on the instruction of the Prophet ﷺ, was covered with palm fronds and prepared so that estranged people who had no homes of families could stay there and dedicate themselves to worship. [t]

587 Abū Dāwūd.

His ﷺ Method of Teaching

The Prophet ﷺ followed, in his way of teaching people and inviting them to goodness, the way of the Holy Qurʾān, in which Allah says: *'Call you to the way of your Lord with wisdom and beautiful counsel, and dispute with them in the better way. Surely your Lord knows very well those who have gone astray from His way, and He knows very well those who are guided'* [16:125].

This holy verse gives us a perfect picture of the manifold forms of invitation which must be extended to different kinds of people; and the sound guidance the verse lays out applies to all kinds of people, its manifested form differing according to their different attributes and types. Among the different types of people are: the elite who seek knowledge of higher realities, the masses of ordinary people, and the stubborn opponents.

For each of these types of people, there is a specific way of speaking to them, calling them and teaching them. He ﷺ would speak to people on the level of their intelligence, and his words would always be appropriate to the situation. He would use with each group the discourse that suited them, and address them in their own language.

Allah ﷻ gifted His Prophet ﷺ with a mighty and awe-inspiring presence, and made his words easy for people's hearts to love and accept, so that he needed nothing more.

Al-Qāḍī ʿIyāḍ said:

> Allah ﷻ cast love into his ﷺ speech and enveloped it with acceptance, and combined for him both awesomeness and sweetness. He never needed to repeat himself, and those who heard his speech never had to ask him to repeat it. He never spoke a word out of place, nor made a slip, nor found himself lost for words.[588]

If we consider these three kinds of people, we find that this verse devotes a unique approach to each of them.

[588] *Al-Shifā*.

The first group, the intellectual elite, should be called and taught with wisdom; that is, with wisely-weighted words and plain evidence of the truth that leave no room for doubt. This is because they cannot be convinced by anything but plain evidence that removes all their suspicions, and wise words that guide them to the way of their Lord.

The second group, the masses of ordinary people, should be called and taught with beautiful counsel; that is, with convincing speech and beneficial expressions in such a way that they can see without doubt that the one speaking to them is sincere and wants what is best for them. They do not need discourse that is especially wisely-weighted, because they are ordinary people, not intellectuals; and they do not need proofs, because they have no suspicions that need righting.

The third group, the stubborn opponents, should be called and taught by means of debate according to the best way, which is the way of gentleness, ease and the use of well-known preambles, so that their rage is abated and the fire in their breasts is extinguished, and they can then return to the way of Allah.

The Messenger of Allah ﷺ would also impart teachings to the Muslims by using a question one of them asked him, which he would then answer for the benefit of all. One example of this is the ḥadīth about righteousness and wickedness. Al-Nawās ibn Samʿān ﷺ said: 'I asked the Messenger of Allah ﷺ about righteousness and wickedness, and he said: "Righteousness is good character, and wickedness is what puts unrest in your heart, and what you would hate for others to discover.'[589] In the same way, women would often come and ask the Messenger of Allah ﷺ questions, and he would answer them.

Thus you can see that the prophetic method of teaching emphasises, in its wise ways, the importance of teaching women as well as men. This shows that Islam encourages that women be nurtured, refined and cultured with a proper religious education to help them to uphold its message.

The Prophet ﷺ would also teach the Muslims by posing questions – not to learn the answers from anyone, but to rouse their interest and inspire in their hearts and minds a desire to discover the truth of the matter at hand, and cause them to recognise its importance.

Muʿādh ibn Jabal ﷺ reported that the Messenger of Allah ﷺ said: 'Shall

589 Muslim.

I not tell you the head of the matter, and its pillar, and its peak?' 'Indeed tell me, O Messenger of Allah', said Muʿādh. He said: 'The head of the matter is Islam, its pillar is prayer, and its peak is struggle.'

This method of teaching which the Prophet ﷺ employed is distinguished by the way it inspired interest in this noble Companion, and pointed to the foundations of happiness in this life and the next: Islam, prayer, and struggle. We can observe that this method of teaching – by asking questions – had been adopted by educators, who present scientific concepts in the form of questions and then provide the answers for them.

He ﷺ would also pose questions for which he did not provide answers, in order to test the knowledge and intelligence of his Companions.

Ibn ʿUmar ﷺ reported that the Messenger of Allah ﷺ said: 'There is a tree whose leaves never fall, and which is like the believer. Can you tell me what it is?' The people began to call out the names of trees of the countryside; 'and it occurred to me,' said Ibn ʿUmar, 'that it was the date-palm, but I was too shy to say it.' Finally, they asked the Messenger of Allah ﷺ to tell them what it was, and he said: 'It is the date-palm.'

Sometimes he ﷺ would be concerned that if he continued to pose questions and teach his Companions, they would become bored or tired. In such instances, he would give them the opportunity to rest and take some time to gather their thoughts until their interest returned, so that the information they had already gathered would take root and be absorbed by their long-term memories. Modern educational institutions are indebted to this rightly-guided way of teaching, since they have ultimately derived their successful systems from this wise prophetic method.

Ibn Masʿūd said: 'The Prophet ﷺ would withhold his counsel from us some days, disliking that we might become bored.'

It was also part of his ﷺ wise method to speak to people on the level of their intelligence and in a way that suited their mental faculties, their natures and their customs; and he would impart his goodly counsel with a spirit of tolerance and ease.

He ﷺ would also speak to people in their own dialects. ʿĀṣim al-Ashʿarī said: 'I heard the Messenger of Allah ﷺ say *laysa min am-birr am-ṣiyām fim-safar*'[590] in the dialect of the Ashʿarī clan, whose definite article was

[590] 'It is not righteous to fast when travelling.' Usually it would be *laysa min al-birr al-ṣiyām fil-safar.* [t]

am instead of the usual *al*.

And in order to emphasise these teachings, he would often repeat what he said three times to make sure it was understood.

In all the commandments and prohibitions he issued, he followed the correct pedagogical method as his Lord taught him, and as was exemplified in the Qurʾān. He would not issue many commandments or many prohibitions all at once, but issued them gradually, bit by bit, so that the people would not become jaded, and so that his teachings would not be overbearing.

An example: When he ﷺ sent Muʿādh ibn Jabal to Yemen, he prepared him with sufficient instruction, and commanded him to follow the way of gradualism with the people there.

From all this, it is clear that the prophetic method of teaching employed many different ways of directing people to the path of light and perfection, and firmly laid the foundations for a good life. Thus Islamic society, with all its different facets, was bound together by the Shariah it received, and guided by the lessons of its Prophet, the Teacher, and the teachings of its Messenger, the Leader ﷺ, so that the Muslims were then granted a clear victory, and were truly '*the best community brought out for the good of mankind*' [3:110].

In the Messenger of Allah ﷺ, we have the best example, and in his Companions we have the finest role-models, so that we may follow his way and adhere to his guidance, until Allah sends upon us blessings from Heaven and earth.

In this, we see also that the prophetic way of teaching did not leave any aspect of the affairs of life and religion without paying attention to it and giving it ample consideration. It laid down the sound foundations upon which the best community stood, and from which was formed the great Islamic state, which spread knowledge and civilisation across the world, from corner to corner.

His ﷺ Perfect Way of Teaching and Guiding

One aspect of the guidance he ﷺ gave in his method of teaching was the art of taking an actual situation and transferring it to an intellectual principle pertaining to faith, ethics, or conduct. This is the best way to affirm a theoretical concept and make it tangible for others.

An example of this was the occasion when he ﷺ saw a woman among some war-captives desperately searching for her child, lost in her anxiety, until finally she found him and cleaved him to her breast, and immediately fell calm. 'Do you see this mother's compassion with her son?', he ﷺ said, and they said that they did. 'Allah is yet more compassionate with His servant', he said. [Or, he said: 'Do you see how this mother rejoices in her son? Allah rejoices even more in the repentance of his servant.']

Another example of this is the ḥadīth narrated by Muslim on the authority of Jābir, who said that the Messenger of Allah ﷺ was walking in the market with people thronged around him when he passed by a dead short-eared goat. He took it up, holding it by the ear, and said: 'Who among you would like to buy this for a dirham?' 'We would not buy it at any price,' they said, 'for we have no use for it.' 'Wouldn't you like to have it for free?', he ﷺ said. 'By Allah,' they said, 'even were it alive it would be flawed, with those short ears – so what use is it dead?' The Prophet ﷺ said: 'By Allah, this world is even more trifling to Allah than this goat is to you.'

In this way, he ﷺ drew from this dead, flawed goat a practical lesson and a prophetic counsel, showing the value and true nature of the life of this world, and how it does not merit all this struggling, covetousness, envy and conflict. He took the physical reality of the goat, and transformed it into an intellectual concept.

The Prophet ﷺ would use every available pedagogical tool to depict and explain truths, illustrating and highlighting their form for all to see.

One day he was speaking about hope, and how strong it always is, for man leaves this life while his hopes and desires are still as high as mountains, although death encompasses him without his perceiving it; he does not sense it until it is upon him, dashing all his hopes and spoiling his plans.

In order to make this truth easier to perceive, he ﷺ drew a figure on the ground for those present to see. Al-Bukhārī narrates that ʿAbdallāh ibn ʿUmar ﷺ said: 'The Prophet ﷺ drew a square, and a line passing through the middle of it and extending out of it, and drew several small lines cutting through the one in the middle. He then said: "This is man, and this is his appointed lifespan, surrounding him; and this part of the line outside the square is his hope; and these small lines are the vicissitudes of time: if this one misses him, another will befall him; and if that one misses him, another will befall him."'

Another aspect of his ﷺ method of teaching and educating was to use allusion when speaking of blameworthy or unpleasant things, by using well-selected words which conveyed the intended meaning perfectly without any vulgarity, so that it was just as well understood as it would have been had he used more direct language.

An example of this is his ﷺ words in the authentic ḥadīth: 'Seven whom Allah will shade in the shadow of His Throne on a day when there will be no other shade: ...a man invited by a woman of good lineage and virtue, but say: "I fear Allah!"'[591]

Observe how he ﷺ alluded to the intended meaning by saying 'invited by a woman', when it is clear that what was meant was that she invited and urged him to commit an indecent act.

Another example of this is what he ﷺ said to the woman whose second husband divorced her without having ever properly consummated the marriage with her. She came and asked him if it was now lawful for her first husband to remarry her, and he said to her: 'No, not until you taste his honey and he tastes yours'[592] – that is, until sexual intercourse has occurred between you; he alluded to this with the euphemism of honey, and to the act of union with the euphemism of tasting.

Another example of this is what he ﷺ said about what necessitates a purificatory bath (*ghusl*), and how the act of penetration necessitates this

591 Al-Bukhārī, Muslim.

592 Al-Bukhārī, Muslim.

even if there is no ejaculation: 'When he sits between her four limbs[593] and enters her, [they] must bathe.'[594]

Another example of this is found in his & words: 'He who guarantees for me that he will guard what is between his jaws[595] and what is between his legs, I guarantee for him that he will enter Paradise.'[596]

Another style he & would employ when teaching was gradualism in giving information and moving his interlocutor from one subject to another, so that he could guide him to what was most appropriate for his situation and what would best solve his problem. He would do all this with a welcoming heart, a kind character, and great forbearance, without ever displaying boredom or weariness. This is embodied in the following ḥadīth:

Abū Hurayra & reported that a man came to the Messenger of Allah & and said: 'I am ruined, O Messenger of Allah!' 'What has ruined you?', he asked. 'I had intercourse with my wife in Ramaḍān!', the man said. 'Can you afford to free a slave?', the Prophet & asked. The man said he could not. 'Could you fast two successive months?', he asked. The man said he could not. 'Can you afford to feed sixty poor people?', he asked. The man said he could not. He sat for a while, and then a basket of dates was brought to the Prophet &, who took it and said: 'Give this in charity.' 'To someone poorer than we are?', said the man, 'for there is no household in town poorer than my own.' The Prophet & laughed until his incisors were visible, and said, 'Go and feed your family with it.'[597]

In this way, the questioner went away having learned a clear and unshakeable truth, and having been made content and assured, and having been made to feel that he was a member of society, and that the community were responsible for him, and cared about him, and experienced his problems with him and looked to solve them with him. Had the Prophet & simply given him the legal ruling all at once by saying, 'You must free a slave, or if you cannot then fast two successive months, or if you cannot then feed sixty poor people', this would not have been incorrect or deficient; but instead he & devoted his whole being to the matter at hand, and asked him, 'Do you have a slave?' (he did not);

---

593   Her arms and legs (in an embrace), or her feet and thighs (*Fatḥ al-Bārī*). [t]
594   Al-Bukhārī, Muslim.
595   I.e., his mouth (by avoiding blameworthy speech). [t]
596   Al-Bukhārī.
597   Muslim.

and 'Could you fast two successive months?' (he could not); and so on, gradually conveying the ruling to him until he led him to a solution which was appropriate for him.

Another of the lofty prophetic methods of teaching was that he ﷺ would always treat questioners with special care, respect, kindness and honour, thereby imparting unto them great confidence and reassurance, so that their awe of the Prophet ﷺ did not prevent them from asking whatever questions they needed to, and his ﷺ great status did not prevent them from expressing what was on their minds. He would be amiable and generous with his counsel, so the questioner felt that the Perfect Educator's ﷺ protection was upon him, guarding him from all sides against anyone who might criticise or find fault with him.

The following ḥadīth illustrates this perfectly; indeed, it was this ḥadīth that suggested this notion to us in the first place. Jābir ibn ʿAbdallāh reported that a Bedouin came to the Messenger of Allah ﷺ and said, 'O Messenger of Allah, about our clothes in Paradise: will we have to make them ourselves?' The people laughed, and the Messenger of Allah ﷺ said: 'At what do you laugh? At one who knows not, asking one who knows? No, O Bedouin, but rather they will be given forth by the fruits of Paradise.'[598]

You see, then, how he ﷺ rebuked them for laughing at the man's question, and told them that there was no reason to criticise him or find fault with his question, and that the one who does not know should be shown attention and appreciation, so that he is encouraged to ask and seek, and motivated to come back and ask again confidently without any shyness or fear. How often shyness and fear of criticism prevent people from discovering important truths!

Another example of this: it is related that a Bedouin came to the Messenger of Allah ﷺ while he was travelling, taking hold of his camel's bridle and saying: 'O Messenger of Allah, tell me what will take me closer to Paradise and further from Hell.' The Prophet ﷺ stopped, looked to his Companions and then said: 'May he be given grace! [Or he said 'may he be guided.'] What did you say?' The man repeated it, and the Prophet ﷺ answered: 'Worship Allah and associate nothing with Him, perform the prayer, give the poor-due, and maintain your family ties. Now, let go of the camel.'[599]

598 Al-Ṭabarānī.

599 Muslim.

You can see, then, how the Prophet ﷺ showed interest in the question, and let his Companions know it and drew their attention to it, asking the questioner to repeat it and praying that he be given grace and guidance.

Another aspect of his ﷺ way of teaching was to represent abstract concepts in concrete language so that those who heard could conceive of them as though they were looking right at them. This causes them to be rooted more firmly in the soul and mind, and thus make a greater and stronger impression.

One example of this is found in his ﷺ words: 'He who begs from the people excessively is only begging for burning coals – let him, then, decide whether to take a little, or a lot.'[600]

So the one who is always asking people for money is not really asking for burning coals; but in the Hereafter it will turn into burning coals to punish him for what he did. The Prophet ﷺ expressed this concept in a way which was closer to something people can conceive of based on their real-life experience, so that it would be all the more effective a deterrent and a warning, and so that the one who engaged in such an act could imagine that he were actually grasping hold of fire.

Another example of this was what he ﷺ said when he saw a gold ring on one of his Companions' fingers: 'One of you desires a brand of fire: let him put it on his hand.'[601]

Another example of this was what he ﷺ said about one who eats from gold and silver vessels: 'He is but gobbling the fire of Hell into his belly.'[602]

Another example of this was what he ﷺ said about the one who rushes and gets ahead of the imam in the prayer: 'His face is the face of a donkey'[603] – Allah be our refuge!

Another instance of this was the Prophet's words, as reported by Abū Hurayra: 'Would any of you, when returning to his family, wish to find there three fat she-camels great with young?' The people said that they would. He said: 'Then the three verses that one of you recites in his prayer are better for him than those three fat she-camels great with young.'[604]

Another example: ʿUqba ibn ʿĀmir ﷺ said: 'The Prophet ﷺ went out and passed us by at the Ledge [*Ṣuffa*], and said: "Which of you would like

600 Muslim.

601 Muslim.

602 Al-Bukhārī, Muslim.

603 Muslim.

604 Muslim.

to go to Baṭḥān [or he said "ʿAqīq'][605] and take two fattened she-camels without committing any crime or severing any family tie?" We said, "We all would, O Messenger of Allah!" He said: "Then why not go to the mosque, and learn or recite two verses of the Book of Allah Almighty; for this is better than two she-camels, and three is better than three, and four is better than four, and so on for any number of camels.'"[606]

Another example of this is his ﷺ words: 'Allah rejoices in the repentance of His servant more than one of you rejoices when he comes across his camel, after having lost it in a barren land.'[607] Muslim's version has it: 'Allah rejoices in the repentance of His servant, when he repents, more than one of you rejoices when, after his camel flees from him in a barren land bearing all his food and drink, so that he despairs of ever finding it, he then comes to a tree and takes shelter in its shadow, having despaired of finding his camel; and then while he is there, it suddenly appears before him, and he takes its bridle, and he says with great joy: "O Allah, you are my slave and I am your lord!", misspeaking because of his great delight.'

The Messenger ﷺ thus compared Allah's acceptance of His servant's repentance, and His contentment, and the great mercy and compassion He has for His servants, with a man travelling in a barren wilderness who loses the camel upon which he was making the journey through that wilderness, and then finds it after having been on the brink of death, and having lost hope of survival. This encourages people to repent, removes any barriers that might dissuade them from doing so, and gives them cause to hope. Alongside His immense power and great glory, Allah is compassionate and merciful, and encourages His servants to repent, and graces them by accepting their repentance, and shows them the way to salvation and happiness in this life and the next.

This ḥadith also alludes to Allah's kindness to His repentant servant and forgiveness of his sins; for when the sinner falls into sin, he falls into the clutches of Satan and becomes his captive, and thus finds himself on the brink of perdition. If, after that, Allah graces him by guiding him to repentance, he emerges from the shadow of that sin and escapes from the clutches of Satan; and Allah welcomes him with His forgiveness and

605 Places near Medina.

606 Muslim, Abū Dāwūd.

607 Al-Bukhārī, Muslim.

mercy. So the comparison here applies to the state of the repentant servant, and the salvation and success he attains on account of his repentance.

The image here is so well-depicted that it succeeds in having all the desired effects: it captures the attention of the listener and stimulates his imagination, senses and thoughts, so that the desired effect is achieved. The image here is that of a man in the desert with food, drink and a camel to ride, who then suddenly loses all of that and is worn out by his search for it until he loses all hope of ever getting it back. He is the very image of hopelessness, and his soul embodies the concept of despair of salvation; and in the midst of his frustration, pain, desperation, and surrender to death and destruction, suddenly there appears his camel, laden with his food and drink. He leaps up like a man possessed and seizes it so it cannot flee from him again, crying out in his joy: 'Allah, you are my slave and I am your lord!', misspeaking in his intense joy. Yet despite his indescribable joy and immeasurable happiness, this man is not more ardent for life, happy to see his mount, or eager to welcome his salvation, than Allah is glad to receive the repentance of His believing servant, and to welcome him back to Him. For if the return of the camel means salvation in this life, then the servant's return to Allah means salvation in the Hereafter, which is what Allah has called him to, and told him to grasp onto and preserve.

This ḥadīth teaches us many things:

- That it is permitted to use parables and examples to explain abstract concepts with concrete ones;
- That we must always watch ourselves closely and be quick to repent, and hope that Allah accepts our repentance;
- That the Lord is merciful, whilst man is often ignorant and heedless of this mercy;
- That hardship comes with ease, and joy with sorrow, and that we must never despair of Allah's mercy;
- That we must be more keen to strive for our religion than for our worldly lives;

- That Allah draws the believers near to Him, and casts the unbelievers far from Him;

- And that unintentional mistakes are accepted and forgiven by Allah.

As for his ﷺ words 'Allah rejoices', in human terms joy means the expansion of the breast caused by a newly-arrived delight; and it is usually a physical delight. Thus Allah says: *'And rejoice not in what comes to you'* [57:23] and: *'They rejoice in this present life'* [13:26].

When applied to Allah, joy is a metaphor for contentment or pleasure (*riḍā*); that is, he is pleased with the repentance, and accepts it. The purpose of these words is to show how quickly Allah accepts his servant's repentance and welcomes him back. So what is meant is the concomitant of joy, namely contentment and acceptance.

By 'barren land', what is meant is a broad expanse of land bereft of water and herbage, where a person fears death.

Directing People to Higher Aspirations

Another aspect of his ﷺ method of teaching and educating was to direct people's aspirations to what was higher and more profound, and to illustrate lofty and profound principles by the use of well-known concepts. An example of this can be seen in his ﷺ words 'Richness is not a matter of material wealth; true richness is richness of soul.'[608]

The concept of richness that most people have is that it means worldly comfort and material wealth; but the Prophet ﷺ alerts us here to a higher way of understanding what richness is, namely richness of soul. This means that praiseworthy richness is not what comes from material wealth and comfort, for many of those to whom Allah grants this wealth do not benefit from what they are given, but rather become obsessed with getting more no matter what the source; and their greed for more makes them no different from poor people, since the greedy person is always poor. Truly praiseworthy richness, according to the folk of perfection, is richness of heart or soul,[609] meaning its contentment with what is given to it, and its satisfaction and pleasure with whatever it has, without any urge to seek more, or desire to ask for more. The soul free of greed is truly a great and delighted soul, blessed with far more fortune, integrity, nobility and worth than the soul of the wealthy man with a poor soul, who is condemned to wallow in base matters and vile deeds because of the ignobility of his aspiration. Such a man sinks in the eyes of others and earns the scorn of their souls, and becomes more lowly in their estimation than the lowliest of people. All in all, the one who is content with what he is given is always satisfied, whilst the one with a poor soul is always lacking, lamenting what he has lost and obsessing in what he might gain.

Those who would like to have rich souls should make firm in their souls the knowledge that the Almighty is the Giver and Withholder, and be

[608] Al-Bukhārī, Muslim.

[609] The author ؒ points out here that different narrations of this ḥadīth have either 'heart' or 'soul'. [t]

content with His decree, and give thanks to Him for His blessings, and seek refuge in Him from the unfortunate turns of fate that He ordains. A poet expressed this by saying:

Seek what is higher from Him who owns you,
And be content with what you have today;
For richness lies in the hearts of men,
And pride resides within their souls.
Many a hard-up man is rich,
And many a wealthy man is bankrupt;
And many a self-sufficient one is dead,
Though he has not yet gone to his grave!

Another example of this is found in his ﷺ words: 'The keeper of family ties is not simply he who returns them; but the true keeper of family ties is he who, if they are cut, restores them.'[610]

The concept of the keeper of family ties that most people have is the one who responds in kind to the actions of his family: if they contact him, he contacts them; and if they cut him off, he cuts them off. But the Prophet ﷺ here gives a different definition for the keeper of family ties, on a higher level than that of the usual understanding people have. According to this higher understanding, the one who receives the reward of keeping family ties, and realises its true virtue, is the one who makes the first move in keeping them, without worrying about what the response is, as people usually do. He ﷺ alluded to this with his words 'but the true keeper of family ties is he who, if they are cut, restores them.' With this, he tells us that the one who repays the kindnesses of others is not truly a keeper of family ties; the true keeper of ties is the one who, when cut off by a relative, actively restores the tie himself. This is an allusion to the higher level of this virtue; for aside from this, if a person is never cut off by any of his relations, and continues to maintain ties with them, he is counted as a true keeper of family ties.

Another example of this is found in his ﷺ words: 'The worst loss anyone can make is that of the man who wears out his hands for the sake of his hopes, yet is not aided by destiny to achieve them, and thus leaves this world with no provisions for the trip, and comes to Allah Almighty

610 Al-Bukhārī, Aḥmad.

without any argument in his favour.'[611]

Generally, 'loss' is understood to be a decrease of capital, yet the Prophet ﷺ used it here in a more universal way, encompassing faith and worship. In this way, he guided us to see loss as being something more profound than mere money, and more valuable than mere social standing.

The meaning of this ḥadīth is that the one who loses out the most is the man who wears himself out with toil and effort in order to achieve his hopes, yet the turns of fate do not help him to get what he wants: wealth, status, prestige, and the like; rather, fate stands in his way and disappoints him. He continues to entertain empty ambitions and false hopes, wishing for Allah to give him what His wisdom has not ordained and His decree has not proclaimed; and when he dies, he leaves this world without any provisions to sustain him on his trip to the next life and benefit him on the Day when the witnesses will come forth and mankind will be judged. The best provision to take with one on the trip to the Hereafter is to keep away from evil deeds, yet this man has wallowed in their foulness and depravity; he has ruined himself by chasing after hopes and neglecting righteous actions, until his heart has become enveloped by the shadows of heedlessness and stamped with the mark of hardness. Fate has not allowed him to achieve his hollow, ephemeral desires, and he remains in a state of defeat, woe and misery until the angel of death finally separates him permanently from his hopes. Every part of him is attached to the world from which he has not been parted, and they pull him to this world even as the angel of death's grip is upon his heart, pulling him to the Hereafter that he does not wish to meet. He is then placed before Allah with no argument in his favour, meaning no excuse to proffer and no valid explanation for why he has been so remiss, wasting his precious life in a search for something base and foul, and turning aside from the worship of his Lord which was the whole purpose of his creation: '*I have not created jinn and mankind except to worship Me*' [51:56]. Al-Ghazālī said:

People like this are like cattle; nay, they are even more errant, for animals were not given knowledge and the ability to resist their passions, whilst these [human being] were, yet have declined to use it. Thus they are truly deficient, and unquestionably responsible for this. A poet said about this:

611 Al-Bukhārī (*al-Tārīkh*); al-Daylamī narrated it without a chain of transmission.

I have seen no greater human flaw
Than the flaw of those who are able to be flawless.

This ḥadīth therefore constitutes a plain and unambiguous warning against giving preference to pleasure and enjoyment, which leads to overindulgence of hopes and negligence of righteous action; now while this may be the attitude of most people, it is alien to the ethics of the believers. This is why it is said that wallowing in the life of this world is the way of the damned.

Another example of this is found in his ﷺ words: 'The most incapacitated of people is he who is incapable of supplicating; and the most miserly of people is he who is too miserly to give greetings of peace.'[612]

The incapacitated person is the one who is weak and unable to perform ordinary activities; but our Prophet ﷺ guides us here to a higher and more profound concept than that, namely that the incapacitated person is the one who is incapable of beseeching Allah, especially at times of dire need, because he has abandoned what Allah has enjoined, and called down His wrath upon himself by neglecting something that is not the least bit difficult for him. This encourages us to call upon Allah.

He ﷺ also said 'The most miserly of people is he who is too miserly to give greetings of peace', telling us that the true miser is one who neglects to give greetings of peace to others. The popular understanding of a miser is that he is the opposite of a generous person, someone who never gives or shows kindness to others; but here, the Prophet ﷺ uses it to describe someone who neglects to give greetings of peace to the fellow believers he meets, whether he knows them or not; for this greeting is easy to give but greatly rewarded, and no one would neglect it but one who is miserly with those deeds which draw one nearer to Allah, and stingy with those acts which earn one reward, and flippant with the outward supports of the Shariah. He ﷺ called such a person a miser because he refuses to give greetings of peace, as the Lawgiver commands; and he called him the most miserly of people, because those who are miserly with money might be broadly excused for it, since money is beloved to the soul and precious to the spirit by human nature and instinct, and thus to give it away requires that one overcome the ego. Giving greetings of peace, on the other hand, involves no expending of wealth, and so the one who

612 Al-Ṭabarānī, al-Bayhaqī.

disobeys Allah by refraining from giving it to those whom he meets is guilty of being miserly with his very words; thus he is more miserly than all other misers.

Supporting Statements With Evidence

ANOTHER ASPECT of his ﷺ method of teaching and educating was that when teaching, he would support his statements with evidence and reasoning in the form of analogy and comparison. This would make his statements clearer, and turn them into arguments and proofs, so that the questioner would be provided with a plain truth which assured his heart and satisfied his soul, and cause him to cleave ever tighter to the truth, as the evidence took root firmly in his soul. The examples we have of these statements are the plainest proof and greatest evidence of this.

One example of this is found in his ﷺ words: '...And for one of you to have conjugal relations [with his wife] is a kind of charity.' 'O Messenger of Allah,' they said, 'will one of us be rewarded for slaking his lust?' 'Tell me,' he said: 'if he were to slake it in an unlawful way, would he thereby be guilty of sin? Likewise, when he slakes it in a lawful way he earns a reward.'[613]

The word used here is *buḍʿ*, which means both sexual intercourse and the private parts; either meaning could apply here. This ḥadīth is evidence that simple lawful things can become acts of worship if they are accompanied by righteous intentions. Sexual intercourse can be an act of worship if one intends thereby to satisfy the right of the wife and give her good companionship as Allah commanded, or to seek a righteous child, or to keep oneself or one's wife chaste and prevent them both from looking at, thinking about, or indulging in unlawful things, or any other righteous intention.

The noble Companions were amazed at this, that a man could go to his wife and slake his lust and enjoy himself, and then be rewarded for it by Allah. It would have been enough for the Prophet ﷺ to say to them, 'Allah has decreed this and ordained it', and that would have been the greatest of proofs, since the word of Allah and the word of His Messenger ﷺ are the only proofs needed. But he ﷺ did not suffice with that, but

613 Muslim.

instead reminded them of the illicit counterpart of this action, which was known to them and obvious to them. In this way, he gave them the opportunity to reflect, think and compare the two similar actions, and base the unknown on the known. Thus he said to them: 'Tell me: if he were to slake it in an unlawful way, would he thereby be guilty of sin? Likewise, when he slakes it in a lawful way he earns a reward.'

Another example of this is found in the ḥadīth narrated by Muslim on the authority of al-Nuʿmān ibn Bashīr, who said: 'My father carried me to the Messenger of Allah ﷺ and said: "O Messenger of Allah, testify that I have given al-Nuʿmān [such-and-such sum of money]." He said: "Have you given the same amount to all your other children as you have to al-Nuʿmān?" He said that he had not. He said: "Then have someone else testify to it." He then said: "Would it please you if they were all equally dutiful to you?" He said that indeed it would. "The answer is no, then", he said.'

By 'Would it please you...', he ﷺ meant: Would it make you happy if all your children were equally dutiful to you, meaning that they were all equal in the kindness they offered you, and in their being careful not to mistreat you, and in the respect and honour they showed you? He said that indeed it would please him. So the Prophet ﷺ said: 'the answer is no, then'; that is, if you really want all that.

Had the Prophet ﷺ simply said to him, 'That is not allowed', it would have been enough, because his ﷺ word is law, and no further evidence is needed. But instead, he ﷺ explained to him the truth of the matter, and showed him the reason why the rule is what it is, guiding him to the evidence by saying, 'Would it please you if they were all equally dutiful to you?' Now it was obvious that such a thing would please him, and thus it became obvious that if he gave to one and neglected the others, they would not strive to be dutiful to him or show him love – that is, if they did go so far as to actually mistreat him! Behold, then, how perfect was the way of educating employed by this noble Prophet and great Messenger ﷺ.

Another example of this was the occasion when a woman of the Juhayna clan came to the Prophet ﷺ and said: 'My mother vowed to make the pilgrimage, but died before she had done it. May I do it in her stead?' He replied: 'Yes, make the pilgrimage for her. Tell me, if your mother had outstanding debts, would you have paid them? Repay your debts to Allah, for Allah is more deserving of fidelity.'[614]

[614] Al-Bukhārī.

You can see, then, how the Prophet ﷺ proved the validity of the pilgrimage she made for her mother by use of analogy, so that her soul would be all the more convinced by having reference to a concept she knew well, and a comparison to something in which there is no disagreement or confusion. There is no doubt that a verdict is strengthened when evidence is provided for it, and that this is more assuring for the soul of the questioner and more likely to win his assent.

Another example of this is the ḥadīth narrated by Muslim on the authority of Abū Hurayra ؓ, who reported that a man of the Banū Fazāra came to the Prophet ﷺ and said: 'My wife has given birth to a black child.' The Prophet ﷺ said: 'Do you own any camels?' He said that he did. 'What colour are they?', he asked. 'Red', the man replied. 'Are any of them grey?' He allowed that some of them were grey. 'Whence came that?', the Prophet ﷺ asked. 'Perhaps it is because of heredity'[615], he said. The Prophet ﷺ said: 'And perhaps *this* is because of heredity.'

Other narrations add that the man wanted to formally renounce his parentage of the child, and that the Prophet ﷺ did not allow him to do so.

Had the Prophet ﷺ simply said, 'Colour has nothing to do with attribution of parentage, as long as the child was born in your bed and the timing fits', it would have been enough. But he ﷺ wanted to show the man the reason for the ruling, so that he would recognise the truth of the matter and adhere to it because it was supported by proof. Therefore he directed him to a comparable matter which he accepted and knew well, so that he could use what he knew as an analogy for what he knew not, and turn his doubt into certainty.

615 The author ؒ explains in a note here that this means this colour had existed in the ancestral line of those camels, and had surfaced for that reason. [t]

The Use of Stories

Another aspect of his ﷺ method of teaching and educating would be to tell stories and use them to explain concepts and clarify issues. A single prophetic story would contain many benefits and lessons; it might pertain to the Oneness of Allah, explaining the virtue of faith in Allah and the necessity of patience in the face of His decree and resignation to His will, and the virtue of repentance and return to Him, and sincerity in one's attitude towards Him, and the virtues of reliance and contentment; he ﷺ might use it to explain how the proponents of Allah's Oneness who came before us were persecuted in Allah's cause. Another story might pertain to general etiquettes and the proper way to interact with people, such as duty to parents, maintaining family ties, kindness to the weak, and other such lofty ethics and noble principles. Prophetic stories are distinguished by their truth: they describe actual events and real personalities, for the one who told them ﷺ was the Honest, Trusted One, who never spoke of his own caprice, but conveyed the revelation that was revealed to him.

The prophetic story always had lofty goals and rarefied intentions, and each one encompassed several benefits and outlined a number of virtues, to which it called us and encouraged us to aspire.

The Story of Those
Who Spoke in their Cradles

A BŪ HURAYRA ♦ reported that the Messenger of Allah ♦ said: 'None spoke in the cradle[616] save three: There was 'Īsā son of Maryam, and there was Jurayj's companion – now Jurayj was a man of worship, who kept a lodge. Once while he was in there praying, his mother came to him and said: "Jurayj!" He said: "O Lord, my mother or my prayer?", and carried on praying, so she went. The next day, she came to him again as he prayed and said "Juraryj!" He said: "O Lord, my mother or my prayer?", and carried on praying, so she said: "Allah, do not let him die until he looks upon the faces of adulteresses!" The Israelites came to know Jurayj for his worship; and a woman of ill virtue and renowned beauty said: "If you wish, I will seduce him." She offered herself to him, but he paid her no heed. She went instead to a herdsman who would come sometimes to his lodge, and offered herself to him, and he had his way with her. She conceived a child, and when she bore it she claimed that Jurayj was the father. They went to him, cursed him, destroyed his lodge, and began to beat him. He asked them what was wrong, and they said: "You fornicated with this jezebel, and she bore you a child!" He said: "Where is the child?" They brought the child forth, and he told them to leave him while he prayed. When he had finished praying, he went over to the child, poked him in the belly, and said: "Boy, who is your father?' The child said: "So-and-so, the herdsman." Upon this, the people approached Jurayj, kissed him and laid their hands upon him, and said: "We will rebuild your lodge from gold!" "No," he said, "rebuild it from clay, as it was", and this they did.

'[As for the third], a baby was being nursed by his mother when a man rode past on a splendid steed, decked out with fine cloth. The baby's mother said, "O Allah, make my boy like him!" The baby left off the breast, looked at the man, and said, "O Allah, make me not like him!", and then went back to the breast and suckled. [The Messenger of Allah

---

[616] I.e., when they were infants.

ﷺ then mimicked the baby's suckling by placing his finger in his mouth and sucking it.] Some people then passed by with a servant-girl whom they were beating, shouting "You have fornicated and stolen!", as all the while she repeated: "Allah is enough for me, and the best of trustees!" His mother said, "O Allah, make not my boy like her!" The boy left off suckling, looked at her, and said: "O Allah, make me like her!" Upon this, the two began to speak to one another. The mother said: "A fine-looking man passed by, and I said 'O Allah, make my boy like him!', yet you said: 'O Allah, make me not like him!' they then passed by with a servant-girl whom they were beating, saying 'You have fornicated and stolen', and I said: 'O Allah, make not my boy like her!', yet you said 'O Allah, make me like her!'" The baby replied: "That man was a tyrant, so I said 'Make me not like him'; and as for her, they accused her of fornicating, though she had not, and of stealing, though she had not; so I said, 'O Allah, make me like her!'"[617]

In this ḥadīth, the Prophet ﷺ tells us the story of Jurayj, a devoted Israelite worshipper, who was so involved in his worship that he did not answer his mother's call or fulfil his duties; so she invoked a prayer against him, which Allah answered, sending to him a woman of ill virtue who invited him to fornicate. He was abused and his lodge torn down, and his mother's prayer came true; but then Allah saved him by the blessing of his worship, and the infant proclaimed his innocence, and his social standing was restored. The Prophet ﷺ then tells us of an ordinary woman who was dazzled by the sight of a strong healthy man on a fine-looking horse, and so prayed to Allah to make her son like him. Yet the child rejected this, and protested it with words Allah allowed him to speak. His mother was then horrified by a woman being punished and humiliated on charges of fornication and stealing, and so prayed to Allah not to make her son like her. Yet the child rejected this, and protested it by saying: 'O Allah, make me like her', explaining that the man was a tyrant and the woman innocent.

With this story, the Messenger of Allah ﷺ illustrates important concepts for us, and calls us to beautiful virtues. Among these are that worldly people judge things by their appearances, whilst people of spiritual insight judge them by their inner beauty; that righteous action is what counts; that judging by appearances does not tell us the truth, but

[617] Al-Bukhārī, Muslim.

only amounts to supposition; and that Allah takes care of inner realities by doing right by the oppressed and giving consolation to the deprived, the exhausted and the downtrodden.

Other lessons of the ḥadīth are the importance of being dutiful to one's parents and giving one's mother her rights and answering her calls; that if two things clash, the most important one should be given preference; and that Allah usually gives his Friends a way out of their grievous trials, as He says: '*Whosoever fears Allah, He will make for him a way out*' [62:2]; and He might send hardships to them sometimes in order to increase them and refine them, which is a kindness.

Another lesson is that ritual ablution is recommended when one wishes to supplicate for important things, and that ritual ablution was known to those who came before Islam; for the narration of al-Bukhārī[618] explicitly states 'so he performed ablutions, and prayed.'

Other lessons of this story are that the saints are vouchsafed miracles; that the miracles of the saints can occur by their choice and their request; and that these miracles can take the form of any kind of supernatural occurrence.

618 The version translated above is that of Muslim. [t]

Explaining Things Using Parables

Another aspect of his ﷺ method of teaching and educating was to explain things by use of parables. The parable is one of the best ways to give a clear image of a concept, and to make it easier for others to comprehend.

Abū Hurayra ؓ reported that the Prophet ﷺ said: 'The parable of the miser and the charitable person is that of two men wearing suits of iron,[619] from their breast to their collarbones. As for the charitable person, every time he gives, the suit expands upon his skin until it reaches beyond his fingertips and drags behind him, covering his tracks.[620] As for the miser, every time he wants to give, the suit tightens, each link cleaving to its place; he wants to widen it, but it will not widen.'[621]

So this is the parable the Prophet ﷺ gave for the miser and the charitable person, comparing them to two men who each want to wear a suit of mail to be protected from his enemy's weapons. Each man puts it over his head to wear it (since mail is first put on the head and the breast, until one puts his arms in its sleeves). He compared the charitable spender to one who wears a voluminous suit of mail that covers his whole body; and compared the miser to one who holds his hands to his neck so that whenever he tries to put it on it catches at his neck and gets no further than his collarbone. This is what 'it tightens' means; it catches and gets stuck. What this means is that when the generous one goes to give charity, his heart is content and his soul at peace with it, and he gives freely; yet when the miser considers it, his soul becomes greedy, and his heart is straitened, and his fist clenches. *'And whoso is guarded against the avarice of his own soul, those – they are the prosperous'* [59:9]. Al-Muhallab said that it means that Allah covers the charitable one in both this life and the next, whilst he exposes the miser. The words 'covering his tracks' symbolise how his sins are effaced. ʿIyāḍ added that this story is a parable, not a real-life incident; others say that it is a metaphor for the way wealth

619 I.e., chain mail. [t]

620 I am indebted to *Fatḥ al-Bārī* for the translation of this phrase. [t]

621 Al-Bukhārī, Muslim.

is increased by charitable giving, and decreased by miserliness.

Another example of this is the Prophet's ﷺ words: 'The parable of the house in which Allah is invoked and the house in which Allah is not invoked is as the living compared to the dead.'[622]

This ḥadīth compares houses with the living and the dead, with respect to whether Allah is invoked in them or not. The one who invokes Allah is compared to the living person, who is outwardly beautified with the light and glow of life with righteous actions and with free will, and inwardly illuminated and beautified with the light of knowledge, recognition and understanding; his heart grazes in the pasture of holiness, and his inner secret resides in the chamber of union. The one who does not invoke, on the other hand, is outwardly defunct and inwardly vacant. Some say that 'the house' here means 'those who dwell in the house'; now one might object to this by saying, 'Those who live in houses are all alive – how, then, can they be called dead?'

I answer this by saying that the 'living' object of this comparison is one who benefits from his life by invoking Allah and obeying Him; it does not refer to actual bodily life. Likewise, the believer is compared to the living, and the unbeliever to the dead, though they are both alive, when Allah says: '*Is he who was dead, and We gave him life…*' [6:122]. Also, to say that the one who does not invoke is outwardly defunct and inwardly vacant seems to work better than to describe his house in this way.

Another example of this is found in his ﷺ words: 'The one who teaches the people what is good and forgets himself is like a lamp which gives others light but burns itself.'[623]

This ḥadīth compares the scholar who enjoins what is good but does not practise what he preaches, benefitting the people but not himself, with a lamp that gives light and burns. What this means is that this scholar burns himself with the fire of the Hereafter, helping others even as he ruins himself. This is true if he does not call others to worldly pursuits – and if he does do that, then he is like a burning fire that consumes both others and itself. There are thus three kinds of scholar: he who saves himself and others, namely he who truly prefers Allah to this world both outwardly and inwardly; then he who damns himself and others, namely he who calls others to worldly things; and then he who

622 Muslim.

623 Al-Ṭabarānī, al-Ḍayyā᾽.

damns himself yet saves others, namely he who calls to the Hereafter and rejects worldliness outwardly, but does not apply his knowledge inwardly. This is a warning to all those who have a mind for remembrance or an ear to hear. The scholars among the Companions were extremely pious and fearful. One day, ʿĀʾisha ﷺ was visited by a young man who had raised an issue with her and asked her about it, and to whom she had spoken. 'What have you done [since we talked]?', she asked him. 'Hah!', he replied. 'Then how many arguments you are providing for Allah to use against us and against you!', she said. And ʿĪsā ﷺ said to his Disciples: 'You work for the life of this world, although you are given provisions therein; yet you do not work for the Hereafter, although your only provisions there will come from your righteous actions.' He also said: 'O scholars of evil, who do not righteous works! You have put this world at your head, and the Hereafter at your feet! Your words are a medicine, but your actions are a disease; like the oleander tree, which pleases those who see it, and kills those who eat it!'[624]

A similar example is his ﷺ words: 'The one who attains knowledge and then does not acts upon it is like the one who gathers a fortune but does not spend it.'[625] Another is his ﷺ words: 'The one who teaches others what is good is like the wick, which gives people light while burning itself.'[626]

This is a parable the Chosen Prophet ﷺ drew for one who does not act upon his knowledge; and it imparts a strong warning. Abū al-Dardāʾ said: 'Woe unto him who knows not; and a thousand woes unto him who knows but does not act!' Al-Tustarī said: 'All people are drunk, save the scholars; and scholars are all perplexed, save those who act on their knowledge.' He also said: 'All this world is ignorance and falsehood, save for knowledge; and all knowledge is an indictment, save for what is acted upon; and all action is dust in the wind, save for what is sincere; and sincerity is incredibly perilous, until one dies with it.' Al-Junayd said: 'If you want to be ennobled by knowledge, and be one of its folk, and be known for it, before you have lived up to its rights, its light will be veiled from you, and it will be an indictment against you, not an argument for you.'

624 This paragraph is from *Fayḍ al-Qadīr.*

625 Al-Ṭabarānī.

626 Al-Ṭabarānī.

In his grace, Allah gave me the fortune to write a treatise[627] on the fundamentals of education in the first Islamic era and the Prophet's ﷺ teaching method, and on some educational theories and principles which can be derived from the prophetic ḥadīth literature, of which we have given a summary in this chapter; and all grace is from Allah.

[627] *Uṣūl al-Tabiyya al-Nabawiyya*, 'The Foundations of Prophetic Education', Majmaʿ al-Buḥūth al-Islāmiyya, 1998.

Part Seven

The Perfection of His ﷺ Law, Which Meets All Human Needs, and Can Be Applied to All Times, Without Any Alteration or Corruption

‘*This day have I perfected for you your religion*’ [5:3]

THE SHARIAH OF ISLAM

THE SHARIAH of Islam is the most perfect, noble and comprehensive message of guidance, and the dispensation with which Allah sealed the revealed Laws of Heaven, making it eternal and ordaining that it remain until Allah inherits the earth. Because of this, it had to be solid and perpetual, strongly built and wisely ordered, able to meet the needs of individuals and the masses.

It is well-known that the Shariah of Islam is built on two great foundations and drawn from two noble sources:

The first is the Book of Allah Almighty, which contains His straight path, His overwhelming argument, and His immutable signs, and is a refreshing spring which quenches the thirst of ignorance.

The second is the enlightening prophetic Sunna, which brings mankind all goodness and happiness in their religious and worldly lives. The Sunna means everything attributed to the Messenger of Allah ﷺ, whether word, deed, or approval. Allah is well pleased with it, and has obliged us to follow it, refer to it, and act upon it. He has commanded us to obey the Prophet ﷺ, and judged that those who refuse to do so are unbelievers, and linked the love of Allah with adherence to his ﷺ Sunna. He has made obedience to the Prophet ﷺ (by following his Sunna) equal to obedience of Allah ﷻ (by following His Qur'ān). He has made it clear that all of the Sunna is from Allah, and that he ﷺ speaks not of his own caprice, but only conveys the revelation that is revealed to him. The Qur'ān is from Allah, and the Sunna is from the Messenger of Allah ﷺ by Allah's command and good pleasure. Thus we may safely say that all of these laws, and classifications of the permitted and the forbidden, are from Allah ﷻ.

THE SHARIAH OF ISLAM AND THE REALITIES OF LIFE

Our Shariah – praise be to Allah – is relevant to any time, and suitable for any generation, and perennially applicable to the changing realities of life. Its legislative foundations are fully capable of providing us with laws which are living, growing and developing, so that people in all their different environments can enjoy justice and security, and lead good and noble lives.

The Shariah has been able to prove its soundness and effectiveness on those occasions when it has had a chance to be implemented in real life. The era of its implementation was a virtuous era in which social justice and human dignity blossomed, and successive generations of mankind were given a beacon showing them the way to goodness and honour. People enjoyed happy lives, and devoted themselves to bearing the message of the world's emancipation from the fetters of injustice, the nightmare of ignorance, and the darkness of error.

The situation of other communities who use systems that contradict this religion is an eloquent testimony to the excellence and perfection of this Shariah; for those communities are ever forced to renounce elements of their laws and systems, and borrow many things from Islam.

The Shariah, then, is broad enough to cover any issue that people might face, set their affairs in order, and meet their needs, however wide their geographic separation might be, and despite their differences of race, culture and nature. No one denies this save one who is utterly deluded.

THE FOUNDATIONS OF PERFECTION AND EXCELLENCE IN THE SHARIAH

Anyone who examines Islamic jurisprudence and its foundations and principles honestly will acknowledge that the Shariah is completely able and well-equipped to order the life of humanity and deal with all their affairs, and that its laws do not follow a single narrow course; rather, they deal with some issues independently, and others collectively according to universal principles. It then leaves those people who have enough knowledge to qualify them for the task of deriving laws to apply these universal principles to individual issues, as they arise.

This is how we can understand Allah's words '*We left nothing out of the Book*' [6:38]; and it is in light of this that we should understand the meaning of development and renewal in the Shariah, which is a pure mercy and a heavenly favour for this community.

Therefore the Law of Islam has a structure which preserves this order, and a form which guarantees total harmony between firm principles and changing temporal circumstances. This order and harmony is the chief agent, as ordained by Allah Almighty, for the preservation of this Shariah and the continued existence of this religion in a way that is free of any meddling, sabotage, corruption or usurpation.

If you know this, then know also that this order and harmony depends, at its essence and its core, on fundamentals which are interconnected and mutually perfecting; they are the crown of the Islamic legislation, a crown resplendent in its majesty and perfection; and they are the pivot on which it is centred; and they are the attributes and foundations of development, renewal and perfection.

ONE: OPENING THE DOOR OF IJTIHĀD

The first of these fundamentals, centres and attributes is the opening of the door to *ijtihād*.[628] Islamic legislation is based on *ijtihād*, for the laws that are explicitly given in the Book and the Sunna are a limited few. Ibn a-Qayyim states, in *Aʿlām al-Mūqiʿīn*, that the verses in the Qurʾān that deal with the fundamentals of law number no more than five hundred, and the ḥadīths that deal with the fundamentals of law number no more than five hundred of all the thousands of ḥadīths that have reached us. Thus the fundamental rulings of this Shariah given to us by the Qurʾān and Sunna are one thousand in number; and this forms the basis of the immense Islamic legislation that remains to this day, continuing to benefit this community.

The Qurʾān taught the Muslims to use reason and to investigate, and to follow the guidance of their scholars and thinkers. Allah Almighty says in His Book: '*When there comes to them a matter, be it of security or fear, they make it public; yet had they referred it to the Messenger and to those in authority among them, those of them whose task it is to investigate would have known the matter*' [5:83].

This is a clear summons to investigation and reasoning; and therefore history tells of the jurists among the Companions, who learned how to apply *ijtihād* to derive rulings and judgements during the time of the Messenger of Allah ﷺ.

History also tells us about the Messenger himself ﷺ, and how he would train his Companions to solve issues and derive rulings, and encourage them to think and reason freely, and fill their hearts with confidence

[628] The word *ijtihad* literally means to strive or to exert oneself. In the Shariah it is a process by which qualified scholars infer jurisprudential rulings from the primary sources of Shariah for scenarios not previously covered. See *Principles of Islamic Jurisprudence* by MH Kamali.

and assurance when they feared to make errors of judgement. When a qualified person employs *ijtihād* and comes to the right answer, he has two rewards; and when he comes to the wrong answer, he has one reward. Allah ﷻ says: '*There is no fault in you if you make mistakes, but only in what your hearts premeditate. Allah is Forgiving, Merciful*' [33:5].

It was in the wake of this enlightened tolerance and broad, noble employment of *ijtihād* that the life of the Muslims proceeded from the time of their first emergence. The Companions ﷺ employed their reason, and the Messenger ﷺ encouraged them to do so and gave them his blessing; and their free souls imbibed the principles of Islam. They differed in their understanding of certain issues and events, but it was the difference of free people, without any bitterness or enmity. They did not resort to name-calling or heckling, nor did they ever think of stifling opinion or restricting thought.

The most eloquent testimony to this was the Prophet's ﷺ assessment of them on the day of Banū Qurayẓa, when he said to them: 'Let none of you pray the afternoon prayer until you reach Banū Qurayẓa.' The time for prayer arrived whilst they were still on the way; some of them said 'We should not pray until we arrive', whilst others said, 'No, we should pray now; that is not what he meant.' The Prophet ﷺ was told about this, and he did not side with either group. Ibn ʿAbd al-Barr said of this: 'This is the way of independent reasoning based on the fundamentals, according to many jurists.' The Messenger ﷺ also encouraged the people he appointed to official posts in their lands to exercise *ijtihād*; and they considered that the greatest blessing Allah gave His servants was to give them understanding of the Qurʾān and the ḥadīths of the Messenger of Allah ﷺ, and understanding of the issues they had to face.

With this complete understanding of the spirit of Islam, and this continuous exercise of reasoning, in an atmosphere of ease, tolerance and freedom, Islamic legislation followed in step with the advances of the Muslims from Arabia to the furthest shores and highest peaks, whatever went on in life. The Muslims never felt that the law was inadequate, nor did they ever have any need – though the world was in their hands – for any laws other than those of their Shariah, nor any lawmakers other than their jurists. Indeed, they not only made laws for themselves, but for the rest of mankind as well, so that Wells[629] could say in his book

[629] H.G. Wells, the author and historian. [t]

The Outline of History that Europe is indebted to Islam for the bulk of its administrative and commercial laws.

Life went on for the Muslims with comfort, goodness, strength and honour, developing alongside the rapid progress of man, thanks to the continuous flow of studies based on free independent reasoning, which was the distinctive mark of the Islamic world, until people strayed from the way of heaven, and their ship sank, sinking one day and surviving the next – but what a wretched, miserable survival it was.

TWO: THE IMPORTANCE GIVEN TO BENEFIT IN THE SHARIAH

One of the focal points of perfection in the Shariah is the importance it affords to benefit. The great scholar ʿIzz al-Dīn ibn ʿAbd al-Salām spoke of this in his book *Qawāʿid al-Aḥkām*, saying:

> All moral responsibilities are meant to give benefit to mankind in this life and the next; Allah has no need of anyone's worship, and is neither benefited by obedience nor harmed by disobedience. And the benefits of the next life can only be attained through the benefits of this life.

Imam al-Shāṭibī said:

> The most widely-accepted view is that the Shariah was made for the benefit of mankind; and this can be ascertained by careful study. Allah Almighty says, speaking of the sending of messengers, which is the basis of the Law: '*[We sent] messengers bearing good tidings and warnings, so that mankind might have no argument against Allah, after the messengers*' [4:165].

Ibn al-Qayyim says in *Aʿlām al-Mūqiʿīn*:

> The Shariah of Allah has, as its chief aim, the benefit of mankind in this life and the next. It is total justice, total mercy, total benefit, and total wisdom. Thus anything that is not just (hence unjust), or not merciful (hence opposed to mercy), or not beneficial (hence harmful), or not wise (hence meaningless), cannot be part of the Shariah.

The eternal Shariah of Allah, then, is a living being [*kā'in ḥayy*] whose rules are meant to uphold the common benefit, as long as this does not involve the breaching of a divine judgement, the violation of an Islamic principle, or the alteration of Islamic law.

THREE: THE RECOGNITION OF COMMON UNIVERSAL PRINCIPLES

Another of the fundamentals of perfection in the Shariah is the recognition of common universal principles.

The Shariah establishes certain common foundations and universal principles, upon each of which is built fundamentals and laws which can be derived by those who have knowledge of the nature of world events by considering what the Lawgiver intended for similar situations. An example of these universal principles is the principle of worship, which states that Allah ﷻ can only be worshipped by those forms of worship He has established. This means that all worship is dependent on direct divine instruction, and can only be learned from Allah; for only He knows what pleases him and what does not. He has made clear in His Book, which He revealed to His Messenger ﷺ, everything connected with this; thus Allah is worshipped by means of His Book, the Sunna of His Messenger, and adherence to the way of the righteous early Muslims.

THE PRINCIPLE OF TRANSACTIONS

The principle of transactions is that 'all transactions are permitted until they are known to be forbidden.' This means that if the Shariah is silent about something, and has issued no commandments, prohibitions or options about it, then it is left to personal opinion. The upshot of all that has been said about this subject is that if the Shariah is silent about a transaction, and it causes no harm, then it is essentially valid. What points to this perspective is that contracts and transactions are based on human customs and conventions; therefore, they can be left to proceed in this way as long as they are not expressly forbidden. Thus Allah says: '*He has made clear to you that which He has forbidden you*' [6:119]. This implies that everything is lawful unless it has been clearly declared unlawful in the Qur'ān and Sunna. Every stipulation, contract, or transaction for which these sources are silent cannot be called unlawful, until some proof that it is prohibited can be produced, or some evidence that it is harmful emerges; for if they are silent about it, this is because of mercy, not forgetfulness. Al-Tirmidhī narrated, on the authority of Salmān al-Fārisī, that the Messenger of Allah ﷺ said: 'The lawful is what Allah calls lawful in His Book, and the forbidden is what Allah forbids in His Book; and if He is silent about something, then He has allowed you it.' Similarly, al-Dāraquṭnī narrates, on the authority of Abū Thaʿlaba, that the Messenger of Allah ﷺ said: 'Allah has obliged *farāʾiḍ* [obligations], so do not neglect them; and He has set up boundaries, so do not cross them; and He has been silent about some things, out of mercy for you, not forgetfulness, so do not go chasing after [a ruling for] them.'

There are many other famous principles which the scholars have collected, ordered, recorded, explained and arranged, and which have been of tremendous usefulness. They include: 'hardship must be alleviated', 'harm must be ended', 'things are determined by their objectives', 'certitude is not annulled by doubt', and 'custom has the weight of law.'

FOUR: THE SUMMONS TO OPENING THE DOOR TO KNOWLEDGE

Another fundamental of perfection in the Shariah is the opening of the door to knowledge by emphasising its virtue, encouraging its acquisition, and stressing the nobility of those who possess it. It could be said that one of the great glories of Islam is how strongly it supports knowledge and encourages its acquisition; and the very first passage of the Qurʾān to be revealed pertained to reading and knowledge.[630]

The place of knowledge in Islam is too well-known to need mentioning, and too vast to encompass; and the verses of the Book and ḥadīths of the Master of Envoys ﷺ contain many clear evidences of the high status Islam affords to knowledge, scholars, and students, and the importance of universal principles.

FIVE: NO OBLIGATION TO FOLLOW ANY PARTICULAR SCHOOL OF THOUGHT

Another fundamental of perfection in the Shariah is flexibility and the absence of obtuseness in the adherence to a particular viewpoint or school of thought in those matters which are the province of reasoning and

[630] This refers to Qurʾān 96:1-5.

opinion. This is because a legal text could have more than one possible meaning, without there being anything to prove decisively which meaning is the correct one, to the exclusion of the others.

Now the way in which one possible meaning of a text is chosen over another is by *ijtihād*, reflection and study. Moreover, study and reflection might result in the alternative meaning being preferred at another time, when it is more beneficial to choose it. The Shariah does not compel us to adhere to the interpretation preferred by a given imam or scholar no matter how times change and circumstances differ; rather, mankind are excused if they differ, and their difficulties may be alleviated. If one of them errs in his qualified reasoning, he is nevertheless rewarded; and the one who comes to the right conclusion is doubly rewarded. This is to encourage them to study and seek out what is most beneficial for all.

This is why there are differences of opinion about these matters and rulings; and this is a mercy from Allah for this community. In His grace with mankind, Allah has caused this difference of opinion to diversify the paths which lead to salvation. Likewise, the low number of legal sources is also a blessing which the Bringer of the Law ﷺ intended: he would even forbid his Companions from asking too many questions, so that things would continue to retain their original ruling of lawfulness.[631]

The imams of this religion and its jurisprudence never obliged people to follow their schools of thought and adhere to them; rather, they had no objections to this difference of opinion, and if any of them saw more benefit in another opinion, he would not hesitate in adopting it.

Abū Ḥanīfa, for example, used to say that charity was superior to performing supererogatory pilgrimages; but when he went on the pilgrimage himself and saw how difficult it was, he changed his opinion. Muḥammad al-Shaybānī had an opinion about impure substances which he changed after he went to Marwā and saw the difficulties people had there.

Mālik, too, changed some of his opinions. And when Imam al-Shāfiʿī, the imam of the famous school, moved from Iraq to Egypt, he ended up establishing a whole new school and renouncing all his old school on all but twenty-something issues.

Because of this, the scholars among the righteous early Muslims would excuse one another when they differed, and would not criticise

631 Ibn ʿĀbidīn, 1/109.

the opinions of others. We should not neglect to mention how Imam Mālik took exception to the Calpih Hārūn al-Rashīd's plan to compel all the Muslims to adhere to his book *al-Muwaṭṭa'*, despite the great care Imam Mālik had taken when compiling it, and the acceptance it had received from the scholars. Malik explained his reason for refusing this by saying: 'The Companions of the Messenger of Allah ﷺ spread out over the lands, and perhaps some of them have ḥadīths which I have not heard and which, if I did hear them, I would change something in my book.' Because of this, the qualified imams of juridical reasoning would forbid those who asked them questions from taking their answers as revealed religion, or making them a cause of sectarianism. Accordingly, some of them would act on the opinion of others, in order to give a dispensation or act in conformity with the Muslims they were with.

An example of this is the story of how Imam Aḥmad (Allah rest his soul), who was of the opinion that cupping or bloodletting vitiated the ritual ablution, was asked: 'If you saw an imam perform cupping and then go to pray without first making ablutions, would you pray behind him?' He answered: 'How could I not pray behind Mālik and Saʿīd ibn al-Musayyib?'

Abū Ḥanīfa and his followers were of the opinion that bleeding necessitates ablutions, but Abū Yūsuf (one of Abū Ḥanīfa's major disciples) saw Hārūn al-Rashīd perform cupping, having been told by Mālik that he did not need to make ablutions after doing so, and Abū Yūsuf then prayed behind him and did not repeat his prayer afterwards.

And it is related that al-Shāfiʿī ؓ left out the *qunūt* supplication of the dawn prayer when he prayed with some Ḥanafīs in their Imam's mosque in the outskirts of Baghdad. Many people said that he did this out of respect for the Imam.

Something else to note is that the scholars among the Companions, Second Generation and those of the righteous early Muslims who came after them would always shy away from calling their legal opinions 'Allah's ruling' or 'Allah's law'; rather, even the most capable and knowledgeable of them would say, 'This is where my knowledge and reasoning has led me: if it is correct, then it is from Allah; and if it is wrong, it is from me and from Satan.'

One counsel that the Prophet ﷺ gave to the commanded of an army was: 'If you lay siege to a people and they want you to let them out according to Allah's ruling, then do not let them out according to Allah's ruling, but let them out according to *your* ruling, for you do not know if you will correctly apply Allah's ruling to them or not.'[632] Ibn al-Qayyim says in *Aʿlām al-Mūqiʿīn*: 'The mufti is not permitted to say "Allah declares this" or "Allah allows this" or "forbids that" when he speaks of something he has found in the book of the scholar whose school he follows; rather he should say "so-and-so says this".'

This was the unique and praiseworthy way, and the sincere and pure spirit, that the imams of the righteous early Muslims ✲ followed; and thus they were more likely to find the truth, and quicker to reach it once they saw it, and firmer to grasp it once they reached it. Their common guiding principle in all this was to return to the truth via the primary sources of virtue. The effect this had on their relations with one another was to foster a spirit of common tolerance, strong love and brotherhood for the sake of Allah and the cause of truth, and cooperation in all that led to Allah's goodly favour and the happiness of the community.

Therefore Allah blessed them in their lives and possessions, and protected them from being wasted in barren, useless debate motivated by nothing but stubbornness and partisanship, however far it may have been from the truth, or however obvious its error.

He also protected them from mutual enmity and jealousy, and from all that corrupts hearts and ruins good works. Thus He benefitted them with their righteous works, and benefitted the Muslims with them too; and their legacies still remain guiding beacons for all those who wish to follow their path, and exemplars for all those to whom Allah grants the gifts He granted them: deep understanding of the religion, eagerness to discover the truth; and an exemplar too for all those who wish to benefit as they benefitted, and succeed as they succeeded.

Perhaps the reason for their success was that they drank from a river both broad and deep: the river of the Book of Allah and the Sunna of His Messenger ✲, from which each of them drinks according to how prepared he is for it, aiming no censure or criticism at any other.

One of them might have understood a verse of Qurʾān or ḥadīth in one way, and another of them in another way; so they would discuss the matter with the utmost etiquette. If they ended up agreeing, then they would praise Allah; and if not, they would each pardon the other and go

---

[632]   Muslim, Aḥmad.

their way, retaining their bond of friendship and love. It should be noted that their difference of opinion was based on their common acceptance of the authority of the text in question, and the obligation of consulting it, and the validity of basing one's worship on it, and its status as a proof, since it is affirmed by unquestionable, mass-transmitted evidence. They agreed that to deny these evidences in the first place – even if some of them might be doubtful individually – is nothing but unbelief, since it amounts to a denial of the unshakeable, certain evidence which it is obligatory to accept.

I would like to draw the reader's attention to something important in which many well-thought-of people err, namely the distinction, in the matter of *āḥād* reports,[633] between the denial of a single report on a particular issue on the one hand, and the wholesale denial of the very class of *āḥād* reports on the other. These people err by asserting that whichever of these two assertions are made in the course of a debate or study, the denier of *āḥād* reports is only guilty of sin, and not unbelief. Yet this is a mistake, or a case of ignorance; for to deny them outright is to deny almost the entire prophetic Sunna. We must make the distinction between denying the *āḥād* wholesale simply because they are *āḥād*, and the denial of individual *āḥād* reports without justification or excuse. We say that the one who denies *āḥād* reports *as a class* is an unbeliever, because in reality he is denying the prophetic Sunna, since most of it is *āḥād*; and the one who denies an individual *āḥād* narration on a particular issue, without having any justification for doing so or any reason for not accepting it, is a sinner. This should be noted.

633 That is, ḥadīths with only one chain of transmission, or with too few chains of transmission to qualify for the class of *tawātur* (mass-transmission). The exact definition of this is a point of difference among the scholars of ḥadīth. [t]

The Meaning of Development in the Shariah

Some people might understand the flexibility, development and dynamism of the Shariah in the wrong way, imagining that Islam does not reject anything new, no matter what it is, as long as it seems to them to be good and beneficial, without holding it up to the standard of the principles of the Law and the focal points of its rulings and evidences, and without carefully examining if this new thing is truly beneficial and good in the first place.

What must be done here is to correct our perceptions, purify our outlook and study the arguments and evidences in great depth, so that we do not fall into evil while intending good; for many of those who desire the truth do not find it. Yes, Islam is broad and expansive; but this does not mean that it accepts every new thing uncritically. The truth of the matter is that Islam accepts some things and rejects others; it contains the lawful and unlawful, and the obligatory and reprehensible. Those who read the books of Islamic writers – may Allah give them success – must, therefore, scrutinise their words carefully and do their utmost to understand what they are saying, without rushing to conclusions that are not correct, and might create delusions and misunderstandings.

The Exact Meaning of *Ijtihād*

Providing an exact definition of juridical reasoning [*ijtihād*] in Islam is not an act of obtuseness, but rather serves to establish its principles, give it vital protection, map out its different paths, systematise its foundational sources, distinguish those who are qualified to exercise it, and get rid of all those false claimants to it, who are like mirages, which seem like water to thirsty people until they reach them and find nothing. Therefore the imams of foundational jurisprudence affirm that since *ijtihād* has such an important place in the Shariah, it requires a great amount of knowledge, extensive experience with the field, and total awareness of the different kinds of legal evidences. Therefore anyone who claims to be qualified for unrestricted (*muṭlaq*) *ijtihād* in these times should examine himself closely and scrutinise his claim; for after careful reflection, he might realise that he is ignorant of the true status of the rank he is claiming for himself, or ignorant of his own true status; and he is not excused for any of this. A man might come forward and with great pomp and pride declare his own right to *ijtihād*, seeking to deduce laws from the Book and Sunna, which are Arabic – yet he does not even know how to read a single sentence without making grammatical slips, and has no knowledge of grammar at all, though it is the key to the Arabic language! By Allah, how can such people claim to be qualified to deduce laws as the righteous early Muslims deduced them, or to be among the ranks of the *mujtahidūn*?

We are not saying that the 'door to *ijtihād* is closed'; nay, it shall remain wide open until the Day of Resurrection – but only for those who are worthy of it, and who have proved themselves qualified to deduce laws, and who have learned what they must learn about abrogating and abrogated texts, and about those things on which there is consensus. Allah's grace is vast, and all gifts come from Him, and Allah is of infinite bounty; indeed, Allah might give any of His servants a special aptitude for the Qurʾān and a sound understanding of the prophetic Sunna, making him qualified to revise certain issues, research certain fields, bring out new understandings, discover new truths, or derive laws for new circumstances and events from universal principles. Yet this alone does not amount to the level of unrestricted *ijtihād*; rather, it makes one a researcher or a thinker. A claim to *ijtihād* from an unqualified person is a 'true word put to false use', and a cause for mischief and strife without any shred of truth; it is to disguise falsehood as truth, discourage people from following the Sunna, and disregard the view of the majority.

How often have the Muslims been subjected to the trial of ignorant men who seek to cause unrest in the religion and criticise the scholars of old, lighting fires of discord and despoiling the reputations of the scholars. They love to raise disputes about everything, chasing after benefits, giving obedience to Satan, having love for material things, desiring roles of leadership, and seeking to divide opinion. They spread confusion among ordinary people, coming to them in the guise of encouraging study, research and demands for proofs, until they finally announce that '*ijtihād* is obligatory, and following the opinion of qualified scholars (*taqlīd*) is forbidden' – and there it is! The ordinary person therefore becomes lost in labyrinths of fanciful 'knowledge' and alleged 'research'; he neither remains as he was, nor do they give him the knowledge he needs to be a *mujtahid* himself. Whoever said that *ijtihād* is obligatory for all people, including those who are laymen, unschooled, or ordinary blue-collar workers? If he would deny that such people exist in the Muslim community, then this is a wilful denial of something that is perfectly obvious; and if he acknowledges that indeed there are ordinary people who need to follow scholarly opinion, then there is no doubt that for ordinary people to follow the opinions of the greatest imams of the first three generation is far better and more appropriate than to follow anyone else; for the Prophet ﷺ attested to their superiority when he said: 'The best of people are my generation, then those that follow them, and then those than follow them.'[634]

This attestation proved true for them ﷺ, which can be seen in how their schools were codified and made distinct, and how their saying and opinions were passed along by their followers with authentic or mass-transmitted reports, from one generation to the next. How can we be told to cease following those scholars, and instead adhere to the opinions of men who do not know the points of consensus, the depths of legislation, or the proper way to derive rulings?

We do not intend here to single out any individual for criticism, or to humiliate anyone, since no intelligent person could be bothered by this, nor any ignorant person be pained by it – wounding a dead body causes no pain. Rather, our intention is to give guidance to the Muslims, and to alert students to the importance of valuing the righteous early Muslims, and to call for unity and cohesion; for this is the most perfect, important and worthy thing to aspire to. We are sorely in need of reunification and the healing of the schism that has taken away our strength and spirit, and allowed the other communities to fall upon us just as hungry people fall upon a plate of food, while we are dazed in confusion.

634 Al-Bukhārī, Muslim.

A False Accusation and Dubious Notion

Some of those people who are remiss in their understanding, having not had a proper Islamic education, entertain the notion that the Shariah of Islam is not up to the task of meeting the needs of humanity in all times and places. They depict the stable definition of legislative power in Islam as a 'limitation', accusing the Shariah of being inflexible and stagnant, and falsely claiming that it is not suited to these times, and cannot keep up with the spirit of the times. They assert that the Muslims need to resort to man-made laws to order their society and their politics, alongside the laws of jurisprudence deduced by the scholars of the early generations of Islam. They explain this by saying that as civilisation spread, science and technology progressed, and lifestyles diversified, new circumstances, problems and issues came into being of which the people of old had no experience, and therefore it is not possible (they claim) to make do with the Shariah alone without something else alongside it, or to suffice ourselves with what it has legislated for us. Therefore they have begun to draw from man-made law, considering it a source equal to the Shariah. They have made the forbidden lawful and the lawful forbidden, according to the views and thoughts they happen to have at this particular time and place, without making any distinction between principles and applications, nor between suppositions and certainties.

Now the emergence of this particular kind of enemies of Islam is by no means surprising or incredible, because the enemies of Islam do not stop at open war and destructive plots which spill blood, violate honour, usurp property and squander rights; but they also wage other wars: wars of lies, falsification, distortion, misguidance, misinformation, propaganda and deceitful fault-finding.

What *is* strange, however, is that this is coming from citizens of our own lands, who speak our own languages, profess Islam and are known as Muslims; thus they proclaim a clear rejection of their own Shariah, even when the enemies of Islam have acknowledged it and attested to its broad horizons. At the 1937 International Congress of Comparative Law at the Hague, where Western thinkers and academics from all over the world gathered, the following points were acknowledged:

1 – Islamic Law is a recognised source of legislature.
2 – Islamic Law is a recognised living law.
3 – It is independent, and not derived from external sources.

We have no doubt that these people, who profess Islam, are the result of one of the most fiendish and dangerous plots of colonialism, aimed at destroying Islamic society and pulling it up by the roots. It has cast into their minds – since they were nursed in its lap and raised in its care – the notion that the greatest cause for the lowly state of the Muslims today, and their lagging behind the advancement of civilisation, is that they are too adherent to their religion, and that this Islamic religion of theirs is incompatible with science, and that adherence to it does not lead to progress and development, but rather is an obstacle to all this. Such is the claim of the enemies of Islam; and this idea has influenced many ignorant people in the Muslim world and inspired them to write things which serve the cause of colonialism. These conspirators fail to discern the huge difference between our religion and theirs, and that not so long ago, their religion and its authorities stood in the way of the European cultural Renaissance, stifled its progress and led the forces of backwardness. This made such people view their religion as a hated enemy. But our religion and its authorities and leaders built the Islamic civilisation that history has immortalised, and they were the ones who roused the world from its sleep and its ignorance, and set the renaissance in motion. Thus we should view our religion as a guiding friend, not a hated enemy.

The great legal and intellectual minds of Europe came forward at an international conference held in Riyadh in 1392 AH [1972 CE] to declare their amazement at the Shariah of Islam and the facts they had learned about it, and the human rights they had seen within it. The President of their commission, Mr Macbride, Professor at the University of Dublin and former Foreign Minister of the Irish Republic, said: 'It is here, in this Muslim country, that Human Rights should be proclaimed, nowhere else.' One of his colleagues said: 'The Qur'ānic prescriptions on human rights are undoubtedly more meaningful than the Charter of Human Rights.'

Conclusion

THE BIOGRAPHY of the Prophet ﷺ and the lives and history of his Companions ﷺ provide us with the best example of the way that summoners to Allah should follow, and the greatest source of their spiritual strength and religious consciousness. From it they can kindle the torch of faith, by which they may then light the censers of men's hearts. In it, they can see a call which was nurtured by faith and sincerity, so that those who bore it were willing to give up their lives, possessions and kindred for it, and happy to endure torment for it, so that it was carried over the earth from East to West, from the furthest shores to the highest peaks. Those who bore it forgot their pleasure, abandoned their comforts, left their homes, devoted their souls, and relinquished their possessions, until certainty had entered hearts and captured souls and minds. Hearts opened up to Allah, and the winds of faith blew strongly, a hurricane of goodness and blessing; and the nation of divine Oneness, faith, worship and piety was founded; and guidance spread through the world; and people entered Allah's religion in droves.

Because of this, those striving for social repair and renewal have always turned to this blessed biography to be an exemplar and a source of revitalisation for the Muslims and for the awakening of their aspirations and the rekindling in their hearts of the fire of faith and religious zeal. It is not merely a question of amassing historical facts, or story-telling; it is a question of witnessing the Islamic reality in its complete practical form, embodied perfectly in its highest exemplar, our master Muḥammad ﷺ and his noble Companions.

The exemplary biography of this Prophet ﷺ and his noble Companions ﷺ illustrates the upright way, the straight path, and the clear model of conduct for those who enjoin goodness and rectitude, and the teachers of guidance and educators; and if they stick to it, it guarantees that they succeed and achieve their aims in the best and most perfect way.

At present, there is a widening state of intellectual distance and detachment from this noble biography and this glorious Islamic history, which produced the likes of those gallant heroes, conquering warriors, world leaders, and teachers of the Islamic civilisation, proud and pious guardians of Islam who guided the world, levelled thrones, conquered lands, educated minds, and established a flourishing Islamic civilisation on the foundations of consciousness of Allah and His good pleasure, and built an Islamic nation stretching from East to West.

This distance and detachment from the prophetic biography is a matter of manifest peril, with grave consequences and evil ends in store for the Muslim community, if we do not turn back to the ways of our former glory and draw our civilisation from the foundational principles of that venerable civilisation. We must form a strong and permanent connection with our heroes and great men, and learn from the history of their lives; for they graduated from the school of the Perfect Man ﷺ. None must be followed but they, and none must be imitated but they, and none must be heeded but they; and we can only be set right by what set them right.

Allah, we ask You to send this religion a trusted ward and a rightly-guided leader who can return us to glory, and inspire in us a rejuvenation, and heal our divides, and raise our banners, and rectify the community, and dispel our woes, and enjoin what is right, and forbid what is wrong, and establish Your rule, and apply Your command, and defend what You hold sacred, and succour Your believing servants. Āmīn!

Muḥammad ʿAlawī al-Mālikī
1st Rabīʿ al-Awwal, 1400 AH.

Works Cited

Tafsīr

1. ʿImād al-Dīn Ibn Kathīr, *Tafsīr al-Qurʾān al-ʿAẓīm*
2. Muḥammad ibn Aḥmad ibn Abī Bakr al-Qurṭubī, *al-Jāmiʿ li-Aḥkām al-Qurʾān*
3. Abū al-Faraj ibn al-Jawzī, *Zād al-Masīr fī ʿIlm al-Tafsīr*

Ḥadīth

4. Abū ʿAbdallāh Muḥammad ibn Ismāʿīl al-Bukhārī, *al-Jāmiʿ al-Ṣaḥīḥ*
5. Muslim ibn al-Ḥājj al-Qushayrī al-Nīsāpūrī, *Ṣaḥīḥ Muslim*
6. Muḥammad ibn ʿĪsā al-Tirmidhī, *al-Jāmiʿ lil-Tirmidhī*
7. Abū Dāwūd Sulaymān ibn al-Ashʿath al-Sijistānī, *Sunan Abī Dāwūd*
8. Aḥmad ibn Shuʿayb ibn ʿAlī al-Nasāʾī, *Sunan al-Nasāʾī*
9. Muḥammad ibn Yazīd ibn Mājah al-Qazwīnī, *Sunan Ibn Mājah*
10. Mālik ibn Anas al-Aṣbaḥī, *al-Muwaṭṭāʾ*
11. Aḥmad ibn Muḥammad ibn Ḥanbal al-Shaybānī, *al-Musnad*
12. Muḥammad ibn ʿĪsā al-Tirmidhī, *Shamāʾil al-Tirmidhī*
13. Aḥmad ibn al-Ḥusayn al-Bayhaqī, *Dalāʾil al-Nubuwwa*
14. Abū Nuʿaym al-Iṣfahānī, *Dalāʾil al-Nubuwwa*
15. Zakī al-Dīn ʿAbd al-ʿAẓīm al-Mudhirī, *al-Targhīb wa al-Tarhīb*
16. Muḥammad ibn Ismāʿīl al-Bukhārī, *al-Adab al-Mufrad*
17. Sulaymān ibn Aḥmad ibn Ayyūb al-Shāmī al-Ṭabarānī, *al-Muʿjam al-Ṣaghīr*
18. Jalāl al-Din ibn Muḥammad ibn Aḥmad al-Suyūṭī, *al-Jāmiʿ al-Ṣaghīr*
19. Shams al-Dīn al-Sakhāwī, *al-Maqāṣid al-Ḥasana*
20. Nūr al-Dīn al-Haythamī, *Majmaʿ al-Zawāʾid*
21. Zayn al-Dīn al-ʿIrāqī, *Takhrīj al-Iḥyāʾ*

Sīra Nabawiyya (Prophetic Biography)

22. Abū al-Qāsim ʿAbd al-Raḥmān ibn ʿAbdallāh ibn Hishām, *al-Sīra al-Nabawiyya*
23. Aḥmad Zaynī Daḥlān, *al-Sīra al-Nabawiyya*
24. ʿAlī ibn Burhān al-Dīn al-Ḥalabī al-Shāfiʿī, *al-Sīra al-Ḥalabiyya*
25. Jalāl al-Dīn al-Suyūṭī, *al-Khaṣāʾis al-Kubrā*
26. Abū al-Faḍl ʿIyāḍ ibn Mūsā al-Yaḥṣabī, *al-Shifā*
27. Shihāb al-Dīn al-Khaffājī, *Sharḥ al-Shifā*
28. Shihāb al-Dīn Aḥmad ibn Muḥammad al-Qasṭallānī, *al-Mawāhib al-Laduniyya*
29. Muḥammad ibn ʿAbd al-Bāqī al-Zurqānī, *Sharḥ al-Mawāhib al-Laduniyya*
30. ʿAbdallāh Sirāj al-Dīn, *al-Shamāʾil*
31. Ibn al-Tallā, *Aqḍiyat al-Rasūl*
32. ʿAbd al-Ḥayy al-Kattānī, *al-Tarātīb al-Idāriyya*
33. Abū al-Faraj ibn al-Jawzī, *al-Wafāʾ fī Faḍāʾil al-Muṣṭafā*

History and Biography

34. Muḥammad ibn Saʿd Kātib al-Wāqidī, *al-Ṭabaqāt al-Kubrā*
35. Aḥmad ibn ʿAlī ibn Muḥammad Ibn Ḥajar al-ʿAsqalānī, *al-Iṣāba fī Tamyīz al-Ṣaḥāba*
36. Ibn ʿAbd al-Barr al-Nimarī al-Qurṭubī, *al-Istīʿāb fī Maʿrifat al-Aṣḥāb*
37. ʿImād al-Dīn Ibn Kathīr, *al-Bidāya wa al-Nihāya*
38. Jalāl al-Dīn al-Suyūṭī, *Tārīkh al-Khulafāʾ*
39. ʿAbd al-Raḥmān ibn Muḥammad ibn Khaldūn, *al-Muqaddima*

Islamic Law and Literature

40. Abī Isḥāq al-Shāṭibī, *al-Muwāfaqāt fī Uṣūl al-Sharīʿa*
41. Jalāl al-Dīn al-Suyūṭī, *al-Itqān fī ʿUlūm al-Qurʾān*
42. Muḥammad al-Safārīnī al-Ḥanbalī, *Ghidhāʾ al-Albāb li-Sharḥ Manẓūmat al-Ādāb*
43. Abū al-Barakāt ibn al-Anbārī, *Sharḥ Qasīdat al-Burda*

Index

A

ʿAbbād ibn Bishr, 18
ʿAbdallāh ibn Jaʿfar, 59
ablutions, performing before supplicating, 292
Abū al-Bakhtarī ibn Hishām, 253
Abū Bakr al-Ṣiddīq
  defence of the Prophet against persecution, 153
  as possessing a pillar of the Pool, 198
  describing the face of the Messenger, 12
  good manners of with the Prophet, 208-209
  position on the captives of Badr, 111, 115
Abū Bakr ibn al-ʿAlāʾ al-Mālikī, Qāḍī, 81
Abū Baṣīr, 148-49
Abū Burda ibn Nayyār, 187
Abū al-Dardāʾ
  on the knowledge of the Messenger, 45
  on those who know but fail to act, 295
  as smiling, 251
Abū Dharr, 259
Abū Ḥanīfa, Imam, 306, 307
Abū Hurayra, 168
Abū Jahl, 73, 153
Abū Jandal, 148
Abū Lahab, 70
Abū Masʿūd al-Badrī, 16
Abū al-Qāsim, prohibition of use of as name, 185
Abū Sufyān, 159, 233-34, 236, 238
Abū al-Ṭufayl, describing the face of the Messenger, 12-13
Abū ʿUbayd, 118
Abū ʿUbayda, 86
Abyssinians, 251
adoption, as not constituting a family tie, 94-95
advice of the Messenger of Allah, 65
āḥād reports, denial of, 309
Aḥmad, Imam, 307
Aḥmad, name of, 180
al-Aḥzāb, battle of, 35
ʿĀʾisha
  on the asceticism of the Messenger, 157
  on Allah's revealing what the Messenger concealed, 95
  describing the face of the Messenger, 12
  on the dignity of the Messenger of Allah, 144
  as envious of Khadīja, 150
  on the fragrances of the Messenger of Allah, 173
  on the generosity of the Messenger, 147
  on the gentleness of the Messenger, 135
  harsh response to Jews, 246
  on how Revelation first came to the Prophet, 104
  interpretation of messengers 'being lied to', 86-87
  on kindness of the Prophet to his family, 247-48
  on the light of the Messenger of Allah, 17
  on the Messenger's fear of Allah, 216
  on the Prophet sewing, 60
  on the Qurʾān as the nature of the Prophet, 204-205
  on the speech of the Messenger of Allah, 48
  on the worship of the Messenger of Allah, 212
Āl ʿImrān, sūrat, 175
ʿAlī ibn Abī Ṭālib
  describing the eyes of the Messenger of Allah, 14

B

E

F

G

H

I

J

K

L

M

N

O

P

T

U

V

W

Y

Z